Ideas and Society

Ideas and Society
India Between the Sixteenth and Eighteenth Centuries

Second Edition

Eugenia Vanina

OXFORD
UNIVERSITY PRESS

OXFORD

UNIVERSITY PRESS

YMCA Library Building, Jai Singh Road, New Delhi 110 001

Oxford University Press is a department of the University of Oxford. It furthers the
University's objective of excellence in research, scholarship, and education
by publishing worldwide in

Oxford   New York

Auckland   Bangkok   Buenos Aires   Cape Town   Chennai
Dar es Salaam   Delhi   Hong Kong   Istanbul   Karachi   Kolkata
Kuala Lumpur   Madrid   Melbourne   Mexico City   Mumbai   Nairobi
São Paulo   Shanghai   Singapore   Taipei   Tokyo   Toronto

Oxford is a registered trade mark of Oxford University Press
in the UK and in certain other countries

Published in India
By Oxford University Press, New Delhi

ISBN 0 19 566864 2

Typeset in New Baskerville 11/13 pt.
by RK Computer Services, New Delhi 110 051
Printed at De Unique, New Delhi 110 018
Published by Manzar Khan, Oxford University Press
YMCA Library Building, Jai Singh Road, New Delhi 110 001

Contents

Contents

Introduction

The historical period examined in the present book is usually construed by readers as a fateful epoch of transition from the middle ages to modern times. Through whatever we have read or heard about these three centuries in human history, we could easily create a more or less vivid picture of an epoch when symbols changed from a feudal castle to a factory. Our memory would prompt us to remember the main historical events of this period, which include great scientific and technical discoveries, masterpieces of art and literature, wars, social turmoil, and three great revolutions (the Netherlands, England, and France). We would remember too, the many illustrious names of that age: Shakespeare and Cervantes, Erasmus and Luther, Raffaello Santi and Rembrandt, Jordano Bruno and Newton, Cromwell and Napoleon, Voltaire and Mozart ... In most cases, these great names belong to Europe. For an educated European (or even a western educated Indian intellectual), a huge part of humanity generally known as the Orient would find no place in this memory except in a very special way. The Orient is thought of as a place to which adventurers flocked to seek their fortune or to overpower the local rulers so that the colonial riches would be appropriated to cement the basis of a new Europe.

These stereotypes colour our perceptions and estimates of medieval history and the epoch that followed it. Thus it is assumed that a feudal lord should own land and exploit peasants; peasants should groan under the yoke and be ready to revolt; religious reformers should think like Luther or, better still, like Cromwell; humanists should follow the luminaries of the Italian Renaissance; and social movements should develop from Watt Tyler to the storming of the Bastille. If the historical reality of an Asian country has little in common with this stereotype, two conclusions generally follow. Either everything deviating from the European canons testifies to the Orient's backwardness and stagnation, or the East has its own way of development, totally different from the western model. The latter conclusion encourages us to look for alternative models of Asiatic societies (and societies other than the western) that are not based on stereotypical assumptions.

Nowadays much is being said about the unity of mankind and the common values of humanity. In that faraway epoch, when peoples of the world were scarcely connected with each other and had no information about their neighbours, humanity was, like now, multifaceted and unified. Unity of societies lies not in following one general model, and diversity—not in negation of common laws of development. These laws or general tendencies of human development are, in reality, numerous and varied and have no one model or standard. Western Europe, which is projected by some scholars as such a standard, seems so only from a bird's-eye view, and different parts of the relatively smaller-sized Britain have shown many peculiarities of development. Yet this diversity gave birth to common laws and tendencies that enable us now to speak and think of a 'world history'. Medieval history of the East and West had different starting points, took different paths, and ended differently but these civilizations, so unlike each other, had many common features, not only in land property, industry, and social processes but also in polity, culture, arts, and ideas.

This book explores the history of ideas and social thought in India during a period, which was a transition to the modern age in the West and a pre-colonial era in the East. People whom the reader will meet here were Indian contemporaries of Erasmus, Hobbes, and Rousseau. The comparison only between India and the West has no special significance and the reader would be right to ask: why not a comparison with China, the Arab countries, Nepal, or the writer's own country? In my view, any such comparison will be most useful and justified too. I have chosen western Europe not because it is a model of 'correct' or 'progressive' development but because the history of ideas in medieval and early modern Europe is well known to scholars and the general public.

Indian studies as a field of research is about two centuries old; exploration of medieval history of India has an even shorter record and can boast only of a few postulates generally accepted by all scholars. Researchers still debate over the beginning and the end of the medieval period in India, the differences between India and other countries in social, economic, and cultural spheres, and whether pre-colonial India was feudal, 'Asiatic', or something else. Because of the efforts of several generations of Indian, British, Soviet/Russian, French, German, Japanese, American, and other scholars of medieval India, the main stages of history, political processes, agrarian and industrial relations, social structure, etc. have been researched into. This vast source material, presented by scholars, their approaches and ideas give opportunity for further discussion and enable us to take at least some steps towards a historical reality.

However, due to several reasons, most studies of the medieval history of India deal with socio-economic and socio-political problems. This holds true for both Russian Indianists and their Indian colleagues, though the latter's scope of research is much wider. Such attention to socio-economic and socio-political problems has nothing strange or wrong about it, since it is connected with the very core of human life and social being. But I do not agree that economy, political life, and social relations are the only criteria of assessing a civilization's level of development and its comparability with other societies. We cannot make a correct assessment of a building if we study only its basement. If we adopt such an approach, we tend to see tools of labour, forms of property, social structure, prices, and goods as main actors in history but Man here is absent—Man with his views on the world around him, on society, on himself, on nature. We shall never get a true picture of medieval India if we fail to consider who a medieval Indian (taking into consideration social, regional, communal, and gender divisions, of course) was, to what extent he/she was unlike a medieval European (a generalization once again, since, apart from social diversity, a medieval Italian and a Briton differed considerably from each other), and to what extent the thoughts and world perception of an Indian were similar to those of the people from other medieval societies. While examining and exploring a society, we should not ignore either the sphere of ideas, or the socio-economic and political processes that influenced people at a specific time. In the never-ending discussion of what is primary and what is secondary in the development of a society, a dialectical approach should not be neglected.

Thus, the task of this book is twofold. First, it takes some steps towards the study of the history of ideas in India from the sixteenth to eighteenth centuries. Second, it makes an effort towards a comparative analysis of some trends in the history of ideas in pre-modern India and some other countries, especially those of western Europe.

A. Gurevich, a well-known Russian scholar of medieval European history, has rightly observed that historical research is a dialogue between two cultural backgrounds, i.e., between the culture of the researched epoch and that of the researcher himself.[1] So my attempt at comparison aims at a better understanding of medieval Indian society by the readers belonging to diverse cultural and temporal backgrounds. It also acknowledges that while the history and culture of medieval India have their own value, they are also a part of world history and culture. For a Briton, the sixteenth century is the age of Elizabeth I and Shakespeare. For a Russian, it is the time of Ivan the Terrible and his associates and opponents. Our common civilization will only benefit if we realize that it was also the epoch of Akbar and Tulsidas. Despite cultural differences, this collective knowledge can enrich world culture and give a wider picture of this epoch.

The socio-political thought and the spiritual and cultural processes in medieval India are the least studied problems of Indian history. As it always happens, the lacunae in our knowledge are often filled by stereotypes. As a result, many people in and outside India may support a statement by the American scholar, Joel Larus, that educated Indians of the pre-colonial times 'concentrated on prayers all too frequently while invaders' legions ripped the country apart', they were 'seeking community with the Universe rather than struggling with mundane problems', and, to sum it up, 'the individual Hindu was concerned primarily with religious and philosophical problems.[2] In more recent studies, S. N. Eisenstadt and Harriet Hartman stressed 'the basic orientation of Hindu civilization away from mundane affairs' while R.S. Sharma noted 'the orientation towards servility, hierarchy, destiny and favour seeking' as the core features of India's 'feudal mind'.[3]

This stereotype has persisted for centuries and has a history of its own, closely connected with the history of ideas in the West and especially the complex trend known as Orientalism. 'Indifference to mundane problems', 'alienation from worldly life', 'aspiration only to the heights of religion and philosophy with no care for reality'—all these features, allegedly characterizing medieval Indians, are differently interpreted to meet different perceptions. Some people interpret these ideas as proof of the backwardness and stagnation of Indian society which was presumably 'sleeping' for centuries, waiting for a jolt (from the West, of course). Others admire this supposed 'unworldliness' of the Indians and want the West to adopt it. These two polar views have similar Euro-centric basis.[4] Such an approach will, at best, lead us to a knowledge of what medieval India did not have and give us no idea of what really was there. The real spiritual world of the epoch and its people, their real concerns and views will remain hidden from us. But if one tries to analyse historical material and compare it with that of the other countries to see India's specific features, it will be noticed that, first, a sage's most mystical revelations may reflect worldly problems, and second, some forms of expression, exotic for the West, may exhibit values and views common to other medieval civilizations.

The historical period selected for this study was a crucial epoch for both Europeans and Indians. For a major part of Europe, it was a period of transition from the medieval to the modern age; for India these three centuries were the end of the pre-colonial period and a beginning of the colonial era. Hence the special significance of the three centuries for India and the world. What was India before it became a colony? What was its stage of historical development? These questions are omnipresent in Indian studies and are significant for the present book too.

The stereotype that still lives in the minds of scholars and the general public is that India spent its medieval history absorbed in a mystical trance or lethargy, in most cases distanced from what is understood as progress or development. It is difficult however to correlate this stereotype with the image of modern, post-

Independence India, with its dynamic development and well-known achievements in economy, social reforms, political democracy, and culture. Many people think that the country owes its modern dynamism to the brief colonial period that lies between 'traditional' and 'modern' India. Without underestimating the western influence during British colonial rule and neglecting its negative aspects too, let us ask, what soil was it in which the seeds of British influence were sown? Only a short period is supposed to divide 'traditional India' from the India of Raja Ram Mohan Roy and other reformers, from the India of the democratic press and first modernist societies. Was a meagre historical space of some decades sufficient to transform the educated elite, that was supposedly 'seeking community with the Universe rather than struggling with mundane problems' into one criticizing medieval legacy, striving for reforms and the country's progress? It is an acknowledged fact that India borrowed much from the West, but we should also question why it could borrow, why it could rethink and reconsider many a tradition and dogma. These questions cannot be fully answered if the whole progress of modern India is attributed only to the influence of the British Raj, which had also been established in many other countries of Asia and Africa, but with somewhat different results. From among a huge number of the former British colonies it was India and not other countries, even from the same subcontinent, that was able to develop, despite many problems and setbacks, a modern economy and a democracy that works. This fact itself testifies that, compared to other countries of the Afro-Asian world, pre-colonial India did have 'something' that enabled its society, albeit in its elitist strata, to rather quickly accept the new ideas. One of the main tasks of the author is to try and fill this lacuna, and also to examine the significance and role of the medieval period in the history of ideas in India.

This is important if we keep in mind that in the India of today the general attitude to the cultural and historical legacy of the past is hardly that of disinterest and remoteness. Great rulers, thinkers, poets, sages, and religious divines of the past are not being relegated to the background as 'classics' to be read at school and quickly forgotten after the exams. Historical legacy forms an inseparable part of present life and culture. There is nothing new in saying that in an average Indian mind, the past and present coexist, sometimes harmoniously, sometimes in conflict. The cultural legacy of medieval India lives on in modern Indian culture as a religious treasure, as a spiritual inspiration, as a foundation for moral and ethical values. Many problems meditated upon by medieval thinkers and sages are vital for modern India also. Some would see this as a proof of the stagnant character of Indian history, but I take a different view. The very fact that many ideas and concerns of medieval thinkers seem modern now, displays the depth of their insight into the crucial problems of the country.

One of the significant developments in present-day India is that the attitudes to and estimates of the country's historical legacy have been and are considerably politicized. Historical problems that one would have expected to be discussed in the quiet and disciplined atmosphere of academic seminars emerge as the core of burning political controversies and even erupt in violent actions. The Ramjanmabhoomi Mandir / Babri Masjid confrontation has been but one example, notoriously known to the world, but many other controversies over this or that historical figure, event, or process have become inseparable from the Indian political scene. The very mode of teaching history to the younger generation is now at the centre of heated debates.

There is nothing strange about the fact that in a country like India various political forces use the country's historical legacy for their specific purposes. This very fact shows, to begin with, that in India the medieval past has not retired to museum displays and book pages, it is very much 'here' and 'alive' and has to be dealt with seriously, since, as we have already seen, sometimes the 'non-academic' mode of discussing a sixteenth-century event affects tragically the lives of so many people who belong to later centuries. It is not for the foreigner to take on a judge's mantle and pass a verdict. But the scholar's role, ethics, and attitude to this array of problems is worth thinking about.

Indeed, what can a scholar, Indian or outsider, do while researching a controversial issue or incident of medieval Indian history and thought? For the present study, this question may first and foremost be applied to the theme of communal relations, or, to be more precise, Hindu–Muslim relations in medieval India. One way would be to be partisan to a certain religious community, to pick up from the historical records only those facts that favour one side and depict the other as the 'villain'. This, no doubt, is unacceptable for any decent, unbiased, professional historian or even just a person who wants peace and amity. And hence such attempts, when made, are met with justified protest and indignation from all people who possess common sense.

But there is another mode of behaviour that historians adopt, generous and well-meaning by intention but rather dubious in its result. From the very beginning of the nationalist school of Indian history up to the present day, there has been a powerful trend of patriotic-minded, secularist history writing by scholars who spare no efforts in showing that Hindu–Muslim relations in medieval India were an example of harmony and brotherhood. Not satisfied with glorifying (and justly so!) the 'proto-secularists' like Akbar and 'great integrators' like *sufi* and *bhakti* saints, they spare no efforts to 'vindicate' even those rulers who, like Aurangzeb, were notorious for their religious fanaticism.

Various methodologies are applied for this purpose. One may, for instance, 'select' the suitable facts and 'delete' the unsuitable, thus portraying a *sufi* saint as an advocate of communal amity and 'forgetting' that his benevolent attitude towards the Hindus and treatment of the Quran as the 'fifth Veda' had a clear-cut purpose of facilitating conversion of the 'unbelieving Hindus' to Islam;[5] similarly for many *bhaktas*, it was important to state the superiority of their religion over that of the Muslims.[6] Another methodology might try to find 'economic' and 'political' reasons for heinous acts like temple destruction and imposition of the *jizya*.[7] There is also the possibility of underestimating the importance of communal problems in favour of socio-economic ones, as a celebrated medievalist was recorded stating, 'It was more social inequality than religious discord. The rulers collected land tax from Hindu and Muslim people, but there was little evidence of religious conflict.'[8] Land tax and social inequality were important aspects of medieval Indian society, but did they overshadow other problems? Is it possible for us now to judge what made people of that faraway epoch suffer more—heavy taxation or sacrilegious demolition of a revered shrine?

The intention behind the above-described approach to medieval history is clear and understandable. Laying emphasis upon communal amity, deletion of 'bad' pages from history and diversion of public attention to other problems must be, according to the scholars who follow this method, instrumental in 'disarming' the communalists and in teaching people the 'good history' instead of the 'bad' one. As a result, a kind of etiquette came into existence that nobody could violate in peril of being labelled a 'communalist'. The present author even had a chance to experience this when the first edition of this book came out in 1996. It was enough to but mention the imposition of *jizya* and temple destruction by Aurangzeb to be rebuked by a reviewer for 'completely depending upon the language and notions of communalist historians'.

The problem, however, is that 'bad' pages can be deleted from history books but not from historical memories of the people who know from an oral tradition about the destruction of a holy place nearby or from a visit to a site like the Qutub Minar where one can see the columns from demolished shrines, which show signs of having been struck by weapons. And when well-meaning and secular-minded historians speak half-truths or distort facts, they create favourable conditions for their adversaries to pose as 'eye-openers' and 'proponents of the truth' and to expound this 'truth' to the public in a way most suitable for their purposes. The present author knows this well from the sad experience of her own country's historical school of the Soviet period. It would be more beneficial for communal amity if people learnt the truth, both 'good' and 'bad', from the professional and secular historians than from the self-styled 'defenders of religion' who would definitely misuse historical facts to provoke communal clashes. And the truth is that in medieval India, like in other epochs, there was the tendency towards communal strife, fanaticism, and discrimination as well as the tendency towards communal amity and cooperation. There were socio-political forces and individuals, both among Hindus and Muslims, who proclaimed the superiority of one community and the subjugation of all others and those who advocated equality of all pathways to God, preached communal amity, and even sacrificed their lives for this noble cause. In some cases, the forces of communal discord took over and this, as numerous examples from history show, resulted in bloodshed and decay, while the most valuable contributions to the Indian socio-economic and political well-being, culture, thought, and arts were made by those who believed in communal amity and did their best to maintain it.

Against this background it would not be out of place to give a second thought to the problem of 'tradition' and its never-ending collision with 'modernity'. In the context of Indian history and society, 'tradition' is complicated and controversial within itself. Indeed, whom should we view as a 'Hindu traditionalist'? Is it a person who strictly follows the laws of caste purity and abhors 'polluting' contacts with the members of 'lower' castes and other communities? Or it is the follower of the teachings of Basava, Kabir, Akho Bhagat, Sarvajna, and a host of other saints who mocked 'pollution' and protested against caste discrimination? How should a Muslim think in order to be labelled 'traditionalist'—like Aurangzeb or like Akbar, like Shaikh Ahmad Sirhindi or Shaikh Nizamuddin Aulia? And the very notion of 'modern' becomes even more controversial if we take into consideration the destructive values proclaimed by some powerful forces with the help of the most sophisticated information technologies.

It seems crucial for the understanding of the 'main code' of Indian history that this country does have a tradition, a thick historical layer of liberal free-thinkers, social reformers, and advocates of communal amity and just a popular common sense of unsophisticated Hindus and Muslims who had through the centuries developed wise and healthy rules of living, rejoicing, and suffering together. An opposite tradition of bigotry and fanaticism has been and is likewise powerful too. In some cases these two approaches could even coexist in one person. Aurangzeb, for instance, resumed *jizya* collection, ordered temple destruction, and at the same time donated wealth to Hindu shrines and created favourable conditions for many Hindu nobles in his court who, during the war of succession, preferred to support him and not the 'liberal and secularist' Dara Shukoh. These two tendencies are both part of India's historical experience; both should be researched into and expounded to the readers.

Now it seems important to suggest a method for this study. Scholars from India and other countries have worked out two methods of research for the history of ideas. One presents a complex study of a certain thinker's views and positions: here scholars also try to project the whole picture of his epoch as reflected by that person's ideas. Such a method would have been suitable for the study of the medieval epoch also, but for the fragmentary character of source material. There is hardly a medieval thinker whose legacy is known in full. Some great minds are known only by name while there are some works or a few lines, belonging to different authors and epochs preserved in archives and elsewhere, still waiting to be brought to light. Another method adopted in scholarly works on the history of ideas is the analysis of different trends and tendencies in the history of thought of a given epoch. For instance, for the nineteenth and twentieth centuries in India (pre-Independence period) one may distinguish between the various ideologies within the national liberation struggle, ideas of religious reform, enlightenment, etc.

This method works for the analysis of the modern period, but is hard to put into practice in the study of a medieval society. Medieval thought has no unified trend, no 'ism', so to say, for differences within each tradition were sometimes many more than outside it. This is sometimes not taken into consideration by scholars, who write on the *bhakti* movement, Sufism, and so on. *Bhakti*, for instance, encompasses saints and poets with totally opposing views. Scholars, who try to look at *bhakti* only as a progressive anti-feudal movement,[9] may be puzzled to find opponents of these progressive ideas within the same tradition.

The very notions of 'progressive' and 'conservative' have special meaning in the context of medieval society and should be handled with care. For instance, two great names in Indian history—Kabir and Abu-l Fazl Allami—are associated with progressive ideas. Scholars universally mention Kabir's criticism of caste inequality and social evils, but very rarely do they pay attention to Kabir's negative attitude to books and knowledge (unless it was a mystical knowledge) and his somewhat fanatical rejection of others' views. Abu-l Fazl, an aristocrat, had no sympathy for egalitarian ideas but he and his followers influenced Indian thought with their free-thinking rationalism and open preference for real scholarly knowledge and research rather than scholastic and theological dogmas. Who of these two, if we judge by the traditional yardstick, is progressive or conservative? We can ask the same question about the European reformers, Muntzer and Cromwell, who are considered more progressive and more towards the 'left' than Erasmus and Ulrich Von Hutten.

No viewpoint can be declared as the only true and valid

approach. My aim is to present an analysis of medieval India from several points of view and, if possible, bring them together. In my analysis of medieval Indian society and ideas I shall base myself on the approaches and views of medieval Indian thinkers as reflected in the source material. If historical research is a dialogue of cultures, it should be held on equal terms. Many discussions, which were held by Soviet/Russian, Indian, and western scholars on the nature of the social system of medieval India,[10] face difficulties because scholars sometimes look into medieval sources only for information and ideas that are interesting to twentieth-century researchers. But medieval authors had different ways of thinking and, if we want to understand them, we must listen to what they say of themselves and on this basis try to find answers for our questions.

Even the small part of source material that is now available to us contains an ocean of ideas and views. Of this, I have selected only those ideas that are relevant to the main aim of the book: ideas and society, i.e., trends of thought reflecting social processes. I have tried to pinpoint some main problems, on which the social thought of medieval India from the sixteenth to eighteenth centuries meditated. From the variety of topics discussed by medieval authors I have selected the following: ideas of state and statehood, religious and cultural relations of Hindus and Muslims, the evolution of social processes and religious reform movements, and the way the Indian mind reacted to the collapse of the Mughal empire and colonial invasion. The structuring of the argument on the basis of these issues was prompted by the literature of the epoch. Thus, the reader will find no special chapter on Sufism and *bhakti,* no special chapter on a particular thinker. Each chapter and paragraph is based on an issue and how it was dealt with by individual thinkers and schools of thought.

This study deals with a relatively small historical period, but while analysing any particular historical process we must bear in mind its sources and historical premises, hence the scope of source material and space of research will inevitably be much wider historically. This will help to understand all the changes Indian society in the medieval and feudal period passed through.

One special point has to be made here. Some readers may ask the author to specify what is meant by the notions 'medieval' and 'feudal' since no accord exists on this subject. For some scholars, pre-colonial India belonged to the Asiatic mode of production; others trace the origins of Indian feudalism back to the times of the Mahabharata while for a number of scholars Marxist terminology has nothing to do with India; they prefer notions like 'traditional society' or stick to divisions like 'Hindu period' and 'Muslim period'. This problem seems so complicated that a reputed Marxist scholar, obviously fatigued by the never-ending discussions, suggested to denote pre-colonial India as the 'medieval Indian system'.[11]

My position here is that the pivotal role in historical studies should belong to the research of concrete reality, otherwise our debates on feudalism, Asiatic mode of production, and so on will be an exercise in rhetoric, like the scholastic disputes of medieval philosophers.

The aim is to attempt a comparative analysis in order to understand the dialectic unity of the general laws of historical development and the special features of each civilization. Keeping in view the relativism of categories, we can call medieval India feudal, if we always bear in mind that it was an Indian feudalism, which might not necessarily have a Watt Tyler or a Cromwell, but still has some ideas, realities, values, processes, and contradictions in common with other feudal societies.

For a historical study, especially for one examining the history of ideas, there is always the problem of adequate source material, which for a historian is like fuel for an engine. For socio-economic and political studies the main bulk of sources consists of documents, chronicles, and notes made by European travellers. Such sources are not always wholly useful for the study, though they should not be neglected.

I have used chronicles, documents, tracts, and treatises not only because they contain information but because they reflect some level of the thought and mind of people. I shall examine the chronicles and ordinances of the Mughal emperors not for facts of concrete politics, but for ideas regarding the state and society. The same approach is applicable to the famous works of Abu-1 Fazl. This celebrated author is sometimes belittled by historians for not being true to reality, for idealizing his royal friend, and for exalting the role of the state. But if one bears in mind the specific features of Abu-1 Fazl's works, these alleged faults will disappear, for the *Ain-i Akbari* and even the *Akbar-nama* are not chronicles, or documents, but treatises expounding the views of the author and his associates. Hence, they reflect in many cases not only documentary facts but the order of things as they should have been according to him. The same approach is applicable to many special treatises like Dara Shikoh's works, *Dabistan-i Mazahib*, and to many works of epistolary literature, like the letters of Akbar, Abu-l Fazl, Aurangzeb, Shah Waliullah, and so on.

One genre of sources, referred to in the present book, also deserves special mention. Works of the biographical genre are used by scholars quite often, but the special features of these works are not always realized in a proper way. Most medieval Indian biographies belong to the genre of hagiography or panegyrics rather than real biography. This is especially true of the writings on various *bhakti* and *sufi* saints. The authors of these works were engaged not in presenting facts, or in creating an individual image, but in working out a legend that would help people in an emotional perception of a religious doctrine and the moral values connected with it, to feel sympathy and veneration for the holy man, to learn from his generosity and zeal. Thus these works have to be approached by historians for the general values they express, and the history of ideas associated with them. It is from this perspective that I have used works like *Janma-lila*, Dadu Dayal's biography compiled by his disciple Jan Gopal. This work seems to hold an intermediate position between hagiography and real biography.

The development of biographical literature reflects an important process of the growth of individual features in literature and culture. I have quoted from a unique source of this type, the *Ardha-kathanaka* by Banarasi Das, a seventeenth century Jain merchant from Agra. Researchers in socio-economic history may find in this work a mine of information on trade relations and the social structure of urban economy. For my study, it is much more important that Banarasi Das was an original thinker with an inquiring mind, who tried to bring elements of religious reforms into Jainism.

Various strands of *bhakti,* Sufism, and Sikhism have left an ocean of literature. Even a brief survey of it would require a huge volume. My study of these sources is based not only on numerous publications and researches on *bhakti* and *sufi* literature in India and elsewhere, but on a well-developed school of *bhakti* and *sufi* studies in the former USSR. Its history started with the Herculean effort of the late Professor A. Barannikov who, as early as 1948, published a Russian translation of Tulsidas' *Ramacharita-manasa* in verse. This was followed by Payevskaya's work on Bengali *bhakti*, studies and partial translations of *Sursagar* into Russian by N. Sazanova and Tsvetkov, Gafurova's translations of Kabir's verses from the *Adi Granth* and *Granthavali*, and Serebryany's researches on and translations from Vidyapati. There are a number of translations and research studies on Amir Khusrau, Bedil, Faizi, Mir Taqi Mir, and other *sufis*.[12] Despite the heavy odds that the Russian scholars had to confront during the last decade of the twentieth century, some new works and translations appeared. In addition to the already translated corpus of *bhakti* literature, the Russian readers can now read Namdev, Tukaram, Mira Bai, and the stories from the Pushti Marg hagiography.[13] A high-level work on the Varkari tradition of Maharashtrian *bhakti*, based upon text researches and field study, has been recently contributed by Glushkova, while Suvorova authored a comprehensive book on the *sufi* hagiography and teachings.[14] This tradition on *bhakti* and *sufi* studies has helped and influenced my perceptions, providing me with valuable source material and reliable methodology.

My attempt to use literary works as sources is not limited to *bhakti* and *sufi* studies alone. A lot of information on the history of ideas is available in the vast literature of the anti-Mughal movements. Texts like *Dasbodh* by Ramdas, *Chatraprakash* by Lal Kavi, *Sri Dasam Granth,* along with romances by Jayasi, Alam, and other poets, lyrics by Akbar's court poets, satirical works of Sauda, and verses, *ghazals*, and poems by Mir, Nazir Akbarabadi, and so on are a rich source of ideas associated with the epoch.

Indian literature of the pre-colonial period is a treasure that has not been fully used by historians. Worse still, there is a sort of prejudice among some scholars against using it for historical studies. First, since the time of Sir William Jones and the first Orientalists there has been a tradition of thinking that while ancient India produced some literary masterpieces, the medieval period could boast of nothing but imitations of Persian or Sanskrit canons. This idea is seen to be corroborated by the fact that many medieval works of literature were written either on classical themes from the

Ramayana, the Mahabharata, and other works or in the developed tradition of ancient writers. Second, though some attempts have been made, there are no special studies on the way literary works should be used as sources of history.[15]

Of course, literary works have some specific features. If modern literature applies sometimes unusual methods of reflecting life, this was more so in the medieval period. The medieval poet was subjective in his views and attitudes. He saw the surrounding reality in a way which was different from that of our contemporaries, but this is what makes medieval literature important for us. Literary works present a unique opportunity to discover the way medieval people saw the world.

There are many reasons to doubt the historicity of events and people depicted in medieval literature. For a poet of this epoch, it was not at all impossible to set his story in some faraway country like China or in some mythical city like Pushpavati or Kamavati. He would, without any hesitation, bring together historical personages who lived centuries apart. He would also make gods and goddesses behave like his peasant neighbours and depict miracles and fantastic adventures. To put it clearly, while reading a medieval romance or a bardic poem, we should not consider the hero's fantastic feats or the ideal king's generosity as a factual documentary, but should note the ideals of heroism and statehood which existed in the author's epoch and to which he wishes to give expression.

Unlike studies on the socio-economic history of India, this book has relatively few references to the European visitors to India. This is partially because the author's aim is to allow India to speak for itself and to make readers, especially in the author's home country, familiar with the treasures of Indian thought and culture. To some extent, it is a quiet protest against the approach of some scholars who base their studies of medieval India totally on European records, which, of course, are very useful as sources, but should occupy their particular place. My position may be somehow justified by the fact that during the period under review European travellers to India were more interested in cloth and spice prices than in the spiritual riches of India. Even those who were observant on this subject (I have referred to Bernier, Tavernier, Orme, and de Laval), were, in spite of their wisdom and insight, separated from

Indian culture by a huge wall of religious superstitions, ignorance, and the arrogance of the representatives of the 'highest' culture and 'most true' religion. In more than one case they were not recording the Indian realities but, as it was convincingly shown by a recent study, contributed to the creation of the imagined India of the colonial and Orientalist worldview.[16] This perception had a lasting impact upon nearly two centuries of scholarship and literary writing on India by not only Europeans themselves, but Indians too who, naturally, studied their country's past from colonial teachers and adopted their approaches. In the first edition of this book the problems of Orientalist perception of Indian history were not paid much attention by the author, and that was a mistake indeed. But the last one or two decades saw a host of high-level works that discuss the origins and development of the Orientalist concepts of Indian history and culture, both as a phenomenon of the Western society as such and as a powerful contributor to the Indians' self-understanding. Therefore I felt it important to refer, albeit briefly, to this problem as applicable to the history of ideas in medieval India.

The author fully acknowledges that her selection of sources has some shortcomings. The most serious of these is an unequal coverage of north Indian sources and those belonging to south India, Bengal, etc. The latter sources were examined mostly in translations, if available. The 'North Indian accent' of the book does not mean that the author is ignorant of the specific features of other parts of India or underestimates the value of Bengali or Tamil thought and culture. It would have been better to undertake a study with strictly delimited geographical, linguistic, and ethnic boundaries but regional studies of medieval India have not reached the necessary level, especially in the sphere relevant to the present study. Another shortcoming that the author fully admits is the use of printed sources only, not manuscripts. This may be natural for a scholar separated from the object of study not only by a long period but by great distance also.

The list of articles and books consulted by the author will require a large space. But it would be unjust not to mention some names to which the author has referred in the book more than once. Several works by Soviet/Russian Indologists[17] other than those mentioned above have been consulted. In the Russian studies of medieval India, researches on socio-economic problems are more numerous than on the history of ideas. Among the latter there are two classical works of Soviet Indology, *Essays on the Social Relations and Political System of the Mughal Empire at the Time of Akbar* (1556–1605) by Antonova (published in 1952) and *Popular Movements in India, Seventeenth to Eighteenth Centuries* by the late Reisner (published in 1961). These books contain an extended analysis of the communal relations during the Mughal period, of the ideology behind Akbar's reforms and his *Din-i illahi*, of *bhakti* and Sufism, and of anti-Mughal movements in Maharashtra and Punjab. The two books draw on a vast mass of source material, though neither of these authors had an opportunity to work in India at that time. Some of their conclusions were later disproved by scholars who had access to new sources. Nevertheless, quite a number of their ideas were corroborated by suitable documentary proofs, and this testifies to the knowledge and insight of these scholars.

It is noteworthy that in Russian Indology even those scholars who traditionally busied themselves exclusively with socio-economic studies began taking a greater interest in the history of ideas in medieval India. This can be said, for instance, of the late Clara Ashrafyan, known for her books *Feudalism in India, Medieval Indian City, Delhi, History and Culture*, etc. It is even more so with the late Professor Pavlov, whose work *Historical Premises for the Development of Capitalism in India* is also known to the Indian reader. As a co-author of the work *Theoretical Problems of World Historical Process,* he contributed a complex study of pre-industrial Asian society, where great attention was paid to the ideas of statehood, religious reform movements, and enlightenment and development of the individual in Asian societies, including India. The work by Polonskaya on the history of Muslim thought is also of great significance. She was the first to bring the thoughts of Waliullah to the Soviet reader and to make the important statement that many trends in the history of ideas in the nineteenth and early twentieth centuries have their premises and foundations in later medieval India.[18] The present writer found it necessary to cite some works by Russian colleagues to familiarize the reader with their views and to help them understand the ideas of the Soviet/Russian school of medieval studies.

It would be impossible to cite all the Indian works that the author has referred to. Indian scholars have done a lot in the field of medieval history of India in general and the history of ideas in particular. There are a number of important studies on the different phenomena and developments in the history of ideas of medieval India and on outstanding thinkers, poets, and saints. However, there has been a certain 'division of labour' between historians and specialists of medieval literature and philosophy. Historians mostly occupy themselves with problems of socio-economic and political life, while philosophers and philologists are busy with literature, culture, and religious tendencies. The same problem exists in the Russian school of Indian studies. However, at present there is a welcome trend towards research into medieval Indian society on an interdisciplinary basis, though in most cases this pertains not to history, but to culture and anthropology studies. A true picture of medieval Indian society can emerge only by the joint efforts of scholars belonging to different fields of knowledge.

Yet the present work would not have been possible without a deep study of the articles and books by a number of Indian scholars of different generations and their viewpoints. Among those whose works were consulted by the author, noteworthy are Kh. A. Nizami, S.A.A. Rizvi, Savitri Chandra Shobha, Krishna Sharma, A.R. Kulkarni, Muzaffar Alam, T. Joshi, J.S. Grewal, J. Correa-Affonso, Harbans Mukhia, D.N. Jha, Irfan Habib, R.S. Sharma, M.G.S. Narayanan, and Kesavan Velluthat, to name just a few. Some of them are known to the author through their work only, others are known personally. To the latter's most friendly cooperation, thought-provoking discussions and generous assistance, and to the assistance of many other scholars and librarians in Delhi, Vadodara, Mumbai, and Pune, the author expresses her most sincere gratitude.

And now a special word to my Indian readers. This book has originally been written for the Russian public, so the author sometimes had to explain in full what is common knowledge in India. Some of the author's views may seem unusual to an Indian reader since the book represents a different historical school. But Indian history is such a vast field that many historical traditions and schools can enrich each other.

Since this book on India has been written by an outsider, an altogether different perception has been brought to bear upon Indian history. Filling this gap is the sincere emotion of friendship and sympathy that the author feels towards India and its people. This book may be considered a small token of friendship and gratitude to the Indian people whose kindness and hospitality has opened the heart of India to the writer. The writer belongs to a country where a friendly attitude towards India is not just a matter of high policy, but a deep-rooted element of the common culture. The author has been brought up in this sympathetic atmosphere, which is the source of her inspiration for working on Indian history and culture.

'Why should a stranger research Indian history?'—someone may ask. The great legacy of Indian thought belongs not only to Indians, but to the whole world. Indian history and culture are valuable in themselves and as a part of world civilization. This book is an attempt to study these two aspects by a scholar from the country which lies in both Europe and Asia. To what extent this effort is successful, I leave the reader to judge.

1 A. Gurevich, *Categories of Medieval Culture*, Moscow, 1984, p. 8 (Russian).

2 J. Larus, *Culture and Political Military Behaviour. The Hindus in Pre-Modern India*, Calcutta, 1979, pp. 9–10.

3 S.N. Eisenstadt and Harriet Hartman. 'Cultural Traditions, Conceptions of Sovereignty and State Formations in India and Europe. A Comparative View', A.W. Van der Hoek, D.H.A. Kolff, M.S. Oort (eds) *Ritual, State and History in South Asia. Essays in Honour of J.C. Heesterman*, London-New York-Köln, 1992, p. 496; R.S. Sharma 'The Feudal Mind' in D.N. Jha (ed.), *The Feudal Order*, Delhi, 2000, p. 467.

4 Discussed in more details in Ronald Inden, *Imagining India*. Cambridge MA-Oxford UK, 1992, pp. 39–47.

5 For such an attitude towards the legacy of the Indian saints see: Kh. A. Nizami, 'Contribution of Mystics to Amity and Harmony in Indian Society', in S. Settar and P.K.V. Kaimal, (eds), *We Lived Together*, Delhi, 1999, p. 148–155. For a more balanced and objective estimate see: Muzaffar Alam, 'Indo-Islamic Interaction in Medieval North India', *Itinerario*, Vol. XIII, 1989, pp. 41–47.

6 This was demonstrated, for example, by a frequent motif in the

bhakti hagiography: a saint meets a Muslim king (mostly Akbar) and fully triumphs over him, making him, as it has been recorded in the case of Dadu Dayal, a follower of *ahimsa*. See: W.M.Callewaert (ed. and tr.), *A Hindi Biography of Dadu Dayal*, Delhi, 1988, p. 54 (English), 103 (Hindi).

7 Satish Chandra, 'Reassessing Aurangzeb', *Historiography, Religion and State in Medieval India*, Delhi, 1996, pp. 155–8.

8 'Madhyakalin dharmik sansar katta nahi tha – Habib' *Amar Ujala*, 17 September 2002.

9 See for instance: R. Pande, 'The Social Context of Bhakti Movement. A Study in Kabir', PIHC, 1986, pp. 230–2; C.Z. Ashrafyan *Medieval City of India, XIIIth to mid XVIIIth Centuries*, Moscow, 1983, p. 141 (Russian).

10 Among the publications that record these discussions, quite a number of works can be mentioned, both individual and collective. For the examples of the latter, see: T. J. Byres and Harbans Mukhia (eds), *Feudalism and Non-European Societies*, London, 1985; S. Bhattacharya and Romila Thapar (eds), *Situating Indian History for Sarvepalli Gopal*, Delhi, 1986; Hermann Kulke (ed.), *The State in India 1000-1700*, Delhi, 1997; D.N. Jha (ed.), *The Feudal Order*, Delhi, 2000; and so on. For the Russian discussions, see: S.D. Skazkin et al. (eds), *On the Genesis of Capitalism in the Countries of the Orient*. Moscow, 1962 (Russian); G.F. Kim and C.Z. Ashrafyan (eds), *Classes and Estates in the Pre-Capitalist Societies of Asia*. Moscow, 1986 (Russian).

11 Irfan Habib, 'Classifying Pre-Colonial India', in Byres and Mukhia (eds). *Feudalism and Non-European Societies*. p. 49.

12 For the most valuable Russian translations and research works on *Bhakti* see: A.P. Barannikov, *Ramayana or Ramacharitamanasa. The Ocean of Rama's Deeds. A Russian Translation in Verse.* Moscow, 1948; E.V. Payevskaya *Development of Bengali Literature, 13th to 19th Century.* Moscow, 1979; N.M. Sazanova, *'The Ocean of Poetry' by Surdas.* Moscow, 1973; Yu. V. Tsvetkov, *Surdas and His Poetry*, Moscow, 1979; Yu. V. Tsetkov *Tulsidas*, Moscow, 1987; S.D. Serebryany, *Vidyapati*, Moscow, 1980; N.B. Gafurova, *Kabir and his Legacy*, Moscow, 1976; N.B. Gafurova (tr.), *Kabir-Granthavali*, Moscow, 1992; G. Aliyev and G. Plisetsky, (trs), *Faizi's Nal-o Daman*, Moscow, 1987; L Penkovsky (tr.), *Bedil's Modan-o Komdeh*, Moscow, 1959; A.A. Suvorova, *The Indian Love Poem (Mathnavi)*, Moscow, 1993.

13 N.M. Sazanova (tr.), 'There is No Life Without Krishna', Moscow,

1993; G. V. Strelkova (tr.), 'Soul is My Measure, Tongue is My Scissors'; 'Namdev's Hymns from the Adi Granth', N. M. Sazanova (tr.), 'Where Beloved Abodes. Select Hymns by Mira Bai', and I. P. Glushkova. (tr.), 'Take God Free! Tukaram's Poetic Autobiography' all in I.D. Serebryakov and E.Yu. Vanina (eds), *Voices from Medieval India*, Moscow, 2002 (Russian).

14 I.P. Glushkova, *Indian Pilgrimage: The Metaphor of Motion and the Motion of Metaphor*, Moscow, 2000 (Russian); A.A. Suvorova, *Muslim Saints of South Asia*, Moscow, 1999 (Russian).

15 Among the successful attempts, an article by Ye. Medvedev 'Medieval Literature as a Source for the History of Socio-Economic Relations in the Feudal India', *The Historiography of the Orient*, Moscow, 1969 (Russian); and a book by Savitri Chandra Shobha, *Solajvin Shatabdi ke Uttarardh main Samaj aur Sanskriti*, Delhi, 1986 (Hindi).

16 Kate Teltsher, *India Inscribed. European and British Writing on India 1600-1800*, Delhi, Oxford University Press, 1995.

17 To avoid misunderstanding it has to be noted here that in the USSR/Russia, words like 'Indology', 'Indologist' do not pertain to a specific period in the history of Indian studies (i.e., late eighteenth early twentieth century Orientalism, closely connected with colonial ideology) but is applied in a very neutral sense to any person professionally engaged in Indian studies.

18 For more details of medieval India studies in USSR/Russia, see by the present author: 'Russian Studies in Medieval Indian History and Society: An Insider's View', *Medieval History Journal*, Vol. 2, No. 2, 1999, pp. 361–86.

1

The State, The Ruler, and The Ruled

No element of a social structure can be a better example of the interaction of different factors of economy, polity, social relations, and culture than the state. The forms and ways of such interaction are determined by the character of a given civilization and the level of its development. One can study the state from various angles: as an administrative/political structure, as an important factor influencing economic, social, and cultural life, and as a mechanism for interaction of different social groups and classes. It is mainly from these angles that most scholars in India, the former USSR, and elsewhere analyse the state in medieval India.[1] But it is as important, and interesting too, to study the state as a complex of ideas, theories, and doctrines, which existed in India during the middle ages, and this will be the main subject of this chapter.

Our study is centred around the India of the sixteenth to eighteenth centuries. But to analyse ideas about the state, peculiar to that period, we should briefly refer to the past traditions and premises on which these ideas were based.

A BIT OF PREHISTORY

The Indians' views of the state were being formed and developed during the whole of the middle ages under the influence of two great and powerful cultural traditions, which can, at the risk of generalizing, be defined as 'Hindu' and 'Muslim'. Each of them consisted of a variety of schools, views and traditions.

The 'Hindu' tradition was based on various schools and theories worked out by ancient and early medieval treatises on *rajniti*—the science of statehood and polity. The principles and methods, followed by these treatises, among which Kautilya's *Arthasastra* is the most celebrated one, gradually turned into a canonic tradition, to which even modern authors considered it necessary to appeal. But the principles followed by the ancient treatises were flexible and the terminology sometimes unclear,[2] so that later authors were able to interpret the ancient legacy in the various ways required by their own time and reality.

A study of the ancient and early medieval political schools of the 'Hindu' tradition is outside the scope of our research. Nevertheless, here we mention some features that played an important role during later periods.

Since earliest times, the state was seen by the Indian experts on *rajniti* as a complex organism, a system that included seven elements like the ruler (*raja* or *svamin*), minister(s) (*amatya*), army (*danda* or *sena*), land or country (*rashtra*), fortresses (*durga*), treasury (*kosha*), and an ally or vassal (*mitra*).[3] Some of these notions, like *rashtra,* were polysemantic: *rashtra* would mean not only land, but people, for, as Sukraniti put it, 'the King will attain no glory without the people inhabiting the land'.[4]

The ruler was the principal element, the core of the system. During the whole of the ancient and medieval times, Indians were sure that the qualities of the king determined the qualities of the state and the way of life of the subjects, their vices and virtues. Sometimes medieval authors, like Somadeva in the great Kashmiri epic *Katha-Saritsagara,* would state that the king was responsible for the misdeeds of the subjects, since he was ignorant in the politics and science of *rajniti* and knew nothing about state management.[5]

Ancient and early medieval treatises and other texts had mentioned more than once that royal power had a divine character and the king himself fulfilled ritual functions. It was to this very idea that the *abhisheka* or enthronement ceremony was fully devoted with all its rituals and sacrifices.[6] But the necessity of royal power was explained by the very mundane reason of having to keep law and order in society. Otherwise, the Indian sages were confident, society would be gripped by violence and chaos. To define such a calamity, Indian authors used the notion *matsya nyaya* or the fishes' justice, meaning that without royal power people would kill and eat the weak and unprotected among themselves like fish.

Such an attitude is ancient and occurs in the Ramayana and the Mahabharata. It was an important idea in medieval times as well. For instance, Somadeva's hero Prince Mrigankadatta visits a village of the Bhils (the forest tribes) and, in a conversation with his friends, notes that though they live in the forest, they have a king of their own. The assumption was that royalty was created by God to prevent people from eating the weak, like fishes do.[7] Says Sukra: 'Without a wise ruler people cannot live, just as a ship cannot move without a pilot'.[8]

It is important to note here that divine character was attributed to the institution of royal power, not to the royal person, who could be addressed as *deva*, compared to gods in panegyrics, or viewed as God's viceroy, but not worshipped as a deity, unlike the Chinese emperor. According to the Indian tradition, the king might possess various qualities, both good and bad, and it is on these qualities that the subjects' loyalty, the fate of the state, and the king's prospects in 'future births' depended. That is why literature and treatises abound in estimates and categories that describe a good or a bad king. To quote Sukra once more, 'The king, victorious over his enemies, taking care of his subjects, fulfilling all rites, generous, charitable, brave, unselfish, acquires liberation after death. The king devoid of these qualities, vicious, cruel, arrogant, attached to violence, lying, debauching, foolish—will enter hell after death'.[9] These definitions are, no doubt, borrowed from earlier authorities, but apart from them Sukra suggests his own concept of *caura-raja,* the 'robber king'. He is a tyrant who not only tortures his subjects, but neglects his duties, fails to maintain law in his country, and does nothing to enrich his treasury.[10]

In the Indian literature of ancient and medieval times, the ruler was a brave and generous king like Rama, Yuddhishthira, and Vikramaditya. These images encompassed all the ideals of the just ruler that were prevalent in that period. Yet, there was a possibility of the king being a tyrant. Some authors even considered it lawful for the subjects to revolt against a tyrannical ruler in the same way that it is 'lawful' to leave a wrecked ship in the sea.[11] The final part of the famous *Mricchakatica* is an interesting example.

What was then the foundation of relations between the ruler and the ruled? It was an exchange of duties or services, by which the king had to protect his people, while the latter had to obey the king and pay him taxes and levies, defined in some treatises as the king's salary (*vetana*).[12]

The king's functions were multifaceted, but protection of the subjects was considered most important. According to Chandesvara, a fourteenth century author from Mithila, 'A king is one who protects'.[13] The history of this idea can be traced to the most ancient times when kings were first and foremost military chiefs.[14] Later on the role acquired many other dimensions. According to medieval sources, the ruler had to protect his subjects not only from foreign invaders, but also from misgivings and from the corruption of local feudal chiefs and officials. 'Let the Raja banish a cruel minister who is hostile to the people'—says Sukra, while Krishnadevarayya, the famous Vijayanagara ruler of the sixteenth century, advised the king to get rid of officers who 'act like jackals, fail to persuade the poverty-stricken peasants from migrating and sell away their grain, cattle and timber'.[15]

Protection of the subjects also meant attempts to improve their economic well-being. Most treatises on the art of *rajniti* advise the king to supply peasants with grain in case of crop failure, protect merchants, organize searches for precious metals and stones, build new roads, bridges, lodges, and water-tanks, protect the travellers from robbers, etc. All this was supposed to enrich the treasury and uplift the people: all authors are convinced, that these two factors are closely connected with each other.[16] Moreover, it was royal duty to offer charity to the beggars, the widows, the orphans and extend patronage to the sages, artists, and poets. It was also considered worthy of a king to donate money and lands to the temples, orphanages, hospices, and seats of learning.[17]

Among all royal duties one was considered the most important and this was the king's protection of *dharma*. *Dharma*, as prescribed by sacred books, was a way of life for every caste and an individual as its member had to follow *svadharma*, i.e., one's own *dharma*. In a wider sense, *dharma* was understood as a general social law according to which every caste and every man possessed the whole sum of rights and duties as it corresponded to his caste status. Protection of *dharma* ensured maintenance of social stability based on each caste's and each man's unswerving obedience to the laws of his caste *dharma*. Otherwise, as it was understood by ancient and medieval authors, *matsya nyaya* would rule supreme to the total destruction of law and order and even *dharma*. When *dharma* is destroyed, the great Maithili poet Vidyapati says in his *Kirtilata*, 'noble men became base, virtuous people obeyed the vicious, servant attacked his master, law and justice disappeared, high-caste people married the low-caste'.[18] This description was, no doubt, borrowed from numerous ancient and medieval texts depicting the decline of *dharma* during Kaliyuga, the Iron Age of Hindu mythology. Gloomy pictures of this kind, according to some scholars, reflected the real social crises of medieval society,[19] but for the present study it is important to note that for the poets of the epoch and their audience, violation of *dharma* implied violence, injustice, and crime.

To protect *dharma,* the ruler, as many authors advised, had to use all methods including violence and punishment. Quoting, no doubt, classical authorities, Krishnadevarayya insisted that a 'wife's attachment to her husband, proper relations between men and women, ascetics subduing their *indriyas,* the lower caste showing deference to the higher, the servant looking carefully to the interests of his master are brought about by the fear of the king's punishment'.[20] All this was, of course, in contrast to appeals for kindness and forgiveness, so frequent in the same texts. The way out of this contradiction was found by equating the king to the father of the family who would be kind to his children and sometimes punish them for their own good. Such an idea was common to many cultures. 'The Raja has to support his subjects' virtues and forgive their misdeeds as a mother forgives her child'— says Sukra, but after several lines he points out: 'The Raja has to punish the subjects' misdeeds like Yama'.[21] Such a combination of kindness and punishment, carrot and stick, was the supposed ideal for the protection of *dharma*.

In historical literature, especially Western literature, there exists a stable idea that the Oriental monarch (or, as it is generally put, the Oriental despot) was the master of his subjects' life and property, that his whims were the only laws. This governed works of the

Western writers of the seventeenth and eighteenth centuries and was, as the Soviet scholar V. Nikiforov rightly observes, an outcome of their attitudes towards their own countries rather than the real practices of the Orient, for to develop a new attitude toward the state that was different from medieval dogmas, they needed the East as a negative model[22] and thus had, as Ronald Inden observed in a more recent study, 'to separate their Self from the Indian Other'.[23] Hence was born the stereotype of 'oriental despotism' which influenced European thought so profoundly that some scholars regard it as the very core of the Oriental state.

It is not the special task of this study to analyse all elements of this concept which has been a pivotal part of Orientalistic thought and colonial ideology.[24] Yet it is necessary to observe that its stability and pervasiveness should have been counterbalanced by a deeper study of the source material. This would have helped us to differentiate 'Oriental despotism' from its Occidental counterpart and to examine if the general and stereotyped notions of 'Oriental despotism' were relevant for all countries of the region and all periods of history. If it cannot be applied so generally, then it is proved to be just an element of ideology or a mere stereotype with no real meaning.

According to the Indian political tradition of the ancient and medieval periods, only undivided power was regarded as stable. Chandesvara was sure that to divide royal power, to share it with anybody meant the ruin of the kingdom.[25] Every Raja had to take advice and support from his close relatives, ministers, religious preceptors, and other members of the state council (*rajya sabha*).[26] But, while fully availing himself of their assistance and support, he was not required to share his power with them. Otherwise, there would always be a risk of becoming a puppet in their hands or even of losing power. Such cases were reported by many sources, and political treatises advised the *raja* to get rid of all those who might claim even a small part of his authority.[27]

There is a very interesting example from a later source. Ananda Ranga Pillai, an interpreter and trade agent to the Governor of Pondicherry from 1742 to 1756, reported in his diary the following episode. One day he asked his patron, Governor Dupleix, to brief him about the political system of Britain and the revolution there. Dupleix did so, of course, without much sympathy for the British.

His explanations made Ananda Ranga conclude that the king of
Britain was a weak ruler, had no 'semblance of power all of which
is exercised by the parliament'.[28] It was only natural that to an
Indian eye the very division of power between the king and some
other institution was a testimony to the weakness of the state, but
it is noteworthy that the Frenchman Dupleix found nothing strange
in such an arrangement, and this was about four decades prior to
the storm of the Bastille.

Does this mean that royal power knew no limits in medieval
India and that the only law was the *raja's* desire? Our answer will
be in the affirmative only if we overlook the most important
element of the law of *dharma*. The law of *dharma* was supposed
to govern not only society, but also the king, who was required
by the ethics and moral values of the time to be obedient to
dharma, to maintain it, but not to reinterpret or change it.[29]

The king had to obey *dharma* even if it was contrary to his
personal interest and feelings. Conflict between the *raja's* personal
emotions and royal *dharma* was not infrequent in medieval
literature. One brilliant example is *Uttara Ramacharita*, a seventh–
eighth century play by Bhavabhuti. The author succeeded in
adapting the story of Ramayana into a drama with tragic elements.
As the story goes, after Sita was rescued from her captivity by
Rama's heroic efforts, he learnt from a spy that his subjects were
critical of his conduct, for, according to tradition, the king had no
right to resume marital relations with a woman who had lived so
long in another man's house. Rama, for whom the voice of his
people was like the voice of *dharma*, sent Sita away to exile
though he had no doubt of her innocence. Bhavabhuti described
with great dramatic skill how Rama's brothers made vain efforts
to dissuade him, and when the spy begged him not to pay attention
to the prating of 'base wretches', Rama stopped him: 'Peace,' he
said, 'the people of my city and my country base wretches?'
Bhavabhuti created a tragic image of a man, whose heart was torn
between love and duty. His family denounced him for such a
cruel decision, even his mother refused to see him but the author
made his hero suffer profoundly: 'I'm treacherously handing Sita
to death as does a butcher his pet bird. I'm an untouchable
criminal'. He even made Rama, like the Shakespearean king
Claudius, see his evil deed staged by actors. Despite the holy

rishis' intervention, Sita was restored to her good name and to Rama only by the verdict of the people personifying the law of *dharma*. In the same play, Rama killed with his own hands a *sudra* who practised asceticism contrary to the laws of his caste. Rama, as the author put it, killed that man, though he was fully aware of the cruelty of this act.[30] Thus the king's conduct was regulated by the tradition and authority of *dharma* and by those who could read and comment upon sacred books.

This theme, of the king being a servant *of dharma*, was touched upon by other authors also but perhaps with less brilliance. Of course, real life offered examples testifying to other kinds of rulers. In many a literary source we find lamentations and complaints that the kings were governed by their own whims and not by *dharma*, that they pursued interests which were contrary to their subjects.[31]

If we put aside some distinctive Indian features, we may suppose that the very concept of 'divine law superior to the will of the king' has much in common with the opinion of medieval Europeans. They were confident that the whole world was ruled by the 'natural law' ordained by God, and the king had no right to alter anything in this divinely ordained order of things. Laws which were passed on from antiquity were considered valid and truthful. The European monarch could not enact a new law, he could only 'recall' or 'discover' ancient laws. Thus in *Erec and Enide*, a twelfth century chivalrous romance by Chretien de Troyes, the celebrated poet and knight, King Arthur says: 'The King has to maintain the law. Let all customs and values be preserved that were observed by our forefathers. You would not approve if I try to impose on you laws alien to our fathers.'[32] Eike Von Repgow, the famous author of the *Saxon Mirror (Sachsen-spiegel)*, the thirteenth century German law-book, found it necessary to mention in the preface of his book that 'the Law expounded hereby, was not invented by me, but has come since ancient times from our forefathers.'[33] For him the antiquity of law and tradition was as sacred as for his Indian counterpart. Those who consider such an attitude to the authorities of the past the exclusive domain of the medieval Indian mind, should know that this very *Saxon Mirror* was used as a law-book up to the eighteenth century in different parts of Germany. Such an attitude seems to be a feature common to all feudal societies, and as we have suggested before, it is in this sphere of values that one may find many more general traces of feudalism, than in forms of land property.

Among these general features, peculiar to the feudal mentality, was the idea of a treaty or, of an 'exchange of services' between the ruler and the ruled. In India as in Europe, the king's protection of his people and the latter's loyalty to the king were dictated by the holy books and traditions. 'Loyalty on both sides was a loyalty to the Law'—this observation made by Dr A. Gurevich is based on Western material and fits medieval India as well.[34]

However, certain differences in interpretation did exist, because this general law was differently understood in India and Europe. Christianity was oblivious of social inequality but, at the same time, made people equal in the eyes of God. A noble knight and a base serf had to pass through the same stages and rituals of baptism, marriage rites, confession, etc. Church rituals and festivals, sacred texts and religious dogmas were the same for all. The order of things sanctified by Christianity, especially in the Catholic countries, had two distinct spheres: secular and ecclesiastical. The first was maintained by the king, the second by the well-organized Church. The two institutions were torn by conflicts, but still contributed to each other's stability. 'God has given two swords to the Terrestrial Kingdom for the protection of Christianity', said the *Saxon Mirror,* 'The spiritual sword behoves the Pope, the secular behoves the King. Who is alienated from the Pope and cannot be subdued by the clerical court of justice, should be subdued by the King's secular court of justice ... Likewise the ecclesiastical authority must assist secular justice.'[35]

In India the situation was different. Each caste not only had its special profession, but also its laws, traditions, rites, sometimes deities and temples. In Europe, sacred texts of Christianity were not accessible to all only because of mass illiteracy; in India only some people were authorized by their caste status to read the sacred books, while others could lose their life for reading them.[36] Under these conditions it was impossible to enact—or—'find' a code of laws that all members of society could follow. Also, ancient and early medieval treatises on law and state policy were not real codes of polity and law, but tracts expounding views of some schools and individuals.[37]

Unlike Europe, no clerical organization that could exercise control over the king and the subjects fulfilling their respective duties existed in India. Of course, the *raja* had to consider the opinion of the brahmans, who acted not only as religious preceptors and experts in the sacred laws, but very often as ministers. But in many cases they depended on the *raja* much more than he depended on them. Moreover, the main principles worked out by the traditional authorities were flexible and thus open to varied interpretations, so the brahmans would easily 'find' or 'recall' a divine ordinance suited to a given situation. At the same time, the caste system being pivotal to society, it did not allow the king and his brahmans to interfere too much in the inner life of the communities if no violation of the general balance or individual *dharma* occurred. An interesting example is the *Sukraniti,* where the author, basing himself on the classical authorities, illustrates this principle: 'For instance—in the South high-caste men marry their cousins, in Madhyadesha high-castes work or practise some craft; all of them eat fish. In the country of Khas (North of Garhwal—author) men marry their brothers' widows. No repentance or punishment should follow this, since it has been a custom through the ages.' All these practices are forbidden by the general Hindu tradition, but, as the writer insists, the above-mentioned castes consider it their custom and the royal power does not interfere, for 'the raja should protect the *dharma* of the kins, castes, *srenis* (guilds) and communities. If he does the contrary, his subjects become angry.'[38]

In medieval Europe too, the power of local traditions was strong.[39] But in any Catholic country such violation of the marriage regulations or eating traditions would have definitely been punished by the Church or the king. In India such breaches of tradition were punishable, only if they were committed by an individual. Then people of his caste were the first to punish him. If a caste, especially a rich and influential one, changed its behaviour and adopted the higher castes' lifestyle, the state would either be indifferent or indeed supportive and the caste itself would 'recall' a legend to provide a divine or historical sanction for changing its *dharma.*[40] As a rule the king's judges and he as a last and higher authority would hear a limited number of cases dealing primarily with state crimes and dangerous felonies like murder. In many cases the state worked as an arbiter in caste disputes. But in most cases and situations the right to execute justice belonged to the caste or community.

In this situation royal power could have but a nominal control over the economic and social life of the society: as a rule, this control existed only on taxes and rent. Craftsmen, for instance, paid taxes to the state, which had some control over this taxation, but neither the king nor the state was really interested in knowing how they manufactured their goods, or how they sold them. Of course, forgery and manufacture of counterfeit products were punishable by the state; sometimes different goods would become the state monopoly, but we know of no Indian ruler issuing an order to 'change the shuttles of the weaving looms', like the Chinese Emperor did.[41] It is noteworthy that prior to the so-called 'Muslim period' and even during it, trade guilds and corporations of cities had considerable autonomy in many important spheres; even more autonomy was enjoyed by the rural communities.[42]

This does not mean, of course, that the order of things was maintained on its own: the main duty of the ruler was to protect and strengthen it by fair means or foul. But the state power did not penetrate to the grass roots. The life of an individual was more influenced and governed by his community rather than by the state or the *raja*. It is interesting to note that in Yuan Chwang's view state principles in India were 'generous' and simple, there was no registration of the families, no forced labour, taxes were not very burdensome and every individual was required to offer only very moderate service to the state.[43] That this picture is too rosy and ideal can be judged from the Indian literary sources of that period, but by this testimony from a Chinese traveller we can gauge how very different the perceptions regarding the state were in both countries.

One can be justified in suggesting that the state built on such principles as mentioned above was quite weak and unstable, and its administrative machinery rather vague and unclear. Analysing the sources of India's ancient and early medieval political traditions, many researchers come to the rightful conclusion that, contrary to the earlier interpretations by Orientalist and Indian nationalist scholars, the state depicted in these sources was neither 'centralized' nor 'bureaucratic'.[44] Strict central power and even 'bureaucracy' could have no place in a state where most spheres of human life depended not on the state, but on caste, community, and kin. The administrative system and territorial division of such a state was amorphous and unclear. Periods of consolidation quickly gave way to long periods of anarchy and disintegration: every small feudal chief, every head of community or caste was much more powerful on his territory than the *raja* at the centre. Kautilya reflected an age-old dream of different regions and lands of the country being ruled by *balisa swami*—foolish lords.[45] But in reality these small rulers were not foolish and used all means in their power to become independent of the central power. To the thinkers of the period, the state territory was like a system of concentric circles: the greater the distance from the capital, the less the influence of royal authority. Many vassal rulers, to say nothing of the subordinate princes, were only formally connected with the central power and their relations with it were limited only to paying tribute and offering their armies for the king's military expeditions. At a greater distance from the centre were 'barbarous' tribes who were outside the binding laws of the caste system; they had to be subjugated and made obedient vassals. Even then they were usually allowed to live according to their own customs. In the eyes of the general Hindu public, they were just another caste with its own rules and *dharma*.

It was with the foundation of the Delhi sultanate that Muslim statehood in India began to develop. It required a political theory of its own which would be based on Islamic principles. At the same time, this theory would have to take into consideration that Muslim rulers had, in India, non-Muslims as a majority of their subjects.

Though such a theory was established, its variance with traditional political schools of Islam deserves a special study. As Alauddin Khilji stated in his ascension *firman*, 'God...made him (the king) the lord of a lasting world...for the exaltation of the faith of Muhammad...to sit on the throne to enforce a common law that is valid forever.'[46] In *Fatawah-i Jahandari*, a tract written by the famous fourteenth century historian Barani, this theory was expounded in an even more elaborate form: 'On the ground that he (the king) protects and promotes the Muslim religion the sins due to his human nature are erased from the record of his life.

The test of the king's faith is that he keeps the inhabitants of his kingdom on the path of Shariat.'[47]

Strange as it may seem at first, these principles have some very important similarities with the Hindu ideas of royal duty. For both the Hindu and Muslim monarchs, their main task was to protect and maintain the divinely ordained order of things. It was not the dogmatic purity and the theological heights of a particular religion that they had to protect (for that brahmans and *ulema* existed) but the social order and values prescribed by it. Both had no rights to alter anything in this order. The whole of Barani's book warns against the introduction of 'novelties', *bidat*, and recommends that the king should withstand them by all means, including violence.[48]

A Muslim king could interfere in his subjects' lives if protection of Islam required it. Many sources testify that some forms of art and craft were prohibited on these grounds (like painting of living creatures) and some other social practices were also regulated by Islamic law.[49] But if everything was in accordance with Shariat, any interference was denounced as an 'innovation'. As far as the non-Muslim subjects were concerned, they were subdued and forced to pay *jizya*. If obedient, they would be allowed to live as they wanted under the protection of the king.[50] Yet Barani, like some other bigoted authors, insisted on 'humiliation of the unbelievers', and even if some Muslim rulers did not molest Hindus for their faith, they prevented them from building new temples and observing traditional festivals.[51]

A Hindu king did not consider promotion of his faith as a duty since nobody could be converted to Hinduism. In medieval Hindu principalities where Muslims lived, the latter were considered as *mlecchas* or barbarians, as people having their own *dharma* but situated outside traditional hierarchy. Islam, in its turn, favoured conversions; however, as historical evidence shows, even the militant Turkish sultans were wise enough not to boost mass and systematic conversion of their newly conquered subjects and a major part of converted Hindus became Muslims not at sword point, but due to other reasons.[52] Despite this, during the whole of the medieval period, Muslims were a minority, and to rule India they had to establish a stronger and more effective administration. But this was hardly possible without utilizing, on a large scale, all traditional institutes, political ideas, and perceptions of society, which were prevalent in ancient and early medieval India. Hence Barani advocated strict hierarchy of hereditary professional groups, though the caste system had no tradition in Islam.[53]

These similarities between 'Hindu' and 'Muslim' concepts of the state and royal duties existed despite many differences in religious practices and cultural backgrounds. In our view, these similarities illustrate some important common laws and tendencies of socio-political development under feudalism, and the fact that nearly similar attitudes prevailed in Europe is also a testimony to this. The pivotal principle on which kingship in the feudal society was based was that the rulers' main duty was to maintain and preserve the social order and moral values prescribed by the holy books of a particular religion. The king was to be the most obedient servant of this sacred order and had no right to alter anything in it. This holy tradition, sanctified by religion, proved to be the 'real despot' and it is only in this sense that we may use the term 'despotism' for both East and West. Therefore, in most cases, the subjects, in obeying the king's wishes, were actually abiding by the sacred law.

Another important feature was common to the 'Hindu', 'Muslim', and 'European' perceptions of the state. The medieval state in this stage of development had much less influence on the everyday life of the people, than did the community, caste, guild, and social group. In the portrayal of the residents of Gokul by Surdas, it is plain that they were practically untouched by any influence of the state though they lived near the capital city of Mathura. The presence of the king in the capital did not affect them except for the evildoers sent by the tyrant Kansa to kill the baby Krishna. 'Dilli dur, dur'—said the Indian peasants for whom their own headman or feudal lord was the *sarkar* rather than the ruler at Delhi. The Russian proverb 'God is high, czar is far' probably reflects a similar situation.

Last, but not least, there is another feature that seems to be common to different feudal civilizations. It is associated with religion but ignores to an extent doctrinal differences between various religions. In a feudal set-up, be it 'Western', 'Muslim', or 'Hindu', there existed within the society a certain privileged religious community or, to be more precise, a socio-religious elite. One could belong to it by birth or in the case of religions other than

Hinduism, by embracing the 'true' faith. As a member of the privileged group which shared its religious beliefs with the king, a person could claim superiority over the subjugated groups. The latter, even if they were rich and socially superior, could at best expect tolerance and non-interference.

In fact, any Christian ruler in Europe was regarded first and foremost as the king and defender of those who professed the 'right' type of Christianity. Others, be they Jews, Muslims (as in Spain), non-Catholics (like the residents of Poland, Austro-Hungary who professed Orthodox Christianity, or Protestants), could hope only for tolerance as a reward for loyalty and submission. In India, a Delhi sultan or a Mughal emperor was considered the king and protector of Muslims, of those who professed the 'true' religion even if he had been liberal to the *kafirs*. His policies had to correspond to the dogmas and traditions of this religion. Likewise a Hindu *raja* was, in most cases, tolerant of his Muslim subjects but he was first and foremost the king and protector of the Hindu *dharma* and all those who observed it.

This similarity of the basic features of the 'Hindu' and the 'Muslim' traditions is important to understand the so-called 'Muslim domination' over India, which otherwise would not have been able to continue for several centuries. Of course, the Hindu princes from time to time renewed their struggle against the *mlecchas*. Even as foes, the invading Muslim kings were treated by the Hindu inscriptions and bardic poems on equal terms with the Hindu rulers. And after the invasion, if a Muslim king was tolerant and wise, he could be easily incorporated into the traditional Hindu political world and even be glorified in the Sanskrit panegyrics.[54] The local rulers, Hindu as well as Muslim, could govern their territories with full freedom while offering their loyalties and armed forces to him. At the same time the administration at the centre had to be flexible enough to keep a balance between the interests of the vassal rulers and the *jagirdars*, between 'promotion of the true religion' and a policy of tolerance for the Hindu majority. 'Muslim rule' was stable and strong, but the states and big empires were as amorphous and loose as the pre-Muslim empires: these two factors were interdependent. The foundation of the Delhi Sultanate was a strong attempt at centralization, but its history was quite short and its disintegration was as inevitable as it was for other states in India and elsewhere at this stage of feudalism.

THE AGE OF AKBAR

In 1556, Akbar, the third ruler of Babur's dynasty ascended the Mughal throne. Akbar began his rule at the young age of 13. He inherited a kingdom comprising only the Agra-Delhi region, Punjab and half-independent Kabul along with some other territories. This kingdom was torn apart by internal feuds and riots and was surrounded by hostile forces. During nearly the half-century of his rule Akbar succeeded, through work, wars and intrigues in doing away with the courtiers who were trying to accumulate power while he was young, and in acquiring the rich territories of Bengal, Gujarat, Kashmir, and Central India. He made militant Rajput princes his allies and relatives, and ruined militarily the mighty power in the Deccan—Ahmadnagar. He managed not only to increase his domain manifold, but also to strengthen his administrative power by great reforms. The historical memory of the Indian people knows this period as 'Akbar *ka zamana*' or the 'Age of Akbar'. While historians dispute and debate about the significance of his reforms, popular culture has defined him as a wise administrator and general, a patron of trade, industries and fine arts with a shining galaxy of poets, scholars, musicians and artists around him. But most significant in the estimate of later generations was Akbar's religious policy based on peace and equality between Muslims and non-Muslims.

Much has already been written on Akbar, his epoch and his reforms. This study has no ambitions of discussing all those aspects of Akbar's policies. Our main object will be to identify some new perceptions of the state that influenced these reforms.

The development of a theory of the state, an important part of Akbar's reforms, is closely associated with the name of Abu-1Fazl Allami, Akbar's *vazir* and friend and one of the most important thinkers of sixteenth-century India. Along with his father Shaikh Mubarak and brother, the talented poet Faizi, he was among the closest associates of Akbar. He was not only one of the main executors of his policy but, in many cases, the brain behind its theoretical formulation. Being a man of education, he had a deep knowledge of different fields of learning in the Muslim and Hindu traditions. His court position and the faith that the emperor reposed in him gave him access to information about the developments in the country and abroad.

Abu-l Fazl wrote no special treatise on state and polity, but his views can be traced from his writings like *Ain-i Akbari, Akbar-nama* and his letters. They are derived in some ways from the views of his Muslim and Hindu predecessors but at the same time contain many new ideas.

From his predecessors Abu-l Fazl borrowed the idea of the divine nature of royal power, for 'royalty is a light emanating from God and a ray from the sun.'[55] This divine light blesses fully not every royal person, but only a 'true' king, and Abu-1 Fazl made a strict distinction between this 'true' king and a 'selfish' ruler (the latter had much in common with the 'robber king' of the *Sukraniti*). The 'true' king, according to Abu-1 Fazl, would not attach himself to the formal insignia of royal power, to lust and pomp, 'for his object is to remove oppression and to provide for everything that is good. Security, health, chastity, justice, polite manners, faithfulness, truth, greater sincerity, etc. are the result.' The 'selfish' king would govern only for the sake of power and vanity, hence 'insecurity, unsettledness, strife, oppression, faithlessness, robbery'[56] would follow.

At first glance, there is no difference between the views of Abu-1 Fazl and the thinkers before him. Moreover, Abu-1 Fazl put even more emphasis on the divinity of royal power and attached to royalty and the king's person some mystical features that were absent in the perception of his predecessors. But Abu-1 Fazl's approach was quite rational and sceptical and if we analyse the thinker's arguments fully, this contradiction can be easily understood.

Contrary to both 'Hindu' and 'Muslim' political thought, the 'true' king of Abu-1 Fazl had to rule according to the requirements of universal good and reason and could, with these purposes in mind, make changes in age-old traditions. Abu-1 Fazl stressed that '(the divine light of royalty) is communicated by God to kings without the intermediate assistance of any one.'[57] He meant that the whole class of the keepers of sacred law, the *ulemas* and *mujtahids,* who for many centuries, like the brahmans before them, had guided the king would no longer necessarily interpret the holy law for him. Unlike his predecessors then, who had no right to introduce any changes into the order of things preserved by the experts in religious and holy law, Abu-l Fazl's 'true king' was allowed to judge for himself and introduce, if necessary, the changes, so feared by Barani.

In this connection some rules enacted by Akbar are notable. These are as significant as his financial and administrative reforms. These regulations prohibited child marriages, matrimonial alliances between close relatives like first cousins, forced marriages, and *sati*. Thus the state, perhaps for the first time, interfered in the sphere which was traditionally the undoubted prerogative of community, caste, kin and family. Muslim rulers before Akbar did prohibit some customs and social practices and introduced rules concerning dress, etc. But these regulations had as their main object 'promotion of Islam and humiliation of the *kafirs*'. Akbar's attempt to interfere in this traditionally independent sphere had a different intention: among the prohibited practices were both Hindu and Muslim customs, and these were prohibited because they were contradictory to common sense and social welfare.

Thus the core of Abu-l Fazl's concept of kingship was that the king should be guided by the principles of universal good and for this he could rise above the regulations of the holy law. This was, no doubt, a blow for the court *ulemas* and *mujtahids* who felt offended and displaced due to the loss of their prerogatives. No wonder that some of them openly accused Akbar of being a heretic and an apostate when he started implementing this scheme.[58]

After a great struggle, Akbar managed to banish from his court some *ulema* who were ardent opponents of his reforms. Others paid lip service to the emperor and remained in quiet dissent. This was helpful as Akbar still needed some support or at least neutrality of the Muslim clergy and high *ulema* to make his effort successful. Thus in the year 1579, the famous *Mahzar* appeared. It was a declaration signed by the court *ulema:* some did it of their own free will, some under pressure. According to this document, the 'true king' was above the *mujtahid* and the experts in the holy law were subordinate to the ruler of the state. Any decree issued by the king 'for the benefit of the nation' was binding on all subjects and, what was more important, this concerned religious matters also. All decrees of the *Sultan-i Adil* or the Just Ruler, had to obey the Quran, but this small reservation was removed by Quranic citations like 'Whosoever obeys the Amir, obeys Me; and Whosoever rebels against him, rebels against Me.'[59]

Thus Akbar's reforms also received a divine sanction. But what is of special interest in the *Mahzar* is the reflection of Abu-l Fazl's ideas which established the priority of worldly power over religious regulations and traditions. Of course, the intention was not to totally subjugate religious institutions and clergy to the state, as it happened in Russia during the reign of Peter the First, when clergymen became government officials. Abu-l Fazl suggested a sort of merger or union of worldly and religious power and Akbar tried to implement it practically. According to some scholars, Akbar's reforms were nothing but an attempt to establish theocracy by investing the king with spiritual power. K.A. Antonova, whose monograph on Akbar was the first work in Russian on the subject and still remains valid in many cases, is of the opinion that Akbar's theocratic aspirations were close to the *Mahdavi* idea of the 'just king'. Since many of Akbar's associates, like Shaikh Mubarak, were influenced by the *Mahdavi* ideas, Akbar utilized this concept of the 'just king' for the purposes of consolidation of his empire and power.[60]

However, the *Mahdavi* influences on Akbar should not be overemphasized. This is because influences of other schools of thought, Islamic and non-Islamic, were also significantly felt. Secondly, if the main purpose of the *Mahzar* was to sanctify Akbar's policies in the eyes of the Muslims, it would have been a bad choice to utilize *Mahdavi* ideas for that. In the eyes of orthodox Muslims, these ideas were heretical, and one has to bear in mind that the *Mahdavi* followers were persecuted in the early stage of Akbar's reign.[61]

Perhaps, the purpose of the *Mahzar* was not so much to sanctify Akbar's policies as to curb the power of the *ulema* who had leanings towards the orthodox Muslim elite. The core of Akbar's policies was somewhat different.

It has already been mentioned elsewhere that the main postulate of the political theory worked out by Abu-l Fazl was the idea of divine sanction for all the innovations made by the 'true king'. If that were the only guiding principle, the whole concept would have led only to an Islamic theocracy. But according to Abu-l Fazl and Akbar himself, this divine sanction was supposed to come not from Allah, but from the Absolute God who was common to all religions and was only worshipped under different names by different creeds. The religious and social aspects of Akbar's reforms will be discussed in the second chapter, but for the present study we must note that these reforms and Abu-l Fazl's political ideas cannot be assessed properly without this most significant principle, that the 'true king' was blessed by Absolute God, for whom there were no 'believers' or 'unbelievers'. As Akbar said in a letter to Abbas, the Shah of Iran, 'It has been our disposition from the beginning not to pay attention to the differences of religion and to regard all the tribes of Mankind as God's servants. It must be considered that Divine Mercy attaches itself to every form of creed.'[62] It can be concluded from this statement that Akbar regarded the king as the worldly and spiritual master of his subjects; as a protector and a supreme authority not only for Muslims, but all subjects, whatever their creed.

This was in complete opposition to a pivotal principle of Hindu, Muslim, as well as European political tradition, according to which the king was, first and foremost, the head and protector of a privileged community of his co-believers while all others could hope only for tolerance.

Akbar introduced reforms like the abolition of *jizya* (poll tax) from the non-Muslims which was economically burdensome and morally humiliating; a ban on forced conversions to any religion; the prohibition of temple destruction; a ban on cow slaughter etc. Moreover Hindu festivals began to be celebrated at the court. For all this Akbar incurred the wrath and condemnation of the orthodox Muslims, who openly accused him of heresy.[63] Akbar's religious reforms culminated in the *Din-i illahi* which is discussed below.

To sum up, the political theory on which Akbar's reforms were based had two new features: priority of worldly power over spiritual power, i.e. priority of the king's decisions which would aim at universal peace and well-being, over the regulations of the holy law. Second, the ruler was seen as a leader and protector not only of the privileged community of co-believers, but of all his subjects, whatever their creed. So his judgement was considered to be above religious differences and dogmas. These principles became pivotal in the concept of the social structure outlined by Abu-l Fazl.

The 'true king' was the centre of this system with *sulhe-kul* as his main purpose. He had to govern society which, according to Abu-l Fazl, was like an organism and consisted of four elements:

'Warriors who in the political body have the nature of fire. Their flames directed by understanding, consume the straw and rubbish of rebellion and strife but kindle also the lamp of rest in this world of disturbances. Artificers and merchants, who hold the place of air. From their labours and travels, God's gifts become universal, and the breeze of contentment nourishes the rose-tree of life. The learned, such as the philosopher, the physician, the arithmetician ..., the astronomer, who resemble water. From their pen and their wisdom a river rises in the drought of the world, and the garden of creation receives from their irrigating powers a particular freshness. Husbandmen and labourers, who may be compared to earth. By their exertions, the staple of life is brought to perfection, and strength and happiness flow from their work.'[64]

Dr Clara Ashrafyan considered this document to be a model of social hierarchy. She observed that despite the caste system, the second place was allotted to craftsmen and merchants, and this signifies the latter's elevation in society due to the development of trade and industry.[65] We have interpreted Abu-l Fazl's ideas differently. His model of social structure is not based on hierarchy at all. He constructed the scheme according to established ideas in the natural philosophy of that epoch. According to these ideas, each living body consisted of four equally significant elements: fire, air, water, and earth. Such an equation of the natural and social structures was common to medieval thinkers elsewhere. Abu-l Fazl might have numbered the elements in any order; so there was no hierarchical structure involved. The main stress was on the equal significance of the four elements, on the necessity of keeping them in harmony, since any imbalance would be harmful for the organism; similarly diseases were also supposed to be caused by imbalanced humours. Abu-l Fazl was not egalitarian; he never meant that a warrior was equal to a peasant or a scholar to a craftsman; he only suggested their equal significance for the state and its well-being.

'And in the same manner that the equilibrium of the animal constitution depends on an equal mixture of the elements, so also does the political constitution become well tempered by a proper division of ranks; and by means of the warmth of the ray of unanimity and concord, a multitude of people become fused into one body.'[66]

This observation by Abu-1 Fazl provides a good picture of his social ideas as consisting of two contradictory positions: different social groups are not equal, but for the well-being of the state they are equally important, and the force which can unite them is the State based on the principles of *sulhe-kul*.

It is against this background that one has to view both Abu-1 Fazl's ideas and Akbar's reforms, one must also take into consideration the unavoidable difference between ideas and real practice. It was only natural that the reforms meant that the state interfered in spheres of life which had hitherto been the domain of caste, kin, guild, and community. For this reason Akbar had to get rid of not only the 'intermediaries' between the king and God, but also the intermediaries between the king and the taxpaying population. Hence the attempt, though unsuccessful, to abolish the *jagir* system and to entrust tax collection not to the *jagirdars*, but to the centrally-appointed officials—*kururi*. Another important step in this direction was a change in the mode of tax and rent payment from kind to cash. The methods of land measurement and tax collection were to be determined not by the community or by the feudal lords, but by rules fixed by the government. For this a uniform system of weights and measures and uniform measuring instruments were introduced; statistical accounts of crops, fertility of land, corn prices, etc. were compiled. Accordingly, the country was divided into *subas*—provinces with a uniform system of administration. A system of ranks—*mansabs*—was introduced for all officials so that a uniform pattern of promotion could be established.[67]

A logical question that arises out of our study is: what kind of a state did Abu-1 Fazl suggest and Akbar put into practice? To find an answer, we have to remember the main feature of the state model (both Hindu and Muslim) before Akbar. At different junctures in their history, when vast empires were established and quickly disintegrated, both 'Hindu' and 'Muslim' political theories suggested that a state was an amorphous, unstable, loosely-knit body.

The history of many medieval societies in Europe is known to embrace three main stages: huge early feudal empires, then their disintegration; a long period of feudal anarchy and separatism of independent principalities, and their bloody rivalry; followed by the establishment of a strong centralized state. (This is only a general scheme, the historical reality was different in each particular country). On the first glance, India witnessed a similar process. After the disintegration of early feudal empires came a long period of feudal disunity which ended in the north by the establishment of the Delhi Sultanate and in the south by Vijayanagar and Bahmani kingdoms. But all these mighty states were not destined for long life and broke into smaller principalities which started to fight among themselves. Then started a new period of centralization with the establishment of the Mughal empire which, though much stronger than its predecessors, followed the same road to disintegration.

Can it be concluded that the establishment of the Delhi Sultanate and the Mughal empire was a process similar to the establishment of the centralized states in Europe? The answer would be in the affirmative if one views the centralized state only as an antonym of the disintegrated state. But by this formal criterion any early feudal empire can be called a centralized state, be it the empire of Carolus Magnus or the Golden Horde. If we look at the centralized state as an important stage in the development of the feudal state which precedes its last, absolutist form, the answer is not so easy.

It is well known that the centralized feudal states in different parts of the globe had many individual features and in each case the historical premises, ways and tempo of this process were different. In some cases aspirations for unity grew as a result of the development of the economy and market connections between different regions and principalities: feudal disunity, never-ending feuds and wars were hindrances to the growing market and developing trade. In other cases centripetal tendencies were stimulated by the growing feeling of ethnic and cultural unity or by some external threat, by the necessity to fight against foreign invaders, as it happened in Russia during the Mongol occupation.

Whatever the premises, forms and ways of this process might be, the establishment of centralized feudal states elsewhere was a result of the internal developments in a society. The atmosphere of feudal anarchy and disunity, the narrowing borders despite the possibility of a growing market were factors that made a strong, centralized state desirable. The strong and united state was seen by peasants as a protection from the oppressions of feudal lords (this was brilliantly portrayed by the Spanish playwright of the sixteenth century, Lope de Vega in his famous play *Sheep's Spring*),[68] by the townspeople as a guarantee of peace and stability required for successful trade; by the people of the arts and sciences as a patron; and by the feudal lords as a possibility to raise their status and power.

All these tendencies were too weak in the India of the sixteenth and the eighteenth centuries. Even in Europe it took a lot of time for a man from Burgundy and a man from Gascony, who spoke one language and worshipped one God to think of themselves as *Frenchmen.* Therefore, such unifying tendencies would almost have been an impossibility in medieval India which was a continent of different languages, cultures, religions, and traditions. Of course, it shared common values and traditions; literary works were translated from one language to another; religious shrines and centres of learning attracted scholars, students, and devotees from faraway regions and played a role similar to the Roman shrines and the famous universities of Padua, Paris, Leipzig, and Toledo. All these were the historical and cultural premises for the unity of modern India. But for the period under consideration these unifying forces were too weak to withstand centrifugal forces, and this helped the invaders' victory.

Invasion in itself was nothing unusual for any medieval society, and in no European state was the centralization process peaceful except, maybe, for Spain where the two kingdoms of Castille and Aragon were united after the marriage of their respective rulers, Queen Isabel and King Fernando. But in India, both the great empires—the Delhi Sultanate and the Mughal empire—owed their establishment to invasion, and the invaders themselves belonged originally to countries living through times of fragmentation.

Due to all these reasons, both the Delhi Sultanate and the Mughal empire before Akbar were models of a state that was different from the centralized feudal one. As mentioned above, the sultans and kings before Akbar were, first and foremost, protectors of the dominant community of their co-believers. The state limited itself only to recovery of taxes from the regions and principalities governed by the vassal Hindu *rajas,* the life of the people of various castes and guilds within these territories was of no great concern to the state, and this was the main cause of the stability of the Muslim power. The quest for new lands and new acquisitions for the treasury led the Muslim rulers to acquire new lands in a manner similar to Harsha and their other Hindu predecessors. But the vaster the empire, the lesser was the possibility of keeping all its vassals in submission; the greater the distance from the capital, the less powerful the central government was. Even during the most peaceful period of the Delhi Sultanate, vassal *rajas* remained semi-independent rulers whose ties with the central power were limited to paying tribute and supporting the Sultan with troops.[69] In the Mughal empire, independence of local chiefs could not be curtailed, despite all efforts. In order to strengthen the base of their own power, the sultans and kings distributed land amongst their vassals but only made them stronger in the process.

According to Dr S. Azimdjanova an Uzbek scholar on Babur, Babur's invasion of India and establishment of the Mughal empire was connected with the consolidation process in the sixteenth-century Central Asia, India, and Afghanistan. These processes made the majority of people living under feudalism 'interested in strong centralized power'.[70] Babur seems to have 'heard' this appeal. Central Asia and Afghanistan are outside the scope of our study, but as far as India is concerned (vividly described by Dr Azimdjanova herself), at the time of Babur's invasion feudal disunity was so rampant that the feudal rulers of India failed to confront Babur with even a small show of unity.[71]

Having settled in India, Babur and his son Humayun made no changes in the state model which was followed by the Delhi Sultanate as well as the Timurid empire. The establishment of the Mughal empire, though not a result of the centripetal tendencies in Indian society, began somehow to stimulate these tendencies. Consolidation of the Mughal power gave, as Dr Clara Ashrafyan rightly observes, 'some order among the disorder'.[72] But all these tendencies were not strong enough to automatically bring about a centralized state. Babur died four years after the invasion and his heir Humayun not only had to spend his whole life fighting against feudal separatism and political rivals, but to live for 15 years in Afghanistan and Iran as a refugee. When Akbar ascended the throne, he had to resist feudal separatism, rivalry at court and bloody rebellions. Because of these reasons, he and some farsighted members of the ruling elite began thinking about the necessity of changing the very model and structure of the state. That in some fields of his reforms Akbar had predecessors like Sher Shah Suri or the Kashmiri ruler Zain ul-Abidin meant that there existed, though in a weak form, some tendencies for centripetal movement. But the main effort towards this was made by Akbar.

It is against this background that one has to view Abu-l Fazl's ideas and Akbar's reforms. The conlusion of some scholars that the main object of Akbar's reforms was to establish a strong centralized state[73] appears to be true but needs further analysis. First, the state which Akbar tried to establish was a significant step forward as compared to the earlier models of Indian statehood, Hindu and Muslim. In such a state, royal power governed by the ideas of *sulhe-kul* would have rivals neither in the *jagirdars*, nor in the *ulema*; there would be administrative borders between the provinces rather than political borders between semi-independent principalities. Such a state could have developed into an 'absolutist' state which is an extreme form of a feudal set-up.[74]

The idea of a strong centralized state was pivotal to Abu-l Fazl's model. In this connection it is interesting to return to his model of the social structure of a state which was a harmony of four equally significant elements (warriors, traders/craftsmen, learned men, peasants/labourers).

This system had nothing in common with any earlier model of social structure followed by any religious community. One also has to bear in mind that the caste system and caste values that existed in India were also adopted by the Muslims.[75] The religious heterogeneity of the Indian population would mean that any specific social group or category mentioned by Abu-l Fazl would either be an abstract notion or connected with a profession rather than a religion. So, who did the social groups of a 'trader', a 'learned man' or a 'warrior' consist of? A trader could have been a Hindu, a Muslim, a Jain or a Parsi. Similarly, a Rajput or a Mughal could become a warrior. The important question that we must address is: why did Abu-l Fazl, who had such a minute knowledge of the religious composition of Indian society, erase all religious difference while analysing social groups in India?

We may suppose that such a scheme was a logical outcome of Abul-l Fazl's model of the state. If it provided that the king was ruler and protector of all his subjects, if he was the highest authority on religious questions, then he would not require intermediaries like *ulema* or brahmans to stand between him and his people. But the ideas of *sulhe-kul* likewise demanded that the state should exercise its authority in the spheres hitherto controlled by caste, kin and community. The king would not have been able to ban child marriages or *sati*, to introduce new calendars, weights and measures, to establish new school curricula except by interfering in the inner life of different communities. It would have hardly been possible when the life of a person in a community was regulated by caste rules. This was the difference between Abu-l Fazl's projects and their practical implementation: if Akbar had tried to press social reforms any further, he would have been confronted by resistance from traditional values and institutions.

One of the distinctive features of the Indian feudal society was the diffused and flexible character of its social structure. In any country's history, a high stage of social development is reached only when the main social divisions are formed. According to Prof. V.I. Pavlov, 'caste system not only was no substitute for the estates' sructure, but was historically alien to it.'[76] One can hold different opinions about the caste system being totally alien to the system of estates which existed in other feudal societies. But it seems clear that the caste system, adopted in India by a considerable part of the population, was inimical to the developent of social groups which would have distinctive attitudes to property, means of production, social status, etc. and, what is more important, common interests in economy, politics and culture. It may seem that when people are divided into innumerable castes, it is easier to govern and the state is politically more stable; but, as it was mentioned above, the state in such a case was bound to be amorphous and loose. The strong centralized state projected by Abu-l Fazl and its implementation by Akbar envisaged that the state model be based on a social structure different from the traditional one. Therefore Abu-l Fazl's model of the state was based not on castes but on social groups like estates in Europe or Russia.

In doing so Abu-l Fazl did not deliberately follow a 'progressive' European model. The system of estates existed not only in Europe, but also in Japan, China, etc. He was too much of a realist to be simply an imitator in his projects; he was an Indian, he thought and acted like an Indian and had no intentions to change the very core of the Indian social structure. But the very logic of his model state brought him to the idea that a new type of state needed a new type of social structure.

It is noteworthy that Abu-l Fazl's ideas worked towards the establishment of a strong centralized state. It is an interesting fact that in medieval Europe too, the stronger and mightier the centralized state grew, the closer it was to absolutist forms and lesser was the traditional 'freedom' of guilds and corporations.[77] If viewed in this light, Abu-l Fazl's state can be regarded as a manifestation of some common tendencies in the development of the feudal state elsewhere.

In our final assessment, Akbar tried to establish in India a centralized state that was based on Abu-l Fazl's ideas. In doing so he progressed a step further than his predecessors, both Hindu and Muslim. It is very difficult to compare ideas that developed in different countries and historical contexts. But some attitudes of Abu-l Fazl and his king seem to be close to the ideas of some Italian thinkers of the fifteenth and sixteenth centuries, who also discussed the necessity of building a centralized state in Italy because it was torn apart by disunity and internal conflicts at that time. Abu-l Fazl's ideas had much in common with the ideas of Janfrancesco Lottini (1512–1572). Much like his contemporary from India, this Italian thinker believed that outmoded laws, established by the forefathers should not guide the policies of the state, but that the law should be modified according to the necessities of time and needs of the state. The law, according to him, should not be considered as divine regulation, but should be formulated by the ruler whose main purpose should be the well-being of his people. Abu-l Fazl would, seemingly, also agree with some ideas of Hobbes, according to whom, only absolute power was fruitful, and the state was to be the highest authority in the affairs of faith.[78] Of course, Hobbes represented a different stage in the development of political thought: he negated the divinity of royal power which Abu-l Fazl had made even stronger, than his early medieval predecessors. Nevertheless, one should bear in mind that the idea of the divinity of royal power was used by Abu-l Fazl for the very practical purposes of enforcing the sovereign rights of the 'true king' to enable him to make changes in centuries-old tradition. These common features and ideas that Abu-l Fazl shared with European thinkers who authored the political theory of a strong centralized state, show that similar perceptions about the feudal state were worked out by thinkers who belonged to different countries and traditions. In Abu-l Fazl, India produced a thinker who was able to respond to the immediate problems of his times and contributed to the development of political thought in the sixteenth century.

'PUTTING THE CLOCK BACK'

Scholars and observers have made different assessments of the results achieved by Akbar's reforms. Some scholars are of the opinion that they were a 'dismal failure' because of Akbar's unsuccessful efforts to 'fuse both communities'. Others insist that Akbar, on the contrary, succeeded in creating a united 'national' state.[79] The latter position was summed up by Jawaharlal Nehru in his celebrated *Discovery of India.* 'Akbar's success is astonishing', said he; it became the cause of the flourishing of Mughal India till the very period when Aurangzeb, with his religious bigotry, 'put the clock back'.[80]

Indeed, it is difficult to formulate a single categorical estimate of Akbar's reforms. From one point of view, he really succeeded in strengthening the empire, in consolidating the social base of his power through his refusal to discriminate against the non-Muslims, abolition of *jizya,* and through his administrative and fiscal reforms. But on the other hand, Akbar failed to abolish or reform the *jagirdari* system; he could not insist on subordinating traditional institutions to the state otherwise mass protests would have followed from both Hindus and Muslims. One has to agree with Dr P.N. Chopra that 'Akbar's well-meant attempt ... touched only a fringe of society, its even tenor continued undisturbed.'[81]

Akbar had a few supporters among the ruling elite. This was a relatively narrow circle of unorthodox 'feudal intelligentsia' which consisted of both communities. The majority of the *jagirdars* would have hardly welcomed the abolition of the *jagir* system and even Akbar's withdrawal of these plans gave them no guarantee of their security; hence they either rebelled openly or supported Salim against his father. However, Hindu feudal rulers like the Rajput princes seemed to benefit from Akbar's policy. The Mughal emperor managed to secure their loyalty through his religious policy and by forming matrimonial alliances with their families. But their support was not always reliable, for many of them still dreamt of the bygone days of independence and glory.

Akbar's reforms were actively supported by the urban traders, moneylenders and craftsmen. In his biographical poem 'Ardha-kathanaka', Banarasi Das gave a graphic description of deep grief and shock, suffered by the urban people when the news of Akbar's death reached them. Banarasi Das was not writing an official chronicle; he was only relating the story of his family many years after Akbar's death; therefore we may trust his sincerity. When the 'orphaned people of the city', who feared for their security, learnt that 'the beloved son of Akbar' has ascended the throne, they rejoiced, hoping that Akbar's successor would continue his father's policy which was quite beneficial for trade.[82] Different kind of hopes were cherished by the orthodox Muslim circles represented by Shaikh Ahmad Sirhindi, an outspoken enemy of Akbar's 'novelties': at the coronation of Salim, who accepted the throne as Jahangir, he wrote: 'If at the very commencement of the new regime Muslim ways are introduced and Muslims regain their confidence, well and good; if. God forbid, it is delayed, the position will be very difficult for the Muslims.'[83] One has to note here that the Shaikh expressed the orthodox *ulema's* view, for the majority of the Muslim community gained much from Akbar's policy of communal peace.

But the Shaikh's position has a special significance. If Akbar's reforms were really a failure, it would be easy for Jahangir, who was in opposition to his father and the author of Abu-1 Fazl's assassination, to abolish or withdraw all Akbar's undertakings. But the new emperor was in no haste to withdraw his father's policies. He tried to withstand feudal separatism and the ambitions of local rulers and with this purpose issued an ordinance forbidding the provincial governors to appropriate royal insignia and powers like distribution of ranks, introduction of new taxes, personal stamps, etc. Jahangir followed in his father's footsteps by patronizing trade and industry, he abolished some taxes and cesses like the road tolls. He was not a supporter of his father's religious policy but was friendly towards the non-Muslims. He promulgated an ordinance banning wine and opium trade. The reason for this, he declared, was not to follow the Shariat, but to assure the social well-being of the community. Such a motive was in agreement with Akbar's traditions.[84]

Shah Jahan, who succeeded Jahangir in the year 1627, was recorded by the historical memory of the Indian people as a king who also followed Akbar's policies. Despite successful wars in the Deccan, which helped to enlarge the empire, the Mughal state under Shah Jahan developed some visible cracks, like the rebellion of the *jagirdars* and vassal rulers, which drained the royal treasury that had already been weakened by wars. In some parts of the empire there were anti-Mughal movements. Under Shah Jahan, the bases on which the Mughal state was formed were reconsidered: the imperial decree on the lunar calendar is a testimony to this. Akbar attempted to introduce for the whole of his domain the solar calendar *illahi, so* that the empire, could be united in a single calendar. It was specially emphasized that the new calendar was neither Hindu nor Muslim but based on scientific data, and Abu-1 Fazl rebuked the 'short-sighted ignorant men who believe the currency of the era to be inseparable from religion.' Such a calendar was used also in Jahangir's times, but after Shah Jahan ascended the Mughal throne, the Muslim calendar was re-introduced. Of importance here is not the calendar itself, but the motive for its introduction as reflected in Shah Jahan's decree on the subject: 'All the royal energies and regal intentions of the lord of the seven climes, Khaqan of the land and sea are directed towards giving currency to the true Muhammadi faith ... And he is not negligent even for a moment in paying regard to the orders and prohibitions of the bright creed ...'[85] This is a clear testimony that under Shah Jahan, the state made a slow but sure return to the pre-Akbar model of the state where the king and the state represented the only 'true' religion while all others could expect only tolerance.

In 1658, Aurangzeb came to power after a bloody war. It was he, who, as Nehru said, put the clock back. Under Aurangzeb the mighty Mughal empire crashed, and there exists a school in historiography which explains the ruin of the empire as a result of the emperor's fanatic bigotry and cruelty, not only towards the *kafirs* but towards the non-orthodox Muslims as well.[86]

Indeed, Akbar's orthodox opponents like Shaikh Ahmad Sirhindi would have regarded Aurangzeb as an ideal hero of their dreams. Aurangzeb waged an uncompromising war with the 'novelties' (*bidat*) wherever he found them. He even rebuked his son for celebrating the Nauroz festival of the Shia Persians. Artists, painters, musicians, even chroniclers were banished from the court. All those who pursued unorthodox practices or propagated heresies were punished severely. Hindu temples were destroyed in different regions.[87]

All the documents and the vast literature of this period present a graphic picture of crisis and destruction. Maharashtra and Bundelkhand, Mevar and many other territories were ablaze with the anti-Mughal struggle. The Sikhs, a peaceful sect of worshippers, with whose leaders Akbar had friendly discourses, took to arms and became a menace for the empire. Even the central regions of Agra–Delhi witnessed anti-Mughal uprisings of the Jats and Satnamis.

One of the most striking documents depicting the tensions of that period is the famous 'letter from Shivaji to Aurangzeb'. Some scholars argue that this letter was authored by the valiant Raja Raj Singh of Mevar who managed to confront the huge Mughal army in the mountains with a small following. The real authorship is of no great importance. Many such messages seem to have been circulated in the India of that time under the names of the celebrated heroes of the anti-Mughal struggle. And to us they are interesting and significant as 'medieval pamphlets' which reflect the tensions and conflicts of that period. Thus it was written: 'Many of the forts and provinces have gone out of your possession and the rest will soon do so too; your peasants are downtrodden, the yield of every village has declined ... The army is in ferment, merchants complain, Muslims cry, Hindus are burned. This infamy will quickly spread and become registered in the books of history that the Emperor of Hindustan, coveting the beggar's bowl, takes the *jizya* from paupers and the famine stricken.'[88]

The fall of the mighty empire, the impoverishment of the rich provinces, the anti-Mughal rebellions can be explained as a result of the bigotry of Aurangzeb who set the Hindus against the regime. But does it really mean that if Aurangzeb had not been a bigot or died in infancy, the disintegration of the empire could have been avoided? Of course, human factors cannot be discarded, especially if one deals with a personality that ruled the country. But to explain the fall of the Mughal empire solely as a result of the bigotry of Aurangzeb is to make reason and consequences change their places.

Aurangzeb's fanaticism was, first and foremost, a reaction to the real process of crisis and disintegration in Mughal society. The mighty empire disintegrated not only because Aurangzeb was a bigot. On the contrary, the fall of the empire was an objective development and the king had no means to stop it. Akbar could abolish *jizya* without doing much harm to his finances because in the well-developed economy of that period he had many channels through which he could acquire wealth for the royal treasury. But when the country was torn apart by wars and rebellion, when local separatism cut one by one all the arteries through which money and wealth came to the capital, *jizya*, often extracted by force, seemed the only possible way to fill the empty coffers of the state. As a contemporary testified, 'What should I write of the violence of *amins* appointed to collect newly imposed *jizya?* They realize crores of rupees, and pay only a small portion to the treasury.'[89]

The disintegration of the empire was seen by Aurangzeb and many of his contemporaries among the Muslim elite as a divine punishment for the preceding kings who had 'abjured Islamic practice and supported bidat'. In a letter to his son, Aurangzeb recalled a prophecy made by a sage to his father Shah Jahan: '... Severe oppression will take place. Justice and gratitude will disappear. Administrators and protectors of the cities will publicly plunder people ... The nobles will support tyrants ... The rights of people will be trampled under foot ... Men of merit, on discouragement and want of appreciation, will abstain from helping to improve affairs. The foolish and inexperienced will manage the state. Sons will afflict fathers, fathers will have no love for sons ... Governors, through their selfish greedy nature will cause corn to be sold dear. The country will be ruined due to the oppressions of rulers. Men will be clad in female dress ... [90]

Such 'prophecies' and 'apocalytic visions' were very common in all medieval societies, where people expressed in these forms, their protest and indignation. But what is significant here is that Aurangzeb himself repeated this prophecy and said that all the sage's predictions came true in his reign. The only way out seen by the emperor and the *ulema* around him, was in fighting the *bidat* and in enforcing the pre-Akbar model of the state. Aurangzeb's policies were a reaction, both political and psychological, to the objective processes of fragmentation and destruction of the empire; the very atmosphere of social turmoil was a fertile ground for reactionary practices like bigotry and obscurantism. It was not Aurangzeb who put the clock back. The clock was moving—but in which direction?

Abu-1 Fazl worked out the model of a strong centralized state, with estates as a basis for social distinctions and the idea of *sulhekul* as a spiritual background. It was this model that Akbar had tried to implement. This very effort, however unsuccessful, is a testimony to the fact that there existed socio-economic, political and cultural premises for the formation of such a state but these tendencies were too weak to become decisive and victorious. Efforts to consolidate the ruling class were unsuccessful. Akbar failed to abolish the *jagir* system. The *mansab* system, introduced by Akbar for all the officials of the empire was, according to Dr Clara Ashrafyan, 'a well-formed system of feudal service, free from all vestiges of pre-feudal norms, gentile links and patriarchal slavery.'[91] Akbar's reforms could have freed the Mughal empire from all pre-feudal norms and divisions and could have played a significant role in the consolidation of the ruling class, but in reality this purpose was not achieved in spite of all efforts to unify forms of feudal property and create a unified system of feudal ranks. The ruling class in every feudal country of this epoch was not a monolith: in Germany of the 1520s, petty knights sided with the rebellious peasants against the mighty lords while in England during the War of the Roses, the British nobility killed their friends and kinsmen who fought under the banners of Lancaster and York. But in India the ruling class was not only divided socially, but also on the basis of religion and ethnicity; there were castes, ethnic groups, kins within each community. There were some consolidating tendencies, which were reflected in Akbar's reforms, but they were too weak to play a decisive role.

According to Prof. V.I. Pavlov, 'efforts to overcome the disunity of the feudal class by means of despotic syncretism (Akbar) or, on the contrary, through Islamic fanaticism ... (Aurangzeb) provided no positive result even for a hierarchic consolidation of the Mughal elite.[92] The idea seems correct, but in reality the policies of Akbar and Aurangzeb were not directed towards the same goal. Their approach to policies and nation-building was very different. Akbar's reforms had an objective purpose (though not realized by the reformers) of bringing the Indian state to a qualitatively new level of development, while Aurangzeb (a ruler, not devoid of some outstanding qualities) had another purpose: to restore the pre-Akbar model of the state which, in the multi-ethnic Indian environment could hardly bring about any consolidation of the estates or social groups.

Most feudal societies which were characterized by a strong, centralized state had an established system of social divisions like estates (feudal nobility, clergy, merchants/craftsmen and peasants) where differences between ethnic groups (e.g. Normans-Saxons in Britain), language, etc. were not significant. In India, this process was accompanied by the consolidation of more unified social formations and groups. The latter development required a lot of historical time even in countries which were ethnically and religiously homogeneous. In India, a Rajput and a Mughal feudal may have shared the same historical context and may have been friends and allies, Hindu and Muslim craftsmen may have realized their common interests but the social composition of India was too complex to be homogeneous.

Nevertheless, it would be wrong to consider the state model suggested by Abu-1 Fazl and the reforms introduced by Akbar as a failure. Akbar could not at that time establish a strong centralized state but his policies provided the basis for the development of Mughal society in this very direction. The impetus given by Akbar's reforms continued for several decades after Akbar's death even under those emperors who had never declared themselves to be Akbar's spiritual and political followers. But the later developments blocked this process completely.

As mentioned elsewhere, the Mughal empire consisted of regions, which were different from each other from the point of view of ethnic, political, communal and socio-economic factors. Despite all efforts made by Akbar and other rulers to establish a unified system of administration, a unified system of calendar, weights and measures and taxes, this diversity flourished. Internal instability, wars and rebellion had a ruinous effect on the market links and bred tendencies of autarchy and separatism.

One may hypothesize that the Mughal empire could have emerged as a centralized state if for a given period of time it had its borders stable. But historical reality was different. More and more territories were conquered by the Mughals. The empire was founded when the ruling class felt no necessity for centripetal movement, for the unity of the country. To secure the obedience and loyalty of the nobles, the Mughal emperors had to invest them with more and more land grants, and even Akbar was forced to continue this practice. This, in turn, required the extension of the borders of the empire. The vanquished, no doubt, sought every opportunity to resume their struggle against the Mughals. *Jagirdars,* whose feudal holdings tended to become hereditary, spared no effort to be independent from the central power.

Mughal invasions, rebellions of the *jagirdars* and vassal rulers and punitive military actions of the Mughal army created an atmosphere of instability and had a ruinous effect on the economy. Under these conditions there was no other way left than to re-establish the pre-Akbar model of the state. The Mughal administration, interested only in recovering tributes and taxes, was only superficially concerned with the inner life of the territories under its jurisdiction. This made for the greater supremacy of castes, clans and communities. When land changed hands frequently in one's lifetime, caste and clan were considered the only stable groups for a man to associate himself with. 'I am a Frenchman, a subject of the king of France', 'I am an Englishman, a subject of the king of England'—thus would a European of the seventeenth century identify himself (with the exception of the Germans and Italians) when speaking to a foreigner, at least. But most Indians of the same period would instead mention their caste, residence, religion, perhaps a name of a local *raja* and some area like 'Mevar', 'Malva', etc. To this we may add, that for many

Indians, both Hindus and Muslims, the Mughals were nothing but foreign invaders despite all their assimilating practices. The Mughal invasion could have inadvertently helped in preserving traditional institutions and practices, since it was quite natural for all those who lived under foreign rule to stick to their traditional practices, to preserve them more rigidly than ever. As more lands and people came under the Mughal dominion, the possibility for the empire to emerge as a strong centralized state became even more remote.

The regional history of Mughal India still needs an exhaustive study. But what seems clear now is that during its early history the empire was a beneficial factor for socio-economic and cultural development of the regions within it but during the later period, it became a hindrance for this development. This was the main cause of the strong anti-Mughal movements.

The fall of the empire was inevitable. For the state that had been established by Akbar, time had moved full circle but for the independent states, altogether new possibilities were opened up. The next few chapters further discuss various perspectives towards theories of the state and the development of the Indian states.

2

'Meeting of the Oceans'

Such was the will of history that medieval India became a meeting place of different religions and cultural traditions, amongst which Hinduism and Islam played the chief roles. Each of these mighty streams was itself a synthesis of cultures, though one belonged to the inhabitants of the subcontinent and the other to the people of the Arab world, Central Asia, Iran, Turkey, etc. No adequate study of medieval Indian society and thought is possible without considering this complex interaction. Quite understandably this period interests scholars of modern Indian history because interaction between various communities at this time led to the gradual emergence of what is now known as Indian culture.

There is no uniform opinion about the result of the Hindu-Muslim cultural and religious interaction and its role in Indian culture. One opinion was vividly expressed by Nehru, who said that the result of this interaction had a positive effect on many spheres of cultural and everyday life. A different stance was adopted by K.M. Panikkar who was sure that despite some interaction 'two parallel societies were vertically established on the same soil. At all stages they were different and hardly any social communication or intermingling of life existed between them'.[1]

This polemic continues to be important in the dispute between the secular and communal elements in Indian thought. The author has no ambitions to make an all-embracing study of the subject and to find answers to all questions. This chapter deals with the processes of the Hindu-Muslim cultural and religious interaction during the period under review, but we need to study some historical premises to analyse the developments that took place from the sixteenth to the eighteenth centuries.

SOURCES AND PREMISES

The period of Indian history that embraces the thirteenth to eighteenth centuries is sometimes called the 'Muslim period'. Nehru rightly observed that such a communal division of history was 'neither intelligent nor correct', and was as wrong as to call the colonial period of Indian history 'Christian'.[2] The reason is that what is now called medieval India, all the pages of its history, all cultural achievements are the common legacy of all Indian people— Hindus and Muslims, Sikhs and Christians, Jains and Parsees, etc.

The Muslims of medieval India, who had their origin in Central Asia, Iran, Afghanistan, Turkey, and the Arab world, preserved their cultural tradition and lifestyle and at the same time assimilated elements of Indian culture. They adopted not only language, customs, and culture, but also some social divisions like the caste system. A significant number of the Muslims were local residents converted to Islam: they acquired all the cultural practices associated with this religion but they also preserved their traditional way of life. 'The Muslims', said the Russian scholar on caste, A. Kutsenkov, 'adjusted to the system of caste interaction and began fulfilling caste functions in it.'[3]

Many cultural practices and traditions of Islam were accepted by the Hindus also, especially by the elite connected with the courts of the Muslim kings. Of course, all novelties were accepted only within certain limits allowed by caste regulations. A *brahman* or a *kshatriya*, who served at the Delhi Sultan's court would never adopt the practice of beef-eating, for instance. But reverence for the traditions of the forefathers would not have prevented him from adopting some of the practices of the Muslim feudals, from the learning of Persian, to admiring the beauty of Rudaki's or Khayyam's *ghazals* or the grandeur of Muslim architecture. Similarly a Muslim, while remaining loyal to his religion, would learn Indian languages, understand the beauty and wisdom of the Ramayana, play Holi with his Hindu neighbours, and see nothing wrong in decorating a minaret like a temple. (Jhulta Minar in Ahmedabad is one of the many examples.)

Of course, Hindu-Muslim relations in the pre-Akbar period did not develop easily and peacefully. The reasons for this were many: for some Hindus, Islam was a religion of the conquerors; differences in cultural and social practices inevitably produced clashes. As the great Maithili poet Vidyapati Thakur put it, 'what was dharma for one, was a mockery for the other.' Vidyapati himself reflected many a contradiction of his epoch: some Muslim practices were for him 'foolish', he was displeased with the Muslims who had 'destroyed temples and built so many mosques and makbaras, that there is no place to step'. But at the same time he admired the justice of a Muslim king and created the characters of two Hindu princes in *Kirtilata*, who seek justice from the Sultan.[4] Some Muslim authors also were very far from tolerant of the 'idol worshippers'.[5]

Nevertheless, despite all these difficulties there were many bases for cultural contacts and interaction, which were equally beneficial to both sides. In this interaction a significant role was played by the city and urban culture. Medieval Indian cities were big centres of trade, industry, education, and culture. The urban population was in many cases mixed, including Hindus, Muslims and followers of other religions. They lived and worked, enjoyed life and suffered together and, as Vidyapati said for the city of Jaunpur, 'here Muslims say "bismillah" and slaughter cattle; there Hindus offer sacrifices to Gods; here they kneel in namaz, there they offer puja; here live Ojhas, there live Khwajas'.[6]

Most cities were administrative centres of one kind or other, and since Persian became the official language, the necessity to know it was understood by many Hindus of different social ranks, especially for the writers and merchants. Indian literature boasts of a number of valuable Persian works which were authored by Hindus. With the purpose of learning Persian, some Hindu boys attended classes in the *maktabs*—schools attached to mosques. But the role of Persian was not limited to official use. Its knowledge, opened to the educated Hindus, the doors to the poetry of Khayyam, Firdausi, Rudaki, Jami, and to wisdom and insight of Muslim scholars.[7] The astronomers, who were heirs of Aryabhata and Bhaskara, studied the works of Rumi and Ulugh Beg, and the disciples of Charaka and Susruta read Ibn Sina.

One of the best results of Hindu-Muslim interaction was seen in the literature of the period. For example the best medieval version of the 'Nal and Damayanti' episode from the Mahabharata is the Persian one by the Muslim writer, Faizi; the celebrated poem by Ja'mi, 'Yusuf and Zulaikha', was translated into Sanskrit by a Kashmiri *brahman*, Srivara.[8] It is to this interaction of the two cultures that Indian literature owes such jewels as Amir Khusrau, Faizi, Rahim, Bedil, Jayasi, Muhammad Quli, Miyan Wali Muhammad, Mir, Sauda, etc. Their *ghazals* and *mathnavis* are full of images from Indian mythology, nature, folklore, and everyday life. Some of them wrote with equal eloquence in Persian and Indian languages and found nothing wrong in addressing Allah as 'Parabrahma' or 'Parameshvar'. Similarly among the Hindu men of letters there were many who knew Persian and wrote in different genres of Persian literature. Even those who remained within the framework of the Hindu traditions were influenced by some Persian modes of expression.[9] In the same way the arts and crafts, architecture and music benefited from the process of cultural exchange during this period.

In the social sphere, at this time the Indian Muslims were not a united social body in either an ethnic, doctrinal, or class sense. They adjusted to the caste system and formed their own hierarchy of castes, sects, clans, and ethnic groups. As a result a significant number of similar professional and social divisions operated in both Hindu and Muslim communities. This was especially true of the cities where the population was mixed. Many professional castes of Hindus had their counterparts among the Muslims of nearly equal status.[10] Such a parallel structure is sometimes seen by scholars as a negative phenomenon, a case for social cleavage and disunity.[11] But there is a possibility of looking at it from another point of view.

The very fact of the existence of a parallel Hindu-Muslim social/professional structure might have helped people of both communities to form the idea that their life and preoccupations were the same in many cases. Of course, each considered his religion to be true and his caste pure. But in the city market a Muslim *julaha* (weaver) had his workshop near that of a Hindu weaver. They lived in similar conditions, worked on the same looms, equally suffered from poverty, wars, and epidemics, were equally exploited by the feudal administrators and moneylenders. Of course, a Muslim might have had some advantages as a 'true' believer in the king's religion, for instance, on the subject of *jizya*. Nevertheless, he was still pressed by heavy taxation like his Hindu counterpart. Thus Guru Nanak, describing the devastating effects of Babur's invasions, specially stressed that it meant death and ruin for Hindus and Muslims alike.[12]

Orthodox people of both communities insisted that their brethren should avoid any communications with *kafirs* or *mlecchas*. But this demand was difficult to fulfil in real life. A merchant, striving for a profitable deal, was much less concerned about the religion of his partner in business; for the Hindu feudal lord, a Muslim *amir* was sometimes closer than a co-believer, and many Hindu princes fought under the banner of Muslim kings against people of their own religion. A Hindu and a Muslim, close in social status, might be good friends. A Rajput source tells the story of a young Afghan feudal lord Farid (the future king Sher Shah), who made friends with a young Rajput prince. Both youths took an oath of friendship and then feasted together contrary to all religious norms.[13]

Rigid traditions were very often violated by the unorthodox intellectuals of the cities. Among the educated urban people, literary circles or salons were very popular. These were generally headed by some luminary of the arts, poetry, or music. The famous statesman and poet of Akbar's court, Abdur-Rahim Khankhanan (pen-name Rahim) headed one such salon. A brilliant and educated man, who had equal mastery in Persian, Hindi, Sanskrit, Arabic, and Turkish (later in Portuguese too), had as guests of his literary circle many celebrated poets and scholars, both Hindu and Muslim. The intellectual elite of Agra flocked to his poetry evenings, where exquisite *ghazals* by Faizi were followed by passionate lyrics by Gang and Keshavdas. Rahim himself wrote both Islamic and Hindu devotional verses.[14] Abu-l Fazl in his biographical notes too mentioned his friendly and intelluectual discourses with men from the Hindu, Jain, Christian, and Buddhist communities.

This phenomenon would not have been possible if the Muslims in India were a unified social body of a ruling elite. Thus there were many instances where religious and doctrinal differences did not play an important part. This seems to be a specific feature of

India, a situation quite different from other medieval countries ruled by invaders (the Ottoman empire with its Christian subjects, for instance).

The idea that a man of a different faith is not alien in god's eyes, if he is virtuous and sincere, developed against this social background. It was expressed and propagated by many saints and poets, who belonged to the religious-reformist schools of *bhakti* and Sufism, as well as by many Sikh gurus. These schools of thought will be discussed at length in the following chapter, but here we have to make a special mention of the fact that the *bhakti*, *sufi*, and Sikh saints played a crucial role in propagating the lofty ideas of communal amity and in denouncing religious hatred and bigotry. Those saints who represented the views of the urban trading and industrial classes were especially outspoken in this matter, since it was in the cities that Hindu-Muslim interaction largely took place. A conclusion was thus reached that god was the same for all devotees and was only worshipped by them under different names; that a true believer and a generous man were equally blessed by him irrespective of their religion.

Same are Mahadev and Muhammad, [may be] called Brahma or Adam,
One is a Hindu, another a Muslim, same land, same way of life!

This couplet is ascribed to Kabir, a weaver from Benares, who was one of the greatest *bhakti* poets and saints.[15] Eknath, a sixteenth-century Maharashtrian saint, authored a beautiful *bharuda* (dramatized poem), *Hindu-Turk Samvad* (*A Conversation between a Hindu and a Muslim*). The poem begins with a sharp confrontation: 'The Turk calls the Hindu "Kafir!"' / The Hindu answers, "I will be polluted—get away!"' The followers of the two religions shower abuses on each other's creed, mythology, and social norms. But ultimately they come to the conclusion that 'Hindu and Muslim both/Are created by God, brother' and proclaim:

'As a matter of fact, you and I are one.
This controversy grew over caste and *dharma*.
When we go to God, there is no such thing.'[16]

For the saints of many *bhakti panths* there existed no 'true' or 'wrong' religions: any sincere feeling towards god, any heartfelt aspiration to see god within one's heart was a true faith for them. Saintliness meant not a blind pursuit of all rituals, not a fanatical animosity towards other religions, but a true, honest and virtuous life dedicated to god. '*Kafir* is one who speaks kaf (evil) and keeps not his heart pure', said Dadu Dayal, one of the most revered saints of Rajasthan. He equated Hindu-Muslim communal animosity to the 'fighting of mad elephants', and, as his biography *Janma-lila* testifies, he suffered equally from attacks by the orthodox elements of both communities.[17] Bhai Gurdas, a famous Sikh poet of Akbar's period, insisted that Rama and Rahim were epithets used for the same god, while *brahmans* and *mullas* fought among themselves over them.[18] Towards the end of the sixteenth century, a *sufi* saint by name Hasan Teli became very popular in the Punjab. He was the son of an oilman, worked as a potter and then became a merchant. Among his followers were Muslims and Hindus from all walks of life. Himself a Muslim, Hasan Teli practised vegetarianism and had a sympathetic attitude towards the Sikhs.[19] Ideas of amity and unity were woven into many works of other *sufi* poets like Jayasi, Daud, Rahim, and Alam also.[20]

Many religious sects were influenced in various ways by the process of Hindu-Muslim cultural interaction. These sects enjoyed wide popularity. From the fourteenth to the sixteenth centuries an important spiritual role was played by an ascetic *sufi* order of *rishis* in Kashmir. Apart from a very Hindu name, they also used yogic practices. Shaikh Nur ud-din, one of their spiritual leaders, said:

Between the brothers of the same parents
Why did you create a barrier?
Muslims and Hindus are one,
When will God be kind to his servants?[21]

The regions of Sind and Gujarat saw the emergence of another very interesting sect—the *satpanthis*. This sect was founded as a branch of Ismailism. But with the passage of time the sect moved further away from its Islamic foundations. *Satpanthi* preachers said that Hinduism and Islam were similar ways of obtaining God, but Islam was a higher stage, while the Quran was the fifth and the last of the Vedas. They had a negative attitude towards idol-worship, but adopted the Hindu postulate of rebirth. They considered that the main aim of human life was to free itself from birth and rebirth and to be united with God, whom they called *Khuda* (a Muslim name) or *Brahma* (a Hindu name). In their works Hindu ideas of transmigration were eloquently interwoven with the Quranic postulates of the Day of Judgement, and hell and heaven. Among the rich literary texts of this sect there is a work called *Jannatpuri* which describes one of their spiritual leaders, Imam Shah, visiting hell and then heaven in the company of one Vir Chandan (something like Dante's Virgilius). While in hell all sorts of sinners are detained, his heaven is populated not only by Muslim righteous men, but by the noble heroes of the Mahabharata.[22]

Thus the process of the Hindu-Muslim cultural interaction and religious contacts developed from the lower ranks or 'bottom' of social life, mostly from the trading and industrial community of the cities. It was a reflection of objective social processes, devoid of any philosophical or theological contemplations. Both communities retained their doctrinal and cultural identity, but at the same time there emerged some common cultural values, and ideas of unity which found popularity among the common people and the educated elite. Interestingly, many hagiographical works on the life of the *bhakti* saints include episodes of the saints' meetings and conversations with Akbar. It is not absolutely certain whether these meetings occurred in real life (though *Janma-lila* had a most detailed description of such a meeting and even mentioned a date—1585)[23] but of interest to us is the very idea these hagiographers wrote about. This literature shows how the ideas of saints who preached communal amity, influenced Akbar and hence his religious policy.

'PEACE FOR ALL'

Now we shall return once more to the age of Akbar, but this time to his religious policies which included the equality of all religions and a ban on all religious discrimination (everybody was given full freedom to profess any religion, to build temples and other places of worship; forced conversion to any religion was forbidden). The emperor was declared the chief authority in all religious matters and was required to be equally benevolent to all confessional groups. Then came the famous *din-i illahi*, which was interpreted by Akbar's contemporaries and later scholars, as an attempt by the emperor to establish a new, composite religion which would embrace elements from all religions of India. Akbar banned cow slaughter, attended court functions with a *tilak* mark on his forehead, worshipped the Sun in the Parsee tradition and heard Catholic masses. A special board was established at the court to translate into Persian, sacred books, scientific texts, poetry and other literature of the Hindus, Parsees, Christians, etc. Among the translated works the *Mahabharata, Ramayana, Atharvaveda, Harivamsa* were mentioned. An effort was also made to translate the Gospel. The feelings of the orthodox *ulema* towards these activities were expressed most vividly by Badauni, the famous chronicler and passionate opponent of Akbar. He was ordered by Akbar to participate in the translation of the Mahabharata, but after every day of this work Badauni 'purified' himself by ablutions and prayers, as he considered the work a great sin.[24]

Akbar's religious policies are still a subject of discussion by scholars. Some historians and scholars follow Badauni and other orthodox observers in accusing Akbar of apostasy from Islam. Others see in Akbar's policies, a benevolent attitude towards the Hindus and even attribute this to the influence of Akbar's Hindu wives.[25] But according to this author, Akbar's religious policies can be best discussed within the framework of his reforms, as a significant new stage in the history of Indian thought and culture.

First, it is necessary to stress upon the difference between the religious policies of Akbar and those of his predecessors. Among his predecessors, both Delhi sultans and Mughals had a reputation for tolerance towards the Hindus. Barani was very critical of the Delhi sultans for being 'mild' to the *kafirs*.[26] The main difference between the policies of Akbar and his predecessors lies in a paradox: they were tolerant while Akbar was not. For tolerance here means that some religions and ways of life were seen as 'wrong', but tolerated. Akbar on the other hand refused to distinguish between 'true' and 'wrong' religions, so his policy was not of a Muslim king's tolerance towards the *kafirs* but of respect towards all religions. This was a new policy not only for India, but for the whole of the medieval world, when for the first time all differences between the believers and *kafirs* were discarded.

Akbar had never abjured Islam, as was specially stressed by Abu-l Fazl.[27] He, like his associates, simply began to look at religion as a private matter, based on internal convictions of every man. According to Abu-l Fazl, 'Through the apathy of princes, each sect is bigoted to its own creed and dissentions have waxed high.' And again he says,

[e]ach one regarding his persuasion alone as true, has set himself to the persecution of other worshippers of God, and the shedding of their blood and the ruining of reputations have become symbols of religious orthodoxy. Were the eyes of the mind possessed of true vision, each individual would withdraw from this indiscriminating turmoil and attend rather to his own problems than interfere in the concerns of others ... If the doctrine of an enemy be in itself good, why should hands be stained in the blood of its professors? And even were it otherwise, the sufferer from the malady of folly deserves commiseration, not hostility and the shedding of his blood.[28]

These are the key words for understanding Akbar's religious policy and the motives behind it. No *kafirs,* but just 'other worshippers of God'. Opposition to religious bigotry and a significant remark that this evil flourished only 'through the apathy of the princes'— these two factors form the bases of Akbar's religious policy.

Indeed, if the main purpose of the reforms was to establish a strong centralized state, if the traditional principle of the domination of one religious group over others was discarded, it was quite logical for Akbar to consider himself not a Muslim king (in a sense of the King of the Muslims) but a ruler and a protector of all his people of different communities. He thus placed trust in the benevolence of the king. In a panegyric to Akbar, *sufi* poet Alam said 'He is a Guru, other people are all his *chelas* [disciples] ... He is a just ruler of the country and guides all—Hindus and Muslims— to the [correct] path.[29] Panegyrics were common at that time, but among all Muslim rulers only Akbar was eulogized as a guru for uniting Hindus and Muslims. This also fits in with Abu-l Fazl's idea of the 'true king' who places the *sulhe-kul* above holy tradition and is the chief authority on religious matters also.

Akbar's approach to religion has one more aspect, which deals not with politics, but with Indian thought and spiritual culture. What he endeavoured to do was not just a political manoeuvre, but a reflection of some deep processes in the development of Indian thought and culture.

We have already made some observations concerning the process of Hindu-Muslim cultural/religious interaction. We have suggested that this interaction took place at two levels. On the more populist level were the sociocultural developments represented by religious reformists, *sufi* and *bhakti* saints, as well as Sikhs, who preached unity and amity of the communities and criticized religious bigotry. Secondly, we have to analyse the views and attitudes of the educated elite who surrounded Akbar at court.

While Akbar, Abu-1 Fazl and their associates shared many ideas with the saints they also differed considerably from the *bhaktas* and *sufis.* This viewpoint was based on rationalism.

India is a home of a centuries-old rationalistic tradition. A special study on the rationalistic principles of Hindu philosophy as reflected by different schools of thought was published in Moscow.[30] Islamic thought also has a strong rationalistic tradition. Abu-1 Fazl was not a philosopher in the strict sense of the word, but he belonged to an intellectual circle which included Akbar, where a rationalistic approach to religion was adopted. For instance, Abu-1 Fazl recorded this statement by Akbar (or, maybe, it was his own thought?): '[t]he superiority of man rests on the jewel of reason'. And further:

Many people think that outward semblance and following Muham-madanism to the letter being profit even if without internal conviction. Hence we, by fear and force, compelled many believers in the Brahman religion to adopt the faith of our ancestors. Now ... it becomes clear that a single step cannot be taken without the torch of proof and only that creed is profitable which is adopted with the approval of wisdom. To repeat the creed, to become circumcised and place one's head on the ground from dread of the Sultan is not seeking after God.[3]

Here the influence of the saints is clearly visible, especially in contrasting the real 'seeking after God' to formal attitudes and rituals of Islam. We should also note here that rationalistic approaches were not totally foreign to the *bhakti* and *sufi* thinkers, and other religious reformers. The Sikh traditions relate the following episode: once the first Guru of the Sikhs was near the bank of the Ganga where some *brahmans* were performing the ritual of offering water to the Sun. Guru Nanak also went into the water and began throwing handfuls of it in the other direction. When asked what he was doing, he said that he was watering his plot of land which was in Kartarpur. The *brahmans* called him a fool and asked how this water could reach the farm which was many miles away from the Ganga. 'But if it can't reach my farm two hundred miles away, how do you expect it will reach the Sun?', asked the Guru.[32] It was the rationalism of commonsense', or maybe an ordinary man's inability to understand the deep religious symbolism of the ritual. The rationalism of Abu-l Fazl and Akbar was based on another principle. Time and again in the *Ain-i-Akbari* and other works, Abu-l Fazl had expressed the necessity of studying natural sciences, for 'no one should be allowed to neglect those things which the present time requires'.[33]

The third volume of the *Ain-i-Akbari* was dedicated by Abu-l Fazl to the geographical, astronomical, historical, philosophical, and ethical doctrines of the Hindus. Compiled by a Muslim, these descriptions may not be altogether correct, but the main aim of the author as spelt out by him is significant: 'that hostility towards this race (the Hindus) might abate and the temporal sword be stayed awhile from the shedding of blood, that dissentions within and without be turned to peace and the thornbrake of strife and enmity bloom into a garden of concord'.[34] The book is full of sincere love for the author's motherland and its people, both— Hindus and Muslims, and of the writer's sincere desire to see them living together peacefully. Mythology, religious doctrines, ethical norms, and the philosophy of the Hindus are described by the author with great respect. His critique was based on reason or on scientific data available in his times.[35] This work by Abu-l Fazl had the features of a truly scientific scholarly analysis. His approach to an alien culture was not that of a worshipper of a 'true' religion, but of a rationalist.

Sworn enemy of religious bigotry and fanaticism, Abu-l Fazl based his arguments on two pivotal principles: monotheism and rationalism. This construction was logically 'roofed' by the ideas of the state and the king aspiring for *sulhe-kul*. The whole doctrine was clearly spelt out by the thinker in his preface to the Persian translation of the Mahabharata. As if especially to irritate the conservative *ulema* he started the preface with the Hindu text-opening formula *Om Ganesay namah*. Abu-l Fazl lamented that the rulers of the past, for fear of the 'babblers', did not dare to take religious matters in their own hands and entrusted these to 'ignorant men who knew nothing but the issuing of *fatwas* and to theologians who failed to understand the real significance of religion'. Only Akbar had the courage to demolish the 'pillars of blind following', so that a 'new era of research and enquiry started'. Furthermore, the author urged that the holy books of different religions be translated, so that people could renounce blind faith and bigotry. Religious fanaticism was for Abu-l Fazl, the sour fruit of ignorance and short-sightedness. In the same preface he criticized the Hindu theologians who had an 'exaggerated and blind faith in regarding even the details of their religion being above question'. He was equally critical about the bigoted *ulema* who have not 'studied books of religion, have no insight into the history of different peoples like Chinese or Indians, nor studied books of the great men of their own religion'.[36]

Abu-l Fazl had a great aversion for religious fanaticism because in his childhood his father was persecuted for being a sympathizer of the *Mahdavi* movement and the whole family had to live in fear of repression every moment. These vivid memories of his childhood played an important role in forming Abu-l Fazl's character and views that were later strengthened by knowledge and research. For him any religion, if professed truly and sincerely, could lead to truth though no religion was free from obsolete rites and unreasonable principles. Shaikh Mubarak, Abu-l Fazl's learned father, was also of the same opinion: 'There is no creed that may not be mistaken in some particular, nor any that is entirely false; if anyone, speaking from his conscience, mentions with favour a doctrine which is at variance with his own sect, his motives should not be misunderstood and people should not denounce him'.[37] For Abu-l Fazl and his associates the main factor on which policies of public welfare were based was reason. With this in view they analysed both Islamic and non-Islamic dogmas, questioning things which were considered absolute and indisputable truths. Once, in a conversation with his courtiers, Akbar questioned the Prophet's ascent to Heaven: 'I really wonder how any one in his senses can believe a man whose body has a certain weight, could, in the space of a moment, leave his bed, go up to heaven ...?'[38] The Jesuit missionary, who had made a lot of fruitless efforts to convert

Akbar to Christianity, lamented:' [h]e shares the common mistake
of the atheists [to be more precise, rationalists] who refuse to
subject reason to faith'.[39]

Around the year 1575 a building called *Ibadat Khana* or the
house of prayers was constructed on Akbar's orders. There Akbar
participated in *zikr* and other rituals of the *sufis*, but later this
building in Fatehpur Sikri was turned into a discussion club where
representatives of different religious and philosophic schools,
discussed in the royal presence, various questions about life and
the spiritual world. It was there, as Abu-l Fazl records, that 'bigoted
ulema and the routine lawyers were shamed'.[40]

The *Dabistan-i Mazahib,* an original encyclopaedia of the
religions and sects of India, written supposedly in the first half of
the seventeenth century, contains a record of some speeches and
presentations made by the debaters of the *Ibadat Khana.* It is
difficult to say whether the author has used documents or witnesses'
records or simply ascribed his own views to the debaters. But
what was recorded by him under the name of an 'enlightened
philosopher' agrees with the ideas of Akbar and Abu-l Fazl (who
were known at that time as *falasifa-i alam*).[41] This is what the
author records about some debates: 'There are particulars in the
(religious) law that reason accounts false or bad; conversations
with God, God's descent into a human being or into a tortoise's
shape ... pilgrimage to a particular edifice, kissing the black stone
... Objectionable sacrifice of animals ... Why is pork eating
objectionable? If on account of this animal feeding on unclean
things, then should not the same be said about poultry?' Further,
he questions the notion of authority:

But the greatest injury is an obligation of human beings to submit to one
like themselves, subjected to ... the imperfectness of mankind, who
nevertheless controls others with severity, drives them like brutes where
he pleases, who takes nine wives and allows his followers four, who
grants impunity to the shedding of blood to whomsoever he chooses. Nor
is it possible to know which of his sayings are correctly his own. ... A
prophet gives to men instruction which they (the low) not understand,
while the intellectual's reason does not approve. So he propagates his
doctrine with the sword.[42]

The fact that these arguments really reflect the position of
Abu-l Fazl's associates can be corroborated by many examples.

Once Shaikh Mubarak was recorded as saying to Birbal, Akbar's courtier and poet: 'Just as there are interpolations in your holy books, so there are many in ours; hence it is impossible to trust either.' The 'enlightened philosopher' of the *Dabistan* was also sure that 'many contradictions exist in the sacred books.'[43]

This was not the only available example of free-thinking in medieval India. As far back as the fourteenth century, Barani expressed horror at the

philosophers and others of bad religion who are opponents of the correct religion and enemies of the Prophet. ... They give way to the sciences of the Greeks. ... They consider that the world is eternal and proclaim it to be such. They do not consider God as having cognition of details. They are disbelievers in the Day of Judgement and the rising of men (from their graves), in the accounting of the Day of Judgement, and heaven and hell, though belief in these things is the basis of the Faith and has been asserted in the three-hundred and sixty revealed books by the prophets. They not only teach their doctrines, but also write rationalistic books. ... Now if such people are allowed to live with honour and dignity in the capital of the King and to promulgate their doctrines and to show preference for the rationalistic over the traditional, how can the correct faith prevail over the false creeds?[44]

The little known sect of *dahariyas* also consisted of such freethinkers. Its spiritual leader is reported to have abused the Prophet and said, 'How can a man be a Prophet who had nine wives?' The Delhi sultan Firuz Shah Tughlaq mentions the total ruin of this sect and punishment of its leaders as one of his achievements and 'God's special favours'.[45] The freethinking of the *bhaktas* and *sufis*, as it will be illustrated in the next chapter, led them to criticize superstitions and unreasonable practices of both religions, and castigate bigoted and immoral priesthood.

It seems that in the age of Akbar, rational freethinking was widespread among the educated elite. One of the pivotal factors of medieval culture in India and elsewhere was a sacred, reverential attitude towards the traditions and practices of forefathers. As Pavlov rightly said, this 'well-established and steadfast character of all socio-psychological norms and behaviour', when 'a full cycle of a human life was repeated without significant changes from generation to generation',[46] was a structural part of the medieval way of thinking not only in the 'Orient', as some scholars may suppose, but in all feudal societies. In medieval Europe, according to Gurevich, 'all that was new, unsanctified by time and tradition caused suspicion. Accusing somebody of the "unheard-of novelties" [what a closeness to Barani] was a dangerous act of social discreditation'.[47] The development of an individual basis of thought was connected in the west with the ruin of feudalism.

In sixteenth century India, feudalism was still far from its end. But some attempts to reconsider the traditional attitudes towards the legacy of the forefathers, attempts at individuality and non-conformism were noteworthy. For instance, a well-known Persian poet, Talib Amuli urged his audience to 'do something new and not copy others.'[48] Also, for the first time, as it seems, plagiarism was condemned; for a medieval writer in India or elsewhere, originality was a disadvantage, sometime as dangerous as a heresy, while to quote some traditional authorities or to rewrite their works was a merit.[49]

In his works and letters Abu-l Fazl repeatedly criticized those who regarded the tradition of ancient times as the only acceptable authority. Among the reasons for the outbreak of religious strife and bigotry he mentioned the following:

the blowing of the chill blast of inflexible custom and the low flicker of the lamp of wisdom. From immemorial time the exercise of enquiry has been restricted, and questioning and investigation have been regarded as precursors of infidelity. Whatever has been received from father, teacher, kindred, friend or neighbour, is considered as a deposit under Divine sanction, and a malcontent is reproached with impiety. Although the few among the intelligent of their generation admit the imbecility of this procedure in others, yet they will not stir one step in a practical direction themselves.[50]

Such an attitude was appreciated by Akbar himself. He was recorded as saying: 'Commending obedience to the dictates of reason and reproving a slavish following of others needs the aid of no arguments. If imitation were commendable, the prophets would have followed their predecessors [i.e. none of them would have been able to found a new religion] ... Many simpletons, worshippers of imitative custom mistake the traditions of the ancients for the dictates of reason, and garner for themselves eternal perdition.'[51]

The literary sources of Akbar's epoch reveal that a new meaning was given to the word 'free'. Traditionally in medieval India this notion had two general meanings: one who was not a slave, a bonded man or a prisoner, etc. and one who acquired spiritual liberation from earthly bonds as a result of some mystical practice. But the 'enlightened philosophers' of Akbar's court called themselves 'free' in the sense of freethinkers, free from superstition and imitative dogmas. Said Faizi:

Islam and non-Islam is the same in the free man's view:
We look equally on the Kaaba and the Temple,
For the Kaaba and the Temple are both mere stones.[52]

Interestingly, Akbar and his friends searched for like-minded thinkers not only in India, but in foreign countries too. In Iran a *sufi* scholar Mir Sayid Safiuddin Ahmad Qashi was executed for heresy and freethinking. In his papers were found letters written by Abu-1 Fazl on Akbar's behalf.[53]

Akbar's religious policy was a reflection and a logical outcome of the processes that were going on in the sphere of ideas. Here the ideas of the saints met with the rationalistic freethinking of the educated intellectuals. Both these trends of thought professed Hindu-Muslim amity and interaction, but each in its own way. However it would be wrong to analyse this amity without taking into account the conflict of ideas that had been caused by these developments. Some scholars opine that conflict of ideas was not a feature of Indian thought of the middle ages, that in the atmosphere of universal tolerance everybody was free to think and to say what he wanted. A well-known opinion of Jawaharlal Nehru that Pavlov quoted to support his thesis was that the feudal 'Orient' knew no conflict of ideas which was one of the proofs of its stagnation.[54]

If one examines the literature of Akbar's epoch one sees a world that was anything but idyllic or stagnant. Polemical debates between different religious sects and communities were common in India from very early times. But the conflict of ideas had never been so sharp and uncompromising as it was under Akbar. For the first time the representatives of one religion, sometimes kinsmen and friends, were divided by their attitudes towards the 'novelties' introduced by Akbar. This can be illustrated by examples from the Muslim intellectual circles of the period, as is vividly shown

by the research of K.A. Nizami and S.A.A. Rizvi. Thus Faizi
suffered the loss of his close friendship with Shaikh Abdul Haq
Muhaddis, a talented writer. The Shaikh could not accept the
ideas of *sulhe-kul*; he showered on his former friend Faizi, several
abuses and accusations of apostasy and heresy, saying that 'the
duties enjoined by the Shara upon the Muslims are not to be
subjected to the test of reason; implicit obedience to all the laws
of Shariat should be the guiding principle of the Muslims' life',
that is why the 'tongues of the people of religion ... seek solitude
in taking (Faizi's) name and that of his disgraceful party'.[55] Even
death was unable to mitigate harshness towards Faizi, and when
he died at the age of 50, Badauni wrote this chronogram:

Faizi the atheist died, an eloquent man uttered the words:
'A dog has gone from the world in an abominable state'.[56]

Justice requires us to note that the radicals also used such
epithets as 'babblers', 'blockheaded fanatics', etc. to describe their
opponents.

A luminary among the opponents of Akbar's policies was Shaikh
Ahmad Sirhindi, a man noted for his religious fervour and
knowledge. He abandoned his bright court career as a protest
against the *bidat* and settled near Sirhind, from where he sent
passionate pamphlets and letters calling for a struggle against
Akbar's apostatic practices, and demanded the protection of Islam
by the sword. He wrote: '*Kafr* and Islam are opposed to each
other. The progress of one is possible only at the expense of the
other. ... One who respects *kafirs* dishonours Muslims. ... They
(Hindus) should be kept at arm's length like dogs. ... The highest
Islamic sentiments show it is better to forego wordly business than
to have contact with *kafirs.*' He urged the reimposition *of jizya*
and lifting of the ban on cow-slaughter, and castigated the Muslims
who participated in the Hindu festivals.[57] Not all of Akbar's
opponents seemed to be of so extreme a disposition, but their
purpose was the same: to return to a society of the pre-Akbar
religious doctrines, to block the way for 'innovations', to suppress
freethinking. Such orthodox views were expressed by the bigoted
elements of other communities also.

Now, four centuries later, when we study the conflict of ideas
in Akbar's time (and we insist on calling it not religious conflict,

but conflict of ideas) we should deal objectively with all the participants of these events. Given our respect for the 'enlightened philosophers', we should for justice's sake note the uncompromising zeal of their opponents, whose very struggle against the policies of the emperor was an act of courage and exhibited some sort of freethinking. Raising their voice against the official ideology, they refused to compromise with it, abandoned high-ranking offices, went to exile and suffered royal disfavour. Historical reality is as contradictory as life itself, and while reading Badauni's book one cannot help appreciating the author's steadfast fidelity to his views, albeit reactionary. The greatness of Akbar's age lies in the very fact that it has enriched India with brilliant intellectuals and thinkers, eloquent writers, uncompromising fighters for 'the idea'. There were outstanding people who formulated opinion on both sides of the conflict, and this adds to the significance of the epoch for Indian culture and history.

In order to unite the postulates and practices of all Indian religions, Akbar promulgated the idea of the 'Divine Faith' or *din-i illahi.* Jesuit missionaries were sure that Akbar 'tried to establish this new faith and himself become God or Prophet'. Badauni was nearly of the same opinion and devoted many pages to the criticism of the emperor and his flattering associates who played upon Akbar's pride and turned his heart away from Islam.[58] But some modern scholars have the following opinion on *din-i illahi:* in an attempt to unite the country, Akbar tried to create a syncretic religion that would unite the elements of Hinduism, Islam, Zoroastrianism, Jainism, etc. This new religion, however, failed to be accepted by the masses and even by the courtiers and did not survive its founder for long.[59]

Some reasons for this failure can be located in the very concept of *din-i illahi.* Judging by the scanty material, which is available now, the *din-i illahi* was devoid of some features important to a religion, like the concept of God, the Holy Scripture, mythology. The main postulate was the idea of the unity of God and validity of all ways of worshipping, if professed sincerely, and if they agreed with reason. Rationalism was thus the pivotal principle of *din-i illahi,* and this also made it different from a religion, since all religions of the world urge people to have faith and believe, not to search and enquire for facts about God. The members of the *din-i illahi* argued that reason and God's will were the same, so whatever was reasonable was true and came from God.

The main postulates of the *din-i illahi*, as our knowledge now suggests, dealt with people's social behaviour and way of life. According to the *Dabistan-i Mazahib*, they were to avoid studying the 'sciences of the Arabs except to astronomy, arithmetics, physics, philosophy' and were not to spend their lifetimes in pursuit of the unreasonable. 'The sciences of the Arabs' meant Islamic theology and scholastics, as Badauni testified. The followers of *din-i illahi* had to take a vow to never be hostile to the people of other religions, to never convert anybody by force into their faith, to never harm living creatures. They also had to avoid eating meat but to allow others to do so if they pleased. At the same time they had to avoid close contact with butchers, fishermen, bird-catchers: these people were considered untouchable by the Hindus and such a regulation might have been aimed at making this code acceptable to Hindu society also. The disciples were advised to be monogamous and to avoid marriage with girls under the prescribed age. Instead of the funeral feast, which was considered unreasonable since the deceased could not himself enjoy it, birthday feasts were recommended. For greeting each other, they had to say 'Allahu Akbar' which meant, at the same time, 'God is great' and 'Akbar and God'.[60] All these regulations validate the estimate of Srivastava that the *din-i illahi* was not a religion at all, but a social order or a brotherhood.[61] Through the *din-i illahi* Akbar wanted to unite not religions, but people belonging to different communities. Most regulations were fully compatible with both Islam and Hinduism in their liberal, non-orthodox forms. Moreover, as Rizvi emphasizes, the new aspirant to the *din-i illahi* had to take a vow: 'I liberate and dissociate myself from the traditional (*taqlidi*) Islam that my fathers practise'.[62] Thus the vow is not to abandon Islam, but to abandon bigotry and blind imitation, which are harmful for any religion or ideology. The very ritual of worshipping god was, in the *din-i illahi*, a combination of different religious practices, was devoid of lavish ceremonies and seemed to be more like an intimate, individual contact with the deity. The followers of the *din-i illahi* remained Hindus and Muslims; they accepted not a new religion, but a new ethic, a new philosophy of life.

Since Akbar's religious innovations were a part of a much broader sociocultural process of Hindu-Muslim cultural interaction, the *din-i illahi* inevitably had many features in common with the ideas of the *bhakti* and *sufi* saints, and was similarly organized.

Both the *bhakti* and *sufi* schools of thought were organized in a characteristic way where communities, and religious orders were guided by spiritual leaders like *gurus* and *pirs*. Akbar became such a leader for his community of the *din-i illahi*. Total obedience, veneration and even deification of such leaders was very common, and so it happened with Akbar.

For the unorthodox intellectuals the aspiration to be part of the *din-i illahi* was a result of bitter disappointment with contemporary forms of religion, in unreasonable practices and ceremonies. As a result a spiritual vacuum was formed which had to be filled (in the atmosphere of a medieval society) only by a religion. And this religion had to be free from superstitions, rituals and all the flaws of the dominant creeds. For the common people, such disappointment in the 'faith of the Brahmans and the Mullas' (not in the religion itself) led to their joining *bhakti* and *sufi* orders. For the intellectual elite a combination of mysticism and rationalism, a mixture of a religious order and an intellectual's club was needed. The *din-i illahi* played this role successfully. Unity among Hindus and Muslims, rejection of communal enmity and discrimination were close to the *sufi* and *bhakti* principles. Thus, the *din-i illahi* elicited the interest and support of vast masses of people.

In our analysis of the *din-i illahi* we should distinguish between the conceptualization and the actual organization of it. As an organization, it was a social gathering simultaneously typical and new for medieval India—a mystical order, a literary club and a circle of 'enlightened philosophers' all rolled into one. But after the death of its members the society ceased to exist. As far as the *din-i illahi* ideology was concerned, it was a part of the wider sociocultural process and as such it continued to develop into different schools of thought.

In the year 1602, Salim, Akbar's heir-apparent tried to rebel against his father. Though peace was established, the sparks of rebellion still smouldered. Anticipating the impending danger, Akbar summoned Abu-l Fazl, who at that time was in the South, to return to Agra. Salim, who was a long-standing enemy of the 'heretic *vazir*, seized this opportunity, and ordered one of his supporters, the Raja of Orccha, to lay an ambush for Abu-l Fazl on the road. Though Abu-l Fazl received some information about the conspiracy, he refused to change his route and hurried to Agra by the shortest road in order to reach the capital as soon as possible. On 12 August 1602, Abu-l Fazl and his small retinue were attacked on the road by the Raja's men. He preferred brave resistance to cowardly escape and was killed along with his escort. It was an irony of fate that a Muslim prince and a Hindu Raja conspired to kill a thinker and statesman whose whole life was dedicated to Hindu-Muslim amity and interaction. The death of a faithful friend was a great blow for the 60-year-old Akbar who was reported as saying: 'If Salim longs for the throne so much, he should have killed me and spared Abu-l Fazl.' Akbar survived his *vazir* by a mere three years.

THE RESISTANCE

In the last part of the first chapter we had discussed that Akbar's policies were abandoned after his death. We also tried to suggest that this process of change was objective and was connected not with the personal likes and dislikes of Mughal rulers, but with such important developments as the growth of centrifugal tendencies, socio-economic development and ethnic consolidation of people inhabiting the mughal *subahs*. These were some of the factors (others to be discussed later) that fuelled the anti-Mughal movements, and all attempts to suppress them by force or by diplomacy proved to be of no avail. The only way to solve the crisis was to re-establish the pre-Akbar model of the state. Aurangzeb's religious bigotry, his merciless suppression of the *kafirs* and radical Muslim elements only added fuel to the fire. The anti-Mughal struggle was considered by many of its supporters as a revival of the traditional Hindu values and as resistance to the *mlecchas*.

If under Akbar the ideas of Hindu-Muslim interaction and amity developed within the framework of the state policy and were fully supported by the ruling circles, under Aurangzeb they were treated as heresy. Also, this spirit of interaction was unacceptable in the atmosphere of the anti-Mughal uprisings. That is why the fate of these ideas under unfavourable conditions, their resistance to the ruling ideology is of special interest to our study.

As in the earlier part of the chapter, we shall discuss the development of the *sulhe-kul* on two planes. The spiritual leaders of *bhakti* and *sufi* communities continued their activity in the lower rungs of the social hierarchy. They denounced bigotry and fanaticism, and preached amity between the religious communities. For instance, a well-known *sufi* scholar, Mulla Mir, was even invited by the Sikh Guru Arjan to participate in the foundation ceremony of the Golden Temple. Great popularity and respect was enjoyed in the first half of the seventeenth century by the *sufi* Shaikh Muhibullah from Allahabad. There were several Hindus among his followers. In a letter to Prince Dara Shukoh he said, 'Justice requires that the thought of the welfare of men should be uppermost in the minds of the rulers, so that people may be protected from the tyranny of officials. It does not matter if one is a believer [i.e. a Muslim] or not. All human beings are creatures of God.'[63] Shaikh Muhibullah's liberal views caused outrage among the bigots. When Aurangzeb came to power, the Shaikh was already dead, but his legacy was so strong that Aurangzeb ordered the Shaikh's spiritual followers to burn his books and to renounce him. Some of these people agreed to do so, but one, by the name of Shaikh Muhammadi refused. He was arrested and died in prison. Rizvi, in his book, refers to this man's bold answer to Aurangzeb. He said that to renounce his master he needed at least to reach a similar level of spiritual development and that much more fire was available in the royal kitchen than in a poor ascetic's, so if the emperor so pleased, he himself could burn the books. Being the Shaikh's pupil, Shaikh Muhammadi also studied Hindu philosophy from the *pandits*.[64] Interestingly, the author of the *Muraqqa-e Dehli* recorded in the first half of the eighteenth century, that one *sufi* Shaikh of Delhi, who was immensely popular and was a follower of Shaikh Muhibullah, had to leave his court position because of that fact. This man was famous for his open criticism of the emperor and the nobles.[65]

Many *bhakti* saints of the period also preached amity and brotherhood of the Hindus and Muslims. Some of the great Bengali spiritual leaders even had Muslim disciples.[66] One of the most popular *bhakti* saints of the seventeenth century was Malukdas, a follower of Kabir. Like Kabir, he wrote devotional songs in both the *bhakti* and *sufi* manner. He denounced the practice of offering sacrifices to God whereby 'he who cuts the throat of one of God's creatures is recorded as a hero'. He said:

Rama is my breath, Rahim is my faith ...
All glorify God—Hindus and Muslims alike.
And God glorifies those, who have solid faith.

Akho Bhagat, the Gujarati saint-poet of the seventeenth century, denounced those who:

Inflict trouble on themselves,
One shouting 'Rama', another shouting 'Allah'.[67]

One would expect that the ideas of Hindu-Muslim amity and cooperation would become redundant in the context of the anti-Mughal movements. The vast and passionate literature of these movements is full of anger towards the 'barbarous Muslims, who have destroyed dharma'.[68] Thus in the poem *Chatraprakash* by Lal Kavi, written in support of the anti-Mughal struggle in Bundelkhand, we read: 'Hindu and Muslim religions are different from each other. They always struggled like Gods and Asuras ... When the Muslim Badshahs sat on the throne, the Hindus' breath was choked, the Vedas lost their sanctity, pilgrimage tax was introduced. The Muslims take *jizya* from every house and do whatever they want.'[69]

We find that even under the unfavourable conditions of Aurangzeb's bigotry and the militant mood of anti-Mughal fighters, ideals of *sulhe-kul* survived, for they were not Akbar's fancy, but a part of Indian culture. Shivaji in his famous letter to Aurangzeb specially stressed that the emperor's policies were equally disastrous for Hindus and Muslims. He also said in this letter that 'Islam and Hinduism were diverse pigments used by the True Painter [God].'[70]

Even the chronicler, who was hostile to the Marathas and their leader was forced by objective facts to note that Shivaji, during the war, tried his best to avoid any insulting action against the Muslims, and if a copy of the Quran was captured by his soldiers, it was supposed to be respectfully restored to the Muslims.[71] Moreover, there were many Muslims among his warriors and supporters.

These people were residents of Maharashtra; they considered themselves loyal sons of this land and compatriots of the Hindu Maharashtrians. One of the famous *sufis* of Maharashtra, Shaikh Muhammad of Srigonde, proudly called himself a 'Marathi speaking Muslim.' He denounced temple demolition by Aurangzeb's administrators and declared himself to be an incarnation of Kabir. The great Maratha saint Ramdas, one of those who inspired the anti-Mughal struggle, wrote a panegyric about this Shaikh. During the Maratha liberation struggle a Hindu poet Devadas addressed the Muslims in the following manner:

We have the same God, brothers.
Says Devadas: there are no differences.[72]

Monotheism and a liberal approach to communal relations was also a feature of teachings of the Sikh gurus. Among the followers of Guru Nanak were both Hindus and Muslims.[73] In the devotional poetry by Nanak and other gurus, Muslim symbols and postulates occurred quite frequently. The Sikh gurus were influenced by the ideas of Islamic monotheism and the community of Sikhs had much in common with the *sufi* orders. By the mid-seventeenth century the Sikhs, who were a peaceful sect to begin with, took to arms and very soon became a great menace to Mughal rule in the North-West. But even at that period many Sikh gurus emphasized that their struggle was not against Islam, but against the Mughal rule. The tenth Guru of the Sikhs, Gobind Singh under whom the movement acquired its most militant from, insisted that 'the temple and the mosque are the same, and it does not matter in what way a man worships God.'[74] He denounced the bigots of both communities who fought among themselves in their ignorance. In his celebrated letter to Aurangzeb, *Zafar-nama* he accused the emperor of cruelty and fanaticism and of not believing in the Prophet and not respecting even Islam.[75] He believed that Aurangzeb's cruelties against Hindus went against the teachings of Islam. There were many Muslims in Guru Gobind's armies. He was very friendly with a *sufi* preacher Pir Buddhu Shah. When the Afghan mercenaries betrayed Guru Gobind, the elderly Pir brought to the Sikh army his sons and disciples, who fought bravely to the end. When Guru Gobind's army was destroyed and he himself narrowly escaped death, some Muslim traders risked their lives to give him shelter.[76] This is a historical truth which is now distorted by those who try to make history a weapon of communal strife.

In the literature of the post-Akbar period the ideas of communal harmony had not withered away. They became even stronger and clearer. Many poets of Aurangzeb's period (though not the court poets) laid special stress on glorifying Akbar. In Akbar's time this might have passed as mere flattery but under Aurangzeb it looked more like a veiled protest against Aurangzeb's policies. Thus Bhushan Tripathi, a celebrated poet from Maharashtra, wrote panegyrical verses in praise of Akbar, but Aurangzeb was 'gloried' by him in the following way:

You have captured your respected father Shah Jahan
As fire captures a butterfly. . .
You have executed Dara, your elder brother.
Says Bhushan the poet: listen, Aurangzeb,
You have acquired a kingdom by bad policy.[77]

Addressing God, the well-known Multani *sufi* poet Bulle Shah said: 'In Brindaban you grazed the cattle, invading Lanka you made the sound of victory, you come again as a Pilgrim to Mecca.'

Bullah, (I'm) a slave of a Muslim
I am a sacrifice to Hindus.
Live in amity with both,
Leave the rest to the Lord.[78]

When the Hindu temples were demolished by imperial order, the *sufi* poet Pemi (real name Barkatullah) wrote:

Hindus and Muslims both possess virtues.
The same torch burns in the temple and in the mosque. [79]

In the year 1686, Krishnaram, a poet from Bengal, wrote a poem titled 'Rayamangal'. The narrative deals with a quarrel between a Muslim and a Hindu deity. Peace is established by the 'Unified God', who is described as follows: 'one half of his head wore a qulah [Muslim headwear], the other a turban, he had a garland and a rosary; his skin was partly fair and partly black, Quran and Puranas were held in his two hands. The two deities became friends.'[80] This simple allegory was well understood in that period.

Thus the ideas of *sulhe-kul* were developed by the *sufi* and *bhakti* saints and their followers on the principle of the Unity of Godhead, with the main accent on sincere religious feeling and not on ritual and dogmas. The saints and their supporters were firm believers in God and that is why they could harbour no ill-will towards the 'other worshipers of God'. All people, including those from a different community, were simply God's creatures to them, and their position was like Fenimoore Cooper's immortal 'Pathfinder', who resisted the negative attitudes of the whites towards the native Americans on the ground that 'if the (American) Indians were a good-for-nothing people, God would never have created them'. Such was then, the view of the simple, reasonable mind.

At the top of the social hierarchy, among the educated elite, this attitude met with a rationalistic and scholarly approach as it did in Akbar's era. A good example of this was displayed by Abu-l Fazl in his study of Hindu culture. Later on, despite adverse circumstances, the rationalistic tendency continued to exist, though our information about it is quite scanty.

One of the greatest rationalist thinkers of the period was Mirza Abdul Qadir Bedil (1644–1721). He was a famous poet, whose Persian *ghazals, mathnavis* and philosophical poems displayed both literary talent and an original, non-dogmatic mind. He was a pantheist philosopher, and made some brilliant observations about the evolution of nature and human society. According to him, 'faith without reason is like a mirror devoid of amalgam'. He especially studied Hindu philosophy and literature (his *mathnavi Modan-o Komdeh* was a Persian version of the Sanskrit *Madhavanal-Kamkandala*) and in his poetry he wrote passionately in support of 'path-illuminating science', advocated studying of the natural and exact sciences and condemned obscurantism and religious bigotry.[81]

Another representative of the rationalistic approach was Prince Dara Shukoh, son of Shah Jahan, and Aurangzeb's unsuccessful rival in the struggle for the throne. Dara Shukoh (1615–59) was an excellently educated man; he knew Arabic, Persian and Sanskrit, and studied Islamic and Hindu philosophy. He was involved in *sufi* mysticism also. Among his close associates and friends were intellectuals of all religious communities and his spiritual preceptors included *sufis,* Kabirpanthi Guru Baba Laldas and Jesuit missionaries.

In his approach to Hindu-Muslim cultural relations Dara was a follower of Abu-1 Fazl. Dara Shukoh made several translations of Hindu religious books into Persian, but most celebrated is his translation of the Upanishads known as *Sirr al-asrar (The Secret of Secrets)* or, in another version, *Sirr al-akbar (The Great Secret).* In the preface of this work Dara stated that the idea of translating the Upanishads was for him a result of a long road to truth-seeking and 'interest in the wisdom of different nations'. Trying to find an adequate explanation of monotheistic principles, Dara, 'turned to the Quran, but the Quran contains only some hints, which are today understood only by a few chosen people', while other theological books on Islam 'only reproduce and comment on each other'. Dara then approached the Gospel, the Torah and the Psalms of David, but was not satisfied as 'these books have only short and vague references to monotheism, and the translations, made by selfish men, do not clarify the right idea'. But in the Upanishads Dara found an 'excellent' exposition of monotheism, contrary to the teachings of the 'shortsighted scholars'. To strengthen this thesis Dara quoted the Quranic dictum that 'there are no tribes without Book and Prophet' and came to a conclusion that studying the Hindu religious books was not against Islam, since these books were 'most ancient' and contained 'the mysteries of Sufic monotheism'. Arguing polemically with the bigoted theologians, Dara observed that 'praiseworthy are those who in our age acquire knowledge independently and get attached to monotheism notwithstanding all scandals, insults and accusations of heresy.'[82] Such an approach was indeed very close to Abu-1 Fazl, who was confident that the Hindu polytheism was just a form concealing a genuine monotheism, which was the same as professed by Islam, so it was wrong for Muslims to scorn Hindus as polytheists.[83]

Some modern scholars are sceptical about the authenticity of such arguments and point out many doctrinal differences between the two religions. But one has to bear in mind Dara's motive which was, to find a proof for the similarity of the two faiths, and to prove the necessity and rightfulness of Hindu-Muslim amity. Dara's translation was, by all standards, a highly scholarly work.

It was from this Persian translation by Dara Shukoh that a Latin version of the Upanishads was written, so that the learned in Europe could get acquainted, for the first time, with Indian religious thought.[84]

Another famous work by Dara was *Majmua al-bahrain* or the *Meeting of the Oceans*; the reader will now guess why we have borrowed this title for the present chapter. The title is very appropriate and indicative of the cultural process of Hindu-Muslim interaction, where two great oceans mingle while preserving their identities. This work by Dara was a comparative study of the main religious and philosophical categories of Vedanta and the *sufis*. The aim of the work was to validate both religions as 'equally searching for God'. Again, a modern scholar would insist that even if Sufism and Vedanta use similar categories, it does not mean that they were based on similar concepts. But one has to bear in mind that for the people of the middle ages verbal categories existed in reality and denoted real subjects (as seen in the discussions between the 'realists' and the 'nominalists', Duns Scotus and Thomas Aquinas). For generations of Indian unitarists the verbal closeness of the words 'Alakh' (a Sanskrit epithet of God) and 'Allah', even 'Ram' and 'Rahim' were valuable proofs of the equal validity of the Hindu and Islamic ways of naming God. Thus Dara made this comparative study of the *sufi* and Vedantic categories to state that 'on the matchless face of God there are locks of both Hinduism and Islam.'[85]

Dara Shukoh repeatedly said that his books were written not for the general public, but for personal use. The reason for this was the fear of the conservative *ulema* who would be infuriated by such contemplations:

If the martyrdom of Imam Husain was the will of God why then blame Yazid? If it was not God's will, what is the meaning of Quranic verse 'God does what he pleases and orders what he desires'? The Prophet went to fight the infidels and the Muslim army was destroyed. The *ulema* declare that it was done by God to teach the Prophet patience, but a Perfect Man needs no schooling.[86]

For Dara this questioning was not a mockery of Islam, it was just an attempt to think independently.

Dara Shukoh lost in the war of succession. He was imprisoned and executed. Aurangzeb wanted to do away with his rival and this was not the only case in Indian history when rival brothers were killed by rulers. But unlike other cases, Dara was executed openly as a heretic and an apostate. In orthodox eyes his crime was that he was 'imbibing the heretical tenets of the *sufis,* declared infidelity and Islam to be twin brothers and wrote treatises on the subjects, and associated himself with Brahmans and Gosains' (Gosains were Vaishnavite preceptors).[87] The people were sympathetic to Dara's views, and in order to save the prince from death, the Delhi craftsmen, traders and common people rose in his defence under the leadership of a soldier by the name of Haibat.[88]

Shortly after Dara's execution, one of his spiritual friends also lost his life on the scaffold. His name was Sarmad. Born in a Jewish family in the Iranian city of Kashan, he accepted Islam and took the name of Muhammad Sayid. Business and trade brought him to India, where he was so enchanted by Hindu spirituality, that he renounced his profession as a trader and began to live as a wandering ascetic. He worshipped God in several ways as prescribed by different religions, glorified both Rama and Allah, said that 'Kaaba and temple are both dominated by darkness' and declared himself 'an idolater, an infidel and one belonging to the Faith. Though I go to the mosque, a Muslim I am not'. Sarmad enjoyed great popularity. When Dara Shukoh, with whom Sarmad had a long friendship, was executed Aurangzeb wanted to see the 'heretic' and asked the prisoner: 'Where is your beloved prince now?' The old man said fearlessly that the prince was present there but not visible to the emperor, 'for you tyrannize even those of your own blood to usurp the kingdom and take away your brothers' lives, and do other barbarities'. Sarmad was tried by the *ulema.* When he was ordered to say the Islamic credo, 'There is no God but Allah and Muhammad is his Prophet', Sarmad only said 'there is no God' and explained, 'I am absorbed in the negative and I haven't come to the positive as yet, why should I lie?' As an apostate and heretic, Sarmad was executed; he met his death as boldly as he had lived, stopping the hangman from blindfolding his eyes. Delhi was strongly guarded that day, since the emperor was afraid of a new uprising.[89]

The ideas put forward by Dara Shukoh were further developed by the Hindu saint and scholar Prannath (1618-94). This man's life was very eventful. Born in a poor feudal family in Kathiawar, he left his house in his early youth and went wandering with some ascetics. He travelled to many parts of India, and visited Muscat also. Back home he took the post of *diwan* in a Hindu principality, but left it soon for the wanderer's life. After visiting Delhi, Prannath sent a letter to Aurangzeb condemning religious fanaticism (another version says he even met the emperor). On being persecuted, he went to Bundelkhand and became one of the spiritual preceptors of the valiant leader of the anti-Mughal struggle, Raja Chatrasal Bundela. His popularity in Bundelkhand was reflected by a saying:

Krishna, Muhammad, Devachanda, Prannath, Chatrasal,
Whoever worships these five, will lose his sorrows at once.[90]

Prannath was well versed in Arabic, Persian, Sanskrit, Hindi, and even seemed to know Hebrew. One of his books, *Qulzum-e Sharif* was written in several languages. He was a wonderful combination of a *bhakti* saint and a researcher. Analysing the sacred books of different religions like the Vedas, the Quran, the Torah, the Gospel, he came to the conclusion that all religions emanate from the same source and hence their similarity: all preach love of God and clemency to man, all prophesy the coming of a Messiah like Moses, Christ or Kalki at the 'end of the world' which would, according to Prannath, put an end to the laws of *dharma* and Shariat and establish peace and justice.

Prannath was a sworn enemy of religious strife and said that 'those whom you call infidels possess all virtues', that 'whatever the Quran says, the Vedas also say'.[91] In his devotional lyrics he comes across to the reader either as a Hindu *bhakta* or as a passionate *sufi*; both religious traditions were used by him with similar eloquence. Prannath's lyrics combined the ideas of the 'enlightened philosopher' and the popular saints.

Both Hindus and Muslims
Should bring their faith to one point.

Unity was one of the main ideas preached by Prannath. He preached not only Hindu-Muslim unity, but the integrity of India, which was not usually mentioned in the literature of this important historical juncture:

Everyone loves best the tongue of his kin,

There are thousands of languages in the world.
People speak differently and have different customs,
It is impossible to count all the languages,
But all of them, taken together, I'll call Indian.[92]

Prannath founded a community that exists even today, mostly in Gujarat. Its members, both Hindus and Muslims, pray and eat together.[93]

Such was the development of the ideas of Hindu-Muslim religious and cultural interaction during the period under review. It worked on two levels that influenced one another. In the lower strata of social hierarchy there were liberal religious reformers of *bhakti* and Sufism, who held that all people were equal in God's eyes and considered the sincerity of one's love for God as a priority over dogmas and rituals. Among the educated intellectuals, the *sufi* and *bhakti* ideas met with rationalistic approach, free-thinking and research. This made possible scholarly comparisons between different religions and the conclusion that all religions suffered from unreasonable dogmas and obsolete rituals. As a result thinkers like Abu-l Fazl, Dara Shukoh and Prannath worked out a theory according to which no religion was able to claim superiority over other ways of worshipping God, and nobody could be considered an 'infidel' for pursuing his own way to the deity. This was, in the realm of ideas and in the concrete policy of Akbar, a significant step forward from traditional 'tolerance', and thus constituted a significant contribution by medieval India to the treasury of world culture and thought.

In this connection it is interesting to compare the attitudes of the Indian thinkers, who supported the ideas of *sulhe-kul* with the European viewpoint. For instance, the documents of the Jesuit missions, who made several fruitless attempts to convert Akbar to Christianity are well-known. A widely acclaimed edition of these documents by Du Jarric was augmented by the 'Letters from the Mughal Court', edited and translated by Correa-Affonso. While reading this material one can feel the elation and joy experienced by the missionaries at the beginning of their activity in Agra. The Jesuits came to a 'barbarian country', ready for sufferings and martyrdom at the hands of the pagans, but in Akbar's court they got an excellent response and hospitality. The emperor himself, Abu-l Fazl and other courtiers displayed sincere interest in the

Christian religion, the missionaries were invited for discussions in the *Ibadat Khana,* they were allowed to preach, build churches and convert to Christianity those who volunteered to accept the new faith. 'God brought us before a very noble and learned King', rejoiced Father Aquaviva in his report; he anticipated glory which would have come to the mission if the mightiest Muslim king had accepted Christianity. But after some time a note of disappointment surfaced in the letters sent by the missionaries: during his conversations with the priests, Akbar asked 'things that were not to the point', he 'doubts everything, so it is not enough to prove to him the mysteries of the faith with scripture, he desires to understand them with reason'. But what the unhappy missionaries, who found in Akbar a convinced rationalist, really discovered was another fact, which was that while the Mughal king quite willingly acknowledged the validity and rightfulness of Christianity, he was sure that other religions were equally valid and truthful. When the Jesuits invited Akbar to see their newly built chapel, he agreed with pleasure, but, to the horror of the missionaries, 'worshipped Jesus first in a Christian manner, then in a Muslim way then in the Hindu manner'.[94] Akbar was faithful to his principles.

The attitude displayed by the Mughal emperor and his associates to the new religion was in total contrast to the attitude of the missionaries to Indian culture and religions. For the Jesuits, Hinduism was mere paganism and Islam a 'mixture of lies and errors'. The learned Europeans could not understand this enigma: if Akbar was not in a mood to renounce Islam for Christianity, why was he so kind to them and why did he study the tenets of Christianity with such sincere interest? They even equated the Mughal king with a boat devoid of a rudder and wandering to and fro in the sea.[95] For Akbar and his associates the way to God was incompatible with fanatical animosity towards the 'other worshippers of God'. This factor, it seems, prevented the missionaries from converting learned Indians of both communities.

It is interesting to compare the *sulhe-kul* with the ideas of the European humanists of that period. For example, the celebrated Erasmus of Rotterdam authored a pamphlet 'The Lamentations of Peace, Banished from Everywhere and Ruined'. This short work was a passionate cry against wars, for peace and friendship among nations. Erasmus expressed indignation at the very fact of waging wars under the religious banner. He was outraged that 'a godless soldier, hired for money to torture and kill, carries the Cross in front of the army like a war emblem'. War under the religious banner was the greatest sacrilege for Erasmus, while peace was considered by him to be the most holy thing. But peace, for which the great humanist appealed so patiently, was only a peace between Christians. Erasmus was very upset at the fact that the Christian powers of Europe waged wars among themselves and maintained peace with the Turks; he even said that if war was such a fateful malady of human nature, this evil should have been used against the Turks. Thus for the great pacifist, war against non-Christians was acceptable, though he emphasized that their conversion to Christianity was desirable by the force of injunctions, benevolent deeds and a rightful life's example, and not by violence.[96] Thus even for the most elevated minds of sixteenth century Europe, to acknowledge the right of non-Christian people to worship God in their own way was untenable. Non-Christian people of the world or religious minorities in Europe could only cherish hopes for a more tolerant attitude.

Moreover, one has to bear in mind that 'the age of Akbar' coincided with the period of bloody religious wars in France and other countries of Europe. The horrific Night of St. Bartholomew was only one small episode in it. The cruelty of these wars between Catholic and Protestant forces was connected with a social crisis, but the toiling masses took part in this struggle on both sides. Many thousands lost their life for the crime of rejecting some rituals and worshipping Christ in French, Dutch or English, not in Latin. India also knew many cases of religious strife, and in Akbar's times, more so in Aurangzeb's, there were many people in all religious communities who would have easily matched Henri de Guise, Catherine de Medicis and Duke Alba, in their religious fanaticism. Despite all this, Indian thought succeeded in positing the ideas of *sulhe-kul* which played an important role in encouraging a more liberal, freethinking and non-fanatical outlook.

3

'The Age of Kali' and the 'Kingdom of Rama'

In our previous chapters we dealt mainly with those trends of Indian thought which were by and large connected with the educated elite. Ideas spread and promulgated among the common people were touched upon only partially, mainly for the sake of comparison. This gap will be filled in this chapter where our attention will be centred on the religious reformist movements, their features and evolution.

While researching on these subjects one comes across many more difficulties as compared to the study of ideas of the state or Hindu-Muslim interaction. The very character of source material changes significantly, we have to deal now not with treatises on polity, or with the works of Abu-l Fazl or Dara Shukoh where the authors' viewpoints were expressed vividly and logically. The only available material for the study we attempt here is devotional poetry with its imagery, complicated system of symbols, allegories and a simplicity that sometimes borders on primitivism. This literature was not written in a scholars' study, or in *Ibadat Khana* discussions, but in the temples and mosques, in the city bazaars, craftsmen's shops and in the fields. In many cases it originated from uneducated people and was passed from one devotee to another orally. The names of many celebrated *bhakti* and *sufi* saints are veiled by the smoke screen of legend. That is why all quotations from Kabir, Dadu, etc. are to be considered not as the illustration of a particular person's views on a subject, but as a viewpoint of many people, perhaps of some social group or community who used the revered name of a saint to express their opinion.[1]

The religious reformist movements and schools of thought in medieval India have been the subject of study of many scholars in India and elsewhere. In the erstwhile USSR there was a well-established school of *bhakti* researchers. Thanks to the efforts of Barannikov, Sazanova, Gafurova, Lamshukov, Tsvetkov, Payevskaya, Glushkova, and others we have studies on the most significant poets of *bhakti* and also valuable translations of their works into Russian. There are also studies on Sufism and translations of some *sufi* literary works by Prigarina, Suvorova, Penkovsky, Aliyev, Baqaev, etc. As far as historical works are concerned, though no special study on Sufism or *bhakti* in historical context is available, scholars like Antonova, Ashrafyan, Polonskaya, Pavlov have touched upon some aspects of the problem in their general work. There exists an established estimate of *bhakti,* with all its differences and arguments, in Soviet Indology. According to Antonova, '*Bhakti* was an anti-feudal movement which in the form of religious reformist ideas reflected the struggle of the toiling masses, which was guided at the beginning by the city and money-lending elite of Hindu society'. In Ashrafyan's view, 'Medieval *bhakti* was an ideology of the townsfolk's protest against the social and caste privileges of religious and non-religious feudals; an movement that grew within the feudal society and was an inevitable result of its development'. As far as Sufism is concerned, the scholars' approach is less unified, and trends of different sociocultural meaning can be distinguished within it.[2]

In this chapter we harbour no ambitions to discuss all the aspects of *bhakti* and Sufism. We shall only chalk out some important problems, and analyse the attitudes of the *bhaktas* and *sufis* in the sphere indicated by the title of this book, *Ideas and Society* (hence some important spheres like mystical practices and doctrinal aspects will be outside our study). We shall also try to look at these ideas against the background of the medieval civilization of the world. But our first step will be to discuss some main characteristics and general principles of *bhakti* and Sufism.

SOME FEATURES OF BHAKTI AND SUFISM

A reader may object to our dealing with these phenomena in one paragraph, or even together. We are not ignorant of the profound differences between religious reformist thought within Islam and Hinduism. But ours is a work of history, not of religion or theology. For the history of ideas doctrinal differences have a meaning, but sometimes they are interwoven with similarities, especially if our main point of interest is not in the doctrinal or mystical, but in the social, ethical and cultural spheres.

Like any other religion, Hinduism offered to its devotees, ways of salvation, which were seen as an individual soul's merger with the Absolute. There were three ways that it offered, as established in the ancient religious texts: *karma,* steadfast adherence to all religious rites, and a life in accordance with the prescriptions in the scriptures; *jnana,* cognition of God through philosophical studies, meditation, study of the holy books (for those whose caste allowed it); and *bhakti,* sincere love and devotion to God, based on deeply felt individual emotion. All these three ways were considered valid, but the first two were supposed to have priority. In early medieval India, especially in the South, some schools of thought that supposed *bhakti* to be the principal way of attaining God started to develop and gradually spread to different regions. Some of them were even critical about the *karma* and *jnana* ways or *margas.* They insisted that neither rituals nor sacrifices, pilgrimages or penance, nor scholarly theological contemplation would bring a man closer to God. The main way suggested by them was a deep, genuine, all-embracing feeling of love towards God. This love was supposed to acquire many forms as for example, the parents' tenderness towards their child, or self-sacrifice and obedience of the slave to his master or a lover's passionate aspiration to obtain his beloved. These feelings, according to the *bhakti* saints, were equally accessible to men and women, to the rich and to the poor, to the *brahmans* and the 'untouchables', to the Hindus and the Muslims. All of them were proclaimed equals in God's eyes and equally protected by him, if they lived virtuously and were sincere in their love towards God. *Bhakti* was a direct link between the Deity and a devotee, a link that had no need for intermediaries like priests, sacred books or rituals.

Many features similar to the *bhakti* doctrines were promulgated by the *sufis*. This closeness is explained by the influence of *bhakti* and *sufism* on each other, though Dr Krishna Sharma was critical about such an approach and stressed that, unlike Hinduism, Islam rejected the idea of a personal God.[3] Such a critique has a point, but one has to bear in mind that this influence could not but exist since both schools developed on Indian soil and many Muslims were converted Hindus. But Krishna Sharma is right to point out that not everything in *bhakti* and *sufism* can be interpreted through this process of influence. Similarities in the *sufi* and *bhakti* approaches had another source: pivotal principles of these two schools of thought were nearly the same from the very beginning. Islam rejects the idea of a personified God, but all *sufi* poets, in and outside India, presented God in their verses as a beautiful lady love and themselves as passionate lovers, sometimes happy, but most often suffering in separation.

Like the *bhakti* saints, *sufi* preachers insisted that the main way to connect with God was not through rituals and sacred texts, but by selfless love for him. They argued that a sincere devotee was not to search for God in books and not to look for proofs of his existence, but to 'dissolve his soul' in sincere love for him. Contrary to the orthodox ideas of God being a dreadful, punishing force, they argued that 'God has a personal love relation with his creatures', that 'God was a living creature and should be loved'. Many *sufis* like the celebrated Shaikh Farid, criticized formal religion and rituals, and emphasized instead one's internal feelings towards God, sincerity of devotion and purity. According to Shaikh Farid, the aim of acquiring *ilm-i shariat* (knowledge of Shariat) was to act upon it and not to harass people.[4] Some *sufis* were quite radical in their rejection of rituals, like the Multani *sufi* poet Bulle Shah, who wrote:

Accursed be prayers, to hell with fasts,
And let profession of faith be damned.
Bullah, I have found God within,
And the world wanders in delusion ...
People advise Bullah: 'Go to the mosque'.
He asks: 'What happens by going to the Mosque,
When prayers don't come from the heart?'[5]

Despite all the doctrinal differences between Islam and Hinduism, *bhakti* and *sufi* preachers had a common basis for their thought: a deep, all-embracing feeling of love for God as a way of salvation. In other words, the inner, emotional meaning of religion was placed above its external forms and attributes. The God of the *bhaktas* and *sufis* was merciful and loving; understood, as they said, the language of the heart and needed neither lavish ceremonies, nor prayers in a foreign language like Arabic or Sanskrit.

Instead of professional priests who were experts on sacred texts and rigid guardians of tradition, *sufis* and *bhaktas* had spiritual preceptors, *pirs, shaikhs* and *gurus,* who helped the people move on the right path of love for God. These spiritual preceptors acquired their status in many cases due to their high moral and religious sentiments, kindness and generosity. Malukdas has depicted most clearly the difference between 'professional' priests and real spiritual leaders:

I have seen the false Mullas, who have no right to read the Quran.
Those Mullas who taught them were also like butchers.
They bring trouble upon their heads, deceiving the Prophet.
I call a true darvesh one who will teach me Rama's charms,
One obtains God, who has no selfishness.
Who has liberated himself from all five elements, is dear to God.
One who gives bread to the hungry, will quickly obtain God.[6]

Both *bhakti* and Sufism were a challenge to orthodox forms of religions. But it is really inadequate to look at them as two homogeneous movements.

The *sufis* were divided into several orders, and the very principles of Sufism were so flexible and all-embracing that varied interpretations of doctrines and ethical norms could be made. Indeed, among *sufis* many rationalists and freethinkers were as well known as their adversaries. For some *sufis* even the slightest attempts at personifying God were unacceptable, while others looked upon God as a living creature. But most vivid were differences in the social and ethical perceptions among the *sufis*. Some considered *fakr* (asceticism) to be the only possible way of life for a *sufi*. They earned their bread by labour or by receiving alms. The Chishti order, especially under such luminaries as Shaikh Farid, Nizamuddin Aulia, etc. was known for its charity and sympathy to the poor: a big part of the community's earnings were given as alms to the hungry, for whom kitchens were especially kept in the *Khanqas*. While *sufis* like Nizamuddin Aulia lived in poverty and said that if their brethren were hungry, food couldn't go down a *sufi's* throat, the Suhrawardis were known for aristocratic attitudes, their leaders accumulated wealth, and accepted *jagirs* from the kings.[7] Some *sufis* shunned any connection with the court and other authorities. As Shaikh Farid put it, 'If you want spiritual elevation, do not mix with the princes'. When Aurangzeb, at that time a prince and the *subedar* of the Deccan, wanted to gift a village to a *sufi* shaikh the latter refused, saying 'the King gives a village and obliges us while God gives us bread without obligation'. When Aurangzeb insisted that his aim was only to gain blessings and bliss, the saint answered: 'If you want bliss and blessings, live a virtuous life and protect the oppressed'.[8] But these very *sufi* principles failed to prevent other *sufis* from accepting land grants, from participating in court politics, or living lavishly. One such shaikh was described by the writer of *Muraqqa-e Delhi* with sarcasm and irony as a 'nobleman in the world of asceticism; his clothes are fine and thin, eatables are prepared for him with great attention'.[9] The liberal *sufi,* Mulla Shah Kashmiri, who was the preceptor of Dara Shukoh and his sister Jahan Ara, lived in poverty, but after his association with the court he had a palace-like *Khanqa,* a garden with fountains, Turkish baths and private cooks.[10] Some *sufis* were friendly and compassionate towards the non-Muslims as they found such an attitude helpful for conversions; others believed in the equal validity of all religions and *sulhe-kul;* but among the *sufis* were also great bigots and haters of the *kafirs.*

Thus within the wide framework of *sufi* principles a space was available for different ideas and interpretations. Ashrafyan has rightly observed that 'the role of sufic ideas in Indian social life can not be determined in a one-sided way: it changed according to the real conditions of the time. The very social layer, which supported this or that sufic order, was very heterogeneous'.[11] This is the reason why these ideas were so popular among people from all walks of life, and not only among the Muslims. In this many-coloured mosaic of ideas anybody could have found something suitable for himself. It was this openness that offered a challenge to the rigidity of official religion. At the same time the flexibility of *sufi* ideas offered possibilities either for a gradual merger with official Islam or for a significant deviation from it.

Our observations on the heterogeneous character of *sufism* are brief indeed but this heterogeneity is an established fact with the majority of the scholars and hardly anyone interprets *sufism* as a unified social and religious movement. We are of the opinion that the same approach should also be adopted to study the *bhakti* movement.

To determine what *bhakti* was, we should start with two general divisions of it into the *sagun* and *nirgun* traditions. *Sagun* means 'having qualities' and possessing a concretized form. Following the general idea of a unified Deity, *sagun bhakti* supposed that God should be worshipped in some anthropomorphous form of either Rama or Krishna. Among the followers of this tradition were such luminaries of medieval Indian culture as Vallabhacharya, the founder of the celebrated 'Pushti Marg' community in Braj. Members of this community consisted of the poets of the 'Ashtachap', among whom Surdas was especially famous, and other great poets like Vidyapati, Tulsidas, Mirabai, Narsi Maheta, the galaxy of Marathi *varkari* saints and the Bengali luminary Chaitanya. For the adherents of this school of *bhakti* the worship of God was expressed by ecstatic love for Rama and Krishna. The devotee here transformed himself either into the tenderly loving step-parents of the baby Krishna, or into his beloved *gopis,* or into Hanuman, the faithful friend and servant of Rama. This perception of God is full of sincere emotion and forms a basis for much beautiful poetry. But at the same time it consisted of premises which brought it very close to the 'official' Hindu cult.

Indeed, if God were *sagun,* if he had human form, and could be depicted through an image, he could have had a life story and could have become the subject of a sacred text; thus temples were needed to worship him. With the passage of time the gap between the *sagun bhakti* communities and the orthodox Hindu cult narrowed. In the early history of the 'Pushti Marg' community in Braj a very simple and modest form of worship was adopted, it embraced only singing hymns to Krishna in folk-language, and the offering of flowers and sweets. Vallabhacharya even opined that lavish ceremonies and loud prayers were to be avoided in order to 'not to disturb God'. But as time passed, huge temple complexes appeared where ceremonies were held eight times a day in a most lavish and detailed way. Temples acquired wealth through donations and land grants made by many rulers, and apart from a great number of priests, the temple complex was attended by musicians, servants, craftsmen and many others.[12] In due course of time other *sagun bhakti* communities evolved and they seem to follow a similar direction.

No less a popularity was enjoyed by the communities and saints of *nirgun bhakti* (*nirgun* means devoid of qualities). Among its most celebrated representatives were Kabir, Ravidas (Raidas), Garibdas, Malukdas, Akho Bhagat, Charandas, Dadu Dayal and others. Early Sikhism had many features similar to *nirgun bhakti*. The adherents of this tradition followed strict monotheism and believed that Rama, Krishna and Allah were the names of the same God, which was understood by them as an Absolute, devoid of any visible form or life story, and hence no temples, rituals and priests were needed to worship him. According to Kabir, God appealed to the devotees thus:

Where do you search for me, oh slave? I am but near you,
Neither in the temple am I, nor in the mosque, nor in the
  Kaaba, nor in the Kailasa;
Neither in the funeral rites am I, nor in asceticism, nor in yoga.
Who searches for me, will find me in a moment. ...
... The abode of Hari is in the East, Allah's abode is the West.
But in your heart, in your heart if you search,
  there you will obtain Karim and Rama.[13]

Unlike the *sagun bhaktas*, who considered rituals and the worshipping of images necessary, the *nirgun bhaktas* rejected all external forms of worship and criticized idolatry. The *Dabistan-i Mazahib* has a story on Kabir's conversation with a woman who wanted to offer some flowers to an idol. Kabir told her: 'In the leaves of the flower the soul lives, and the idol to whom you offer flowers is without feeling, dead, without consciousness ... so the condition of the flower is superior to that of the stone'.[14] The whole of the *nirgun bhakti* literature objects to '*patthar puja*' or stone worship.

Pantheism was the main feature of the code of beliefs of Kabir and his followers. They preached that God was omnipresent, dwelled in a true devotee's heart, so there was no need for temples, rituals, sacred books, pilgrimages, penances:

Tirthas are just water, there is nothing in it, do you understand?
Image of God is a mere stone, brother, it can say nothing, do
    you understand?
Puranas and Quran are words, remove the veil from your soul;
Kabir judges by experience: all this is just trumpery, do you
    understand?[15]

Doctrines like these brought *nirgun bhakti* close to sufism. Hasan Teli from Punjab said that there was no need to go to the Kaaba for a devotee who worshipped it a hundred times a day in his heart. This thought was common to many *sufis*.[16] Thus it was not accidental that many sects of the *nirgun bhaktas* were respected and joined by the Muslims.[17]

The God whom the *nirgun bhaktas* followed and worshipped needed no temples and rituals, and no professional priests. Since very early times Indian literature in Sanskrit, Prakrit, Persian and modern Indian languages had a tradition of criticizing and satirizing the ignorant, foolish and arrogant *brahmans* and *mullas*. The *bhakti* saints played an important role in continuing this tradition, but they did it in different forms. For many believers in *sagun bhakti* only priests who were bad, immoral, ignorant and hypocritical were worthy of derision.[18] For the *nirgun bhaktas* like Kabir the very form of traditional worship merited criticism. If all the external forms of religion were nothing but 'trumpery', if no temples and images were needed, then there was no necessity for professional priests and for reading sacred books in Sanskrit and Arabic.

Pandits make false discourses.
If (you) say 'Rama', will the world change?
If (you) say 'sugar', will your mouth become sweet?
If (you) say 'fire' will fire sparkle?
Will you quench your thirst by saying 'water'?
Will you fill your stomach by saying 'food'?
Living with a man, a parrot repeats the name of Hari,
Knowing nothing of Hari's greatness,
Then flies away to the forests and forgets.[19]

This juxtaposition of the external forms of religion to its inner meaning, of 'words' to divine revelation acquired in the heart, of 'dead stones' to the Absolute God was the pivotal feature of *nirgun bhakti*, which in its development distanced itself from orthodox Hinduism, though influenced by it. The most consistent follower of this tradition was to feel himself Hindu and Muslim at the same time, and sometimes neither a Hindu nor a Muslim. So it was not by accident that *nirgun bhakti* gave birth to a new religion—Sikhism.

Our observations on the *sagun* and *nirgun* traditions of *bhakti* should not make the reader think that the first tradition was 'conservative' and the second 'progressive'. Such terms are very difficult to apply to medieval schools of thought. Indeed, if *nirgun bhakti* was in its most radical form a significant deviation from 'official' Hinduism, one also has to note that the very idea of the Absolute God, devoid of any visible qualities, could have brought the *nirgun bhakti* close to some other *margas* like contemplation and philosophical meditation. *Sagun bhakti* was oriented more towards a human, emotional feeling for God who was worshipped in the attractive human form of Rama or Krishna. This contradiction was illustrated by an episode from the 'Sursagar', a poem by the greatest 'Ashtachap' saint-poet Surdas.

The episode is as follows. When Krishna left the village of Gokul, his step-parents and loving *gopis* for his new career as a hero and destroyer of the tyrant king Kansa, he sent to the grief-stricken *gopis* his friend Udho, to explain to the lamenting beauties of Gokul that their beloved Krishna was an Absolute God and so their passion for the handsome 'flute-player' was nothing but an illusion. But the village beauties (and Surdas himself) could not think of Krishna as an Absolute, a philosophical category. With some irony they question Udho: 'Where does your nirgun God live? Who are his father and mother, what is his image and clothes?' The only *bhakti* available to them is their tenderness towards the charming baby who stole their butter and their passionate love for the handsome youth who played beautiful music on his flute.[20] Udho's debate with the *gopis*, which this learned friend of Krishna loses to the simple village women is a vivid illustration of the differences between the two schools of *bhakti*. These polemics, however, never developed into contradictions or hostility to each other: the literature of each tradition treated the followers of the other with respect.

Both *sagun* and *nirgun bhakti* have enriched Indian literature, thought and culture with many masterpieces, and have played an important role in developing the modern languages of different people of India. All the traditions of *bhakti* form an inseparable part of Indian culture and mass consciousness.

Both traditions of *bhakti* were a challenge to the orthodox religion because many moral, social and ethical categories were critically reviewed by the saints. For instance, the traditional idea of the mundane world being *maya* (illusion) and God being the 'Reality', was reconsidered by the *bhaktas*. God was, according to them, dissolved in the mundane being, hence to know God there was no need to renounce the world in the way the ascetics did. For Kabir, asceticism was a part of the same 'trumpery' since it meant living in the caves, shaving one's head, bathing in some sacred places, etc.

You became a sadhu, put on four garlands—so what?
You look nice from outside, but inside you is rubbish.[21]

It is important to note here, that criticism of the ascetics did not mean for the *bhaktas* an acceptance of hedonism. A true *bhakta*, no doubt, had to renounce the world, but he had to do so internally rather than outwardly. For if God was everywhere, what was the need of going to the forests and caves to find him? The Sikh gurus inherited the negative attitude towards ascetic practices from the *bhakti* saints. There is a poem by Guru Gobind Singh that sounds like a quotation from Kabir:

You wander in the woods? So do the deer.
You live in silence? So do the trees.
You are celibate? So are eunuchs.
You wander barefoot? So do the monkeys.
You live on grass, vegetables and desire no wealth—
So does the cow, the ox.
You sit in meditation—so do the crane, the cat, the wolf ...
You cry out God's name, so does the jackal in winter.[22]

Most *bhakti* saints saw the right path to God in the normal life of a householder. A true devotee had to have God in his mind while going about his daily life. The ethics of *bhakti* were by and large, a commonsense compromise between worldly life and a renunciation of it: earn yourself a modest living by your labour, but aspire not for wealth and lavishness; be well-established among the people, but never be arrogant, aspire not for fame and glory; have wife and children, but avoid passions; take care of your body, but never forget that it is a temporary dwelling for your soul. Among the famous *bhakti* saints many were traders and craftsmen: Kabir the weaver, Dadu the carder, Namdev the tailor, Raidas the cobbler, Akho, Narhari, Haridasa the jeweller, Malukdas and Tukaram the traders; some sources say that Surdas was a peasant; so were Kumbhandas and Krishnadas. This definitely influenced the attitude of the saints to life and humanity. They interpreted the surrounding world and even religion from a toiler's point of view. That is why they commented equally on wealth and pauperism, on hedonism and asceticism. A simple and open-hearted householder with his 'honest poverty' or modest well-being was their social ideal. Nanak also said that great kings with their fabulous wealth were nothing compared to a worm who had God in his heart. He emphasized too that a pauper should not be revered as a preceptor because only one who earned his living by some honest toil and shared his bread with his neighbour could know the right path to God.[23]

Because they took the viewpoint of a common man, the saints had a rather scornful attitude towards bookish knowledge. 'I say what I have seen with my own eyes, and you say what is written in a book'—Kabir was reported as saying to the learned and so 'whatever was written by the Mullas and Pandits, I threw away and took nothing from it.'[24] This scorn was mainly reserved for those who tried to reach God through some theological studies or philosophical contemplation. But any knowledge, with the exception of the mystical cognition of God, was seen as a sinful attempt to decipher the divine mysteries. The Gujarati saint poet of the fifteenth century, Narsi Maheta equated searching for truth in the books to throwing out corn and eating the husk; for the Marathi saint Ramdas, too vast a knowledge led to the sin of pride.[25]

A significant feature of the *bhaktas'* attitude to God and the world was simplicity, sometimes close to primitiveness. Instead of theological categories that only a chosen few could understand, they addressed the devotees in a very simple language; their hymns were close to folk songs, their modes of expression easily understood by the illiterate: 'without money goods can't be taken from the shop, without a boat man not cross the sea, without serving a Guru, there is total full loss', or: 'Rob, if you can, but rob Rama's Name only.'

The world of *bhakti* is a world of medieval India's common people; the *bhakti* poetry is a reflection of the feelings of the people, the only source which enables us now to hear the voices of the medieval Indian bazaar, the craftsmen's shops, the peasants' huts. This world was, however, complicated, contradictory and variegated. The way of *bhakti* was open to people from all walks of life, people of many moods and ideas; hence many differences existed in mystical practices, views and attitudes of different saints. For instance, unlike many *bhakti* thinkers, Chaitanya considered asceticism a necessity and being a Krishna worshipper, practised only one ritual—*sankirton* or the chanting of God's name by all members of the community.[27] Apart from the traders and craftsmen, peasants and other poor and illiterate people there were among the followers of *bhakti,* well-educated members of the upper ranks of society and this too influenced the *bhakti* attitudes and views.

Nothing testifies better to the heterogeneous character of *bhakti* than its attitude towards social problems. Most saints belonged to the downtrodden classes or lived among them, and this was reflected in their social protests. Despite all differences, they were united in denouncing their contemporary world as cruel, unjust, full of grief and sorrows. It almost seems that the poets of *bhakti* competed among themselves in depicting the dark side of the world, using a traditional image of *Kaliyuga*—the Dark Age of Indian mythology. 'Times are horrible, rulers are merciless, their judgement turned into foolery. No crops for peasants, no alms for beggars, no trade for merchants, no jobs for servants. Destitute people ask one another: "Where to go? What to do?"', lamented Tulsidas. Nanak was even more outspoken: 'This age is like a drawn sword, the kings are butchers, goodness has taken wings and flown into the dark night of falsehood'.[28] Denunciation of the dark side of life became a sort of canon in Indian poetry, but each poet tried to make his *Kaliyuga* a living picture of the injustices and cruelties of his age. Heroes of bardic and heroic literature were beautiful and lavishly dressed, they fought their enemies, who were equally elegant *rajas* or some monsters and earned glory and a beautiful princess as a reward. *Bhakti* poetry had a different, lyrical hero: a poor and downtrodden man, either toiling day and night to save himself from a beggar's fate or just a pauper, hungry, dressed in rags.[29] His enemies were cruel kings, unjust and lustful officials, moneylenders, hunger and disease.

Why is *Kaliyuga* so merciless and what has to be done to improve the plight of the people? This question rose inevitably, but the answers provided by the thinkers of *bhakti* as they reflected on the subject were widely different. This gives us vast material for the study of their social attitudes, since the saints not only denounced the evils of *Kaliyuga,* but also created utopias that reflected the social ideals of the many schools of *bhakti* thought.

One of the greatest utopias of this kind was the *Ramacharitamanasa* by Tulsidas, an epic poem of great literary merit. Tulsidas hailed from a poor *brahman* family; he was an orphan and learned many bitter lessons from a life of poverty, disease and humiliation of all kinds. His literary works were deeply connected with the Hindu tradition and at the same time reflected the life of the common people. His descriptions of the dark side of the *Kaliyuga* were graphic and tragically realistic. The main reason for all the evils of *Kaliyuga* was, for Tulsidas, the society's deviation from the sacred traditions of the *varnashrama,* where 'people of despised castes make the high-born bow at their feet', and *shudras* ask 'how is it that we are inferior to the twice-born'.[30] Hunger, poverty, cruelty of the kings and officials were explained by Tulsidas as being the punishment for the people's refusal to strictly observe caste laws. This postulate seems to contradict one of the main principles of *bhakti* according to which all people were equal in God's eyes. Tulsidas never renounced these principles of *bhakti,* but succeeded in uniting them very naturally and eloquently with his social ideas. With this in mind, Tulsidas, Surdas, and other Vaishara poets introduced into his epic the episode of Shabari. While wandering in the forests, Rama and his companions Sita and Lakshmana became guests of a tribal woman Shabari. In order to serve some fruit to her guests the hospitable woman selected the best, but being ignorant of the rules of etiquette and hygiene, she bit every fruit to make sure it was ripe. Despite the fact that the fruits, touched by the low-caste tribal woman were a contamination according to traditional Hindu practice, Rama partook of them with thanks, and so did his wife and brother. Thus the poor tribal woman in her sincere feeling of hospitality towards Rama became equal to the high-born *kshatriyas*. According to Tulsidas, people of different castes were equal to Rama but each of them had to obey strictly the laws of caste dharma.[31]

The social ideals of Tulsidas were vividly reflected in his utopian *Ramrajya* the kingdom of Rama, where all people lived happily, there were none who were grief-stricken or destitute, and everybody could obtain all they needed free of charge; all were pure-hearted, loyal to the law and devoid of hypocrisy.[32] The very notion of Rama's kingdom became a part of the Indian culture of different epochs, and many national leaders (Gandhiji is an example) used it to illustrate a social ideal. Tulsidas's *Ramrajya* was a blend of *bhakti* and caste harmony. Rama here appeared in two roles—as a merciful protector of loving *bhaktas* and as a mighty king who followed the sacred laws sanctified by the ancient sages. This 'Kingdom of God on Earth' was an alternate world to the evil and disordered one of *Kaliyuga,* and it was a specific feature of Tulsidas' utopia.[33]

Quite different from this was the social utopia of Surdas. In his celebrated poem 'Sursagar' the great poet of Braj created an idyllic image of Gokul, the village where Krishna was brought up in the family of the headman Nanda. The residents of Gokul were kind, simple-hearted and good-natured shepherds and milkmaids, they lived peacefully and happily in harmony with nature and among themselves. In this ideal community everything worked harmoniously. Krishna's stepfather Nanda was very different from the real village headmen: he worked with the villagers and was wise and just. His family members also lived peacefully with other villagers, worked with them, and when Krishna during play, tried to bully the other boys, he was rebuked by his playfellows who said that they were all equal and there was no one high nor low among them.[34] Sazanova, the first translator of 'Sursagar' into Russian, said that Surdas saw worldly heaven in the patriarchal and idyllic village community, where neither inequality nor exploitation existed.[35]

The villagers of Gokul lived happily since all of them were sincere *bhaktas* of Krishna, and this happiness, according to Surdas, was unacceptable to the mighty king Kansa. Krishna, as seen by Surdas, was a God and protector of the poor and the downtrodden. He refused king Kansa's invitation to a lavish feast and partook, instead, of some simple vegetables in the untouchable Vidura's hut because Vidura was a true devotee. Surdas stressed that for Krishna it did not matter whether you are a beggar or a Raja.[36] This idea seems close to what Tulsidas had expressed in his Shabari episode and elsewhere, but in the works by Surdas these egalitarian ideas were more clearly spelt out. At the same time Surdas' world was limited to the borders of the village and whatever was outside it—the cities, the state and its authority and other people—found no place in his utopia; all hostile forces like Putna came from outside to destroy the idyllic world of Gokul. When Krishna grew up and left the village, it was the end of utopia, for outside the happy island of Gokul the cruel world of *Kaliyuga* began. Thus if the kingdom of Rama was an ideal state, established by a well-educated man, the utopia of Surdas was the heaven for villagers who seldom left their native place.

There exists an example of another utopia, different from those mentioned before, and this was idealized by Raidas/Ravidas who was a cobbler from Varanasi and lived in the fifteenth century. Raidas/Ravidas was an ardent devotee of *nirgun bhakti*. His utopia was the city of Begampur, 'The City of No Sorrows', where 'there is no place for griefs and troubles, one has not to pay taxes, there is no fear, no disease, no sorrow'. It is in this ideal city that Raidas/Ravidas called upon the downtrodden to 'obtain a beautiful motherland' for 'there were no people of the second and third sort. ... All may go where they please, and no place is forbidden to them'.[37]

In this poem the social ideals and dreams of the city tradesmen and craftsmen were clearly expressed. The 'City of No Sorrows' would have even been agreeable to Tulsidas too but for one important thing which the great author of the 'Ramacharitamanasa' would not have accepted—that in Begampur all people were equal, and 'no place was forbidden to them'. Raidas/Ravidas was a *chamar*, to whom a thousand-year old tradition gave no access to palaces and temples. Even in the twentieth century this social discrimination has remained a problem for many *dalits*.

The utopia of Raidas/Ravidas reflected the views of radical *bhakti* saints as well as *sufis* who were close to the common people. They were openly against caste inequality. The great Gujarati saint-poet Akho Bhagat said: 'Only fools are proud of their caste ... (They say that) the high-born are close to God, while the low-born are far from him. But however tall a man might be, he will never touch the Sun.' He even predicted that observers of *varnashrama* would be unhappy and childless.[38] Purandara, a famous saint from Karnataka, said: 'What does it matter to what religion or caste one belongs if he knows Atmabhava ... Tell me, to what caste does Narayana belong, of what caste is life, love and fine sensibility?' Another poet from Karnataka, Sarvajna, said: 'When light enters the Pariah's dwelling, is it also an outcaste? Oh, talk not of high castes and outcastes. We all tread the same mother Earth.' Sharp criticism of caste inequality was offered by Chaitanya and his followers in Bengal and Orissa.[39]

Many *bhakti* preachers, as well as Sikh gurus, were of the same opinion. But most outspoken in this matter was Kabir. He dared to ask the high-born why he was a *shudra* while they were *brahmans* and *pandits*. Did that mean that they had milk in their veins while he had blood? He also insisted that all castes were holy for him and the *chamar* Raidas/Ravidas was a saint.[40] Guru Gobind Singh was sure that 'He (God) was devoid of caste marks of any kind ... All men have the same caste.' He followed the creed of the celebrated founder of Sikhism, who insisted that 'In God's court caste is of no account. Castes are a mockery, name a mockery.'[41]

While reading Kabir, Raidas/Ravidas and other *bhakti* saints of such radical social views, one notices a very important fact. The social ideal of these saints was in many aspects quite opposite to that suggested by Tulsidas and other saints, though all of them professed the same postulates of *bhakti*. Tulsidas's dream of caste harmony in *Ramrajya* was rejected by Kabir, Raidas/Ravidas, Akho and Sarvajna. And Kabir's bold question 'Why are you a brahman, why am I a sudra?' sounds apocalyptic for Tulsidas, in whose view the deviation from *varnashrama* laws was the main reason for the evils of *Kaliyuga*. And here thus a question arises: can *bhakti* be defined as a movement?

Just as Sufism embraced a variety of ideas, with the name *sufi* given to men of different social, ethical and even doctrinal ideas, *bhakti* too was open to many interpretations. The very principle of all people being equally dear to God was used both for denouncing the caste system and for glorifying it. Thus *bhakti* was, in our view, not a movement, but a complex of movements, schools of ideas and trends. The same view was expressed by Savitri Chandra and Krishna Sharma. The research methodology and spheres of interest of these scholars are different from ours, but the conclusion that they reach is similar.[42] The ideology of social protest, with which some Soviet and Indian scholars associate *bhakti*, was significant, but not the only direction *bhakti* took, for the heterogeneity and contradiction of ideas within *bhakti* were many.

The notion of *bhakti* as a movement is untenable because of other reasons too. Even for its most radical thinkers, who combined *bhakti* with social protest, the main aim was to save an individual soul, not improve society, and one has to agree with Savitri Chandra that 'its objective was individual salvation and mystical union with God rather than a change in the living conditions of the masses'.[43] One of the main postulates of *bhakti* was the people's total dependence on God's will which was seen as an unexplainable and unperceivable 'whim' or 'play' of God's *lila*. Surdas in some of his verses from *Vinayas* even mildly reproached God for his *lila*, in which a brave lion may die of hunger while a python easily fills its stomach.[44] Hence the only way for the downtrodden was to hope for God's mercy by submissiveness, meekness and sincere *bhakti*. As far as the greedy and unjust, sinful and stupid were concerned, they would sooner or later be punished, if not in this life, then after death. Many saints in their poetic works gave severe warnings to kings, like the one by Nanak:

Of kings, subjects, rulers none shall remain,
... Storehouses filled with wealth in a moment became empty.
Steeds, chariots, camels, elephants,
Gardens, properties and houses ...
Tents, beds and pavillions—where shall they be recognized? ...
Emperors pass away, but God ever flourishes.[45]

Mercy for the oppressed, punishment of the oppressors were thus entrusted only to God, while the true *bhaktas* had to tolerate all sorrows and to love God sincerely. The way to the 'Kingdom of Rama' was through the soul of an individual man. The world was seen as a field of battle between good and evil, not between men and society.

PREMISES AND PERSPECTIVES

After we have defined some specific features of the religious reformist schools of thought and shown that both *bhakti* and Sufism consisted of complexes of ideas and trends, heterogeneous in both a doctrinal and an organizational sense, we have to analyse the origin of these schools of thought and the paths of their evolution. Our attention here will be focused mostly on *bhakti,* since Sufism was acquired by India initially in an existing form.

According to some scholars, medieval *bhakti* emerged as a response to the invasion of Islam. According to K.M. Panikkar, *'bhakti* ... provided balm to the bleeding soul of Hinduism in Northern India during the period of Muslim occupation'. Similar views on *bhakti* were held by Joshi, Krishna Rao and others.[46] Such an estimate does not agree with the facts of history, for if *bhakti* was a response to the challenge of Islam, then we cannot account for the development of *bhakti* in many regions of India especially in the South, much before the Muslim invasion.

Bhakti indeed was an answer to a challenge, but not to the challenge of Islam. It owed its development to many important changes in Indian society and culture. These changes occurred very gradually, sometimes in different directions, and none of them can be defined as the only important one.

For those who seek and fail to find in medieval India some changes equivalent to medieval Europe, claim that Indian society of the middle ages was stagnant and never-changing. But if we look at India on its own terms and treat all similarities and differences with Europe not as deviations from the 'progressive model', we would inevitably see that there were changes and developments, though only gradual. They influenced different spheres of social life and had a clear bearing on the history of ideas.

First, significant changes occurred in the traditional caste hierarchy. Development of industries and trade raised the social status of traders and craftsmen, especially in the cities. While in the early medieval period most craftsmen were treated as low-caste and untouchable, in the later period some castes like the weavers, jewellers, armourers, cloth-printers, etc., began to play a significant role in city life, and became members of the city elite. As a result of technical development and division of labour in different crafts, many artisan castes were split into sub-castes, and this also affected the caste hierarchy in the cities. Many tradesmen managed not only to acquire significant wealth, but to occupy high administrative posts and play an active role in political life directly or indirectly.[47]

Second, some changes were taking place in the rural communities also. There the rural elite of the landowning class and the rich peasants grew in influence and even acquired feudal status and ways of life, aspiring as our sources testify, to more and more.[48] At the same time many sources describe and decry the degradation of some *brahmans* having to take up occupations incompatible with their high status, like working as clerks to the Muslim administrators or even as accountants in the shops of traders, etc.[49]

The elevation of status for some castes might have brought about some growth of self-consciousness and pride. These feelings are expressed in the verses of Kabir, Raidas/Ravidas, and Akho. They expressed pride in their professions and proclaimed themselves as not being inferior to the brahmans and other high-born castes. *Bhakti* seems to be an embodiment to this growing self-respect. Raidas/Ravidas expressed it as follows:

Oh people of the city, everyone knows
That I am distinguished as a chamar by caste,
All gunas or Ram and Govind are in my heart ...
And the chief brahmans bow to me since
Ravidas obtained protection in God's name.[50]

It can be assumed that in order to raise the status of particular castes, the Sanskritization process was appropriated and some castes would even 'recall' the story of their more elevated origin.[51] But this was not always easy and not everybody was able, like the great Maratha leader Shivaji, to acquire royal status and to use his military might to solve matters. The contradiction between the growing self-consciousness of the lower castes and their traditionally despised status was difficult to solve at that time by means of orthodox Hinduism. These people needed 'their own' Rama or Krishna, who would not scorn an untouchable's food and for whom 'it does not matter whether you are a pauper or a Raja'. Having no access to the Vedas, they needed their own sacred books, easily readable by a graduate of an urban *muhalla* school and understood by the illiterate. They also needed 'their own' spiritual preceptors who would say like Prannath:

God is not scornful of any one,
He is merciful to the poor
And even the Lord, King of Kings,
Was from among the begging Jews [Christ].[52]

The spiritual preceptors, among whom were craftsmen, traders, peasants and impoverished people, composed in the common languages their numerous 'Ramayanas' and 'Mahabharatas', which might not have been totally in accordance with the classical texts, but helped any weaver or *chamar* not to feel inferior to people of higher castes.

This process was not the only one that helped in the development of *bhakti* and other religious reform schools of thought. One can suppose that the ideal system of the *Manusmriti* never existed in reality, but one cannot help acknowledging that with the passage of time Indian society moved further away from the ancient traditions and ways of life sanctified by the holy books.

The advent of Islam made the situation even more complicated. Living within a well-defined caste structure, the Muslims got involved in an intricate system of social division and ethnic groups. The dogma of Islamic practices, cultural traditions and values influenced the Hindu society in various ways and vice versa. All this led to the traditional outlook of both communities.

The development of *bhakti* was closely connected with the development of medieval culture, especially the urban culture. In the streets and bazaars of the thickly populated cities, people of all castes and religions rubbed shoulders with each other in everyday business, sorrows and joys. Vidyapati says that in the city throngs 'one's caste mark was transferred on the other's forehead; Brahman's *janeu* found itself on an untouchable's neck'.[53] It became more and more difficult to maintain one's caste purity, though the basic idea survived.

Another significant aspect of cultural life at this time was the crisis in traditional Sanskrit knowledge. In the states ruled by the Muslim kings, Persian became the official language. To read, write and speak Persian as well as vernacular languages became a matter of prestige and career opportunities, and, many *brahmans* and *kayasthas* preferred this type of education to the traditional one. The sphere for using Sanskrit, already narrow, became more so. Most urban craftsmen and traders were educated in local schools and in vernacular languages; they also needed some Persian to converse with the Muslim administrators. In many literary sources Sankrit was criticized while local languages were praised. Vidyapati authored many a work in Sanskrit, including the celebrated *Purushapariksha,* but in his preface to *Kirtilata* he stressed that 'Sanskrit is known only by a small number of people, while the mother tongue (Maithili) is pleasant to all.' Many saints praised the 'simple folk tongue' and even proclaimed its superiority to Sanskrit. [54] All this made it necessary to render the holy texts into vernacular languages. This was in accordance with the *bhakti* doctrine which insisted that God understood the language of a pure heart.

One can also study the sociocultural premises of medieval Indian life from a conservative point of view. In the eyes of an orthodox Hindu, the rajas of the 'Moon' and 'Sun' dynasties, related to the epic heroes, became vassals of the *yavanas* and even married their own daughters to them. Tradesmen, artisans and peasants began to claim high status thus upsetting the social order. Brahmans, the repositories of sacred knowledge, began to lose their holiness, served the Muslim kings and even began to read Persian *ghazals.* An orthodox Muslim would also have seen the many deviations from the holy traditions as tragic. The people of that time reacted very differently to social changes. Some damned the 'heresies' and *bidat* and became more orthodox, struggling to preserve the sacred values. Others felt that the way out of the injustices of *Kaliyuga* lay in reconsidering the orthodox traditional religious and social practices. Yet another way was to try and unite these extremes and follow a middle path. This encouraged the development of the religious reformist schools of thought.

We shall here chalk out some features of the development of *bhakti* (as far as Sufism is concerned, one has to be brave indeed to match the work of Rizvi).[55] Till the end of the sixteenth century and the beginning of the seventeenth century the only way of promoting *bhakti* ideas was through the numerous sects, communities, and fraternities, which evolved around a spiritual leader. These sects were to some extent comparable to the *sufi* orders, but devoid of strong discipline and hierarchic organization. Such sects were open to people of all castes, social orders, sex and religion. These organizations met with different fates in history. Some failed to survive their founders, others are flourishing even today. But as a rule, all of them suffered gradual transformation. For instance, the community founded by Prannath split into two sects: one of them (*dhami*) refused to reject caste differences, the other (*pramani*) remained faithful to the ideas of Prannath and rejected caste distinctions.[56] Many followers of different *bhakti* saints either returned to orthodox practices or tried to combine them with *bhakti*. This was entirely in keeping with the insistence of the saints on fulfilling obligations to family life and professions. In the medieval society, where a social being was defined only as a member of some caste or community, even the most radical *bhakti* communities either dissolved or got transformed into castes. And even now we have *kabirpantis* or *raidasis* as sub-castes.[57]

Despite this, the influence of the *bhakti* communities was very strong. They played a great role in the development of not only social thought and religion, but also music, literature and fine arts. Many *bhakti* preachers as well as *sufis* travelled throughout India and spread their ideas in different regions. On the one hand, as Ashrafyan has rightly observed, the spread of the *bhakti* ideas to different parts and ethnic groups of India testifies to their similar social development.[58] On the other hand, the spread of *bhakti* became a part of India's cultural integrity and unity.

The influence of *bhakti* extended not only to Sufism, but even to a religion that seemed to be insensitive to reformist ideas, Jainism.

Among the Jains an important reformist was Banarasi Das of Jaunpur. He wrote the biographical poem 'Ardhakathanaka'. This poem is interesting as a description of the commercial and family life in the sixteenth and seventeenth centuries, and also as a history of the author's spiritual search. Banarasi Das was a well-educated and intelligent man, a poet and thinker, who assimilated many features of *bhakti* in to his own ideas. From his youth he had an enquiring mind and was sometimes sceptical about Jain and Hindu rituals.[59] At the beginning of the eighteenth century a Jain monk Meghavijaya reported on Banarasi's, reformist attitudes (this source was translated into English and added by Dr Mukund Lath to his edition of the 'Ardhakathanaka'). His critique can be illustrated by such question as: 'What was the original form given to the precepts by Tirthankars and what is the fashion in which they are observed now by the monks and householders?' He also asked 'whether a man, who observes the practice in its external form with mind full of impure thoughts may achieve his goal?' (The latter sounds like a quotation from Kabir or Nanak.) Banarasi Das organized a sect, with mostly merchants as followers, and said that it was profitless to perform rituals and only the real truth was valid; he refused to respect and worship idols, mocked the belief in miracles, and criticized lavishness of ceremonies. Meghavijaya called him a man who proclaimed his independent views (*svamata*) and noted that his ideas were popular.[60]

Thus approximately up to the first half of the seventeeth century the main key to the development of *bhakti* ideas was through the sects and fraternities, peaceful gatherings of submissive followers of *nirgun bhakti* or *sagun bhakti*. Feudal authorities, both Hindu and Muslim, who were sympathetic to these sects, sometimes granted them lands and money.[61]

These sects and communities existed for many centuries and some of them flourish even today. But by about the mid-seventeenth century the religious reformist schools of thought moved onto a new stage. From the traditional practice of peaceful discussions and preaching the ideology of *bhakti* became transformed into the ideology of anti-Mughal struggle. This process coincided with the crisis and disintegration of the Mughal empire. The growth of opposition to Aurangzeb's policies as well as the ethnic consolidation of some peoples of India led to freedom movements which were in need of some doctrinal, religious and ethical basis. Such a basis was provided by *bhakti* ideas, which were transformed to meet the new requirements.

We do not plan to analyse in detail the anti-Mughal movements. Much has been written on them, including the late Reisner's book *Popular Movements in India, Seventeenth and Eighteenth Centuries* which became a classical work of Soviet Indology. Published as long ago as 1962, this book remains valid and though a lot of new material has been brought to light, many ideas of the author seem to correspond to the new data. In this present work we shall draw the reader's attention to the anti-Mughal movements mostly from the point of view of their ideology.

Maharashtra was not so developed economically as, for instance, Gujarat or Bengal, but it was here that the process of ethnic consolidation began quite early and met with great success. As early as the twelfth century the Marathi language had pushed Sanskrit out of the administrative and literary spheres. A significant role in the cultural development of the region and in heightening the people's self-consciousness was played by Dnyaneshvar (end of the thirteenth century) who wrote a Marathi version of the Bhagavadgita. After him Marathi literature developed rapidly, and one of the main themes was praise for the Marathi language and patriotic pride for Maharashtra. Mukteshvar, a seventeenth century poet said: 'Maharashtra is the most important of all lands and even gods fear it and are put to shame by it'.[62]

Maharashtra was an important centre of *bhakti*. Of special significance was the *varkari* panth. This school of *bhakti* worshipped the local deity Vithoba who was supposed to be an incarnation of Krishna. The main centre of *varkari* tradition was the city of Pandharpur, to which the devotees still make annual pilgrimages. This school of *bhakti* gave birth to a galaxy of poets like Namdev, Narhari, Bahinabai, Cokha Mela, and of course, Eknath and Tukaram.[63] As observed by Reisner and some Indian scholars, Maharashtrian *bhakti* had the biggest support in the villages, since urban life in Maharashtra was not so developed as compared to other parts of India. Because of this reason, as Reisner says, *bhakti* there was closer to the ideas of Tulsidas, than to those of Kabir (mainly in social aspects).[64]

Maharashtra was conquered by the Mughals long after other parts of India had been annexed; the Mughals after a long and bloody struggle, wrested it from the rulers of Bijapur and Ahmadnagar. The people of Maharashtra put up a brave fight, and had in the person of Shivaji (1630-80) a bold and talented leader and a spiritual preceptor, who played a great role in creating a climate for the anti-Mughal struggle.

Ramdas was a saint poet of *sagun bhakti,* a devotee of Rama. He insisted that Rama protected all people equally and was even bold enough to publicly support a *brahman* who incurred the wrath of his caste for taking as his guru, a man who belonged to a low caste. He is reported as saying: 'What is your purity that becomes impure by mere touch? ... Really speaking, the body itself is full of impurities, and there is no purity of Brahman and no impurity of Shudra'. At the same time he rejected egalitarian ideas in social spheres, disapproved of the mixing of castes and unequal marriages and insisted that *varnashrama* was to be preserved. Like Tulsidas, he created his own 'Kingdom of Rama' of 'Anandavanabhuvana', where Rama was the only ruler, under whose sceptre 'the community will be so rich that there will be no need of theft ... life will be healthy, without disease ... There will be many palaces to stay in and God will rejoice seeing them ... There will be no fool because of the lack of education. Arts and sciences will be taught to enrich the life of man. ...'[65]

Ramdas travelled a lot as a wandering preacher and devotee, and, as he himself said, was filled with deep sympathy for the plight of the people and hatred of the Mughal invaders who 'rob and kill, loot the temples, enslave the people, rape women, convert people by force'.[66] And in Ramdas' poetry and preaching, *bhakti* began to be associated with patriotic ideas. But for this he had to reconsider some of the principles of *bhakti,* the ideas of meekness, humility and patience. Tukaram, for one, preached humility and submissiveness to his followers, for 'an elephant may crush an army, but an ant survives'.[67] Ramdas rejected this postulate: 'How long are we to live in bondage? How can I call you a noble man when you sit quietly while our house is on fire?'[68] One should take special notice of the meaning of the word 'free'. *Mukti* meant for Ramdas not only spiritual liberation, but freedom of the Marathas from the Mughals. The freedom struggle here for the first time was thought of as a social and religious duty, as active *bhakti*.

Most *bhakti* saints rejected asceticism but were equally against any striving for glory, as this would lead to the pursuit of *maya*. In the 'Dasbodh', one of the major works by Ramdas, this traditional postulate was not accepted: the poem breathed into men vitality, action in life, energy and a strong feeling of self-respect, which never passed into selfishness. 'Never stop your efforts, never be afraid of odds ... Be not separated from people, never be idle, be dependent on nobody'. Without renouncing the main ideas of *bhakti,* Ramdas laid special stress on human activity; he acknowledged the right of a man to aspire to happiness and fame. He was confident that not only 'God's lila', but man's own efforts would be effective and bring success. 'Listen, poor man, do something yourself to be happy', he insisted.[69] This is but one more testimony to *bhakti's* flexibility. Ramdas's social ideal was a devoted *bhakta* who was loyal to God and his country, fearless and active, very unlike a submissive insect:

Oh coward, why are you seized with fear?
Cast your fear away, gather your courage.
If Rama put his hand on your head,
Even Yama's anger should not be feared.[70]

In the doctrines of Ramdas the central place was occupied by the idea of 'Maharashtra dharma'. This was the idea of liberation from the Mughals and consolidation of all the Marathas. Ramdas applealed to Shivaji and his heirs with the words that became the main slogan for the anti-Mughal struggle in Maharashtra: 'to unite all the Marathas and to promote 'Maharashtra Dharma'. This patriotic slogan has been and is still being interpreted differently, but in Shivaji's time it seemed to signify more regional and ethnic consolidation than restoration of the purity of the Hindu values and statehood. No doubt, some Marathi and Sanskrit texts of the subsequent period did portray Shivaji as a protector of Hindu *dharma*, cows, and the Vedas, but at the same time, in the construction of the Maratha state, Shivaji aptly used the political and institutional legacy of the Mughal empire and Muslim kingdoms of the Deccan.[71]

It has been accurately observed by some scholars like I.M. Reisner and P.V. Ranade that one of the most important social processes that spearheaded the Maratha movement was the feudalization of the rural elite who began to press for a dominant role in Maharashtra and thus inevitably clashed with the Mughals. The Maharashtra *watandars* were strong enough politically and economically to become the rulers of an independent state. Here the ideology of the 'Maharashtra Dharma' with its clear appeal for ethnic consolidation and for re-establishment of traditional values of *dharma* helped, according to Ranade, 'the dominant group of the Maratha *watandars* to consolidate its position among its own people and expand its power over India'.[72] Of course, the Maratha feudals and common people had somewhat different aims and ideals, but the ideas of 'Maharashtra Dharma' as well as the preachings of Ramdas became a meeting point for all the aspirations of the Maratha people. Huge masses of peasants, who fought bravely and died under the banners of Shivaji would have hardly done so if they had no interest, economic as well as cultural, psychological as well as religious, in joining Shivaji.

It will be incorrect to label the Maratha movement as a conservative one, though its social and political ideals went back in history to the sacred books of the Hindus. For India the liberation struggle of the Marathas, under the banner of 'Maharashtra Dharma' and inspiration from *bhakti,* was an important example of freedom struggle, which played its role in the colonial period also.

The development of the anti-Mughal struggle in the Punjab and the ideology of this movement was very different from the Maratha liberation war. The reasons for this were social, cultural and ethnic, but this happened mainly because the Maratha and the Sikh movements were based on different schools of *bhakti.* As mentioned elsewhere early Sikhism was a school of *nirgun bhakti,* close to Kabir and Raidas/Ravidas. Nanak, like them, professed strict monotheism, rejected rituals and all forms of external worship, and criticized caste inequality. The main social base of the Sikhs were tradesmen and craftsmen from the Punjab and some other regions of northern India. Thus it is not surprising, as I.M. Reisner notes, that 'in many images and comparisons, willingly and frequently used by the Sikh gurus, one feels something of the salesman's counter'.[73] This 'something' was in the very spirit of early Sikhism, its social and ethical ideal being the hardworking and patient householder who lived in a modest style and was always thinking of God. Preserving all the main principles of *nirgun bhakti*, Sikhism gradually acquired a strict organization, headed by the hereditary gurus, who were like living Gods for the common Sikhs. Even when the Sikhs were peaceful sectarians and lived in accord with the Mughals, the gurus slowly accumulated great power and wealth, the main source for the latter being the tithes, which all members of the community had to pay to the guru through his agents—the *masands*. The *masands* also acquired petty feudal status and kept in submission the rank-and-file Sikhs whose number grew day by day.

By the end of the sixteenth and the beginning of the seventeenth centuries, the Sikh communities were headed not by modest preceptors like Guru Nanak, but by lords or kings, whose lifestyles and stature were not very different from those of the Mughal rulers. The city of Amritsar founded by the Sikhs as their main religious centre became the capital of a state within the state. A clash with the Mughals was unavoidable, and the immediate cause of it was Guru Arjun's support of the rebellious son of Jahangir. After Arjun was tortured to death in Delhi, the Sikhs took to arms and succeeded in beating back several punitive expeditions of the Mughal army.[74]

Some scholars are of the opinion that the peaceful or militant form of the Sikh movement depended on the Mughal emperors' friendly or hostile attitude to it and on the gurus' attitude which after Nanak's death became more and more warlike.[75] Such an approach is however superficial. It seems more likely that the Sikhs took to arms because of reasons similar to the reasons that armed the Marathas, as well as other people of the Mughal empire.

At the same time the development of the armed struggle of the Sikhs and the ideology of this movement were very different from the Maratha movement. If in Maharashtra the process of feudalization of the rural elite was a catalyst, the Sikh community took to arms when a similar process within it had already reached a high stage of development and led to a theocratic state. Moreover, in this state feudal disintegration was visible, for the *masands* became the real feudal chiefs and claimed independence from the guru saying that if they had their way, there would be no guru at all.[76] It has to be added that the Sikh movement was, from the very beginning ethnically heterogeneous, since many downtrodden people from different parts of India found refuge in this community. Therefore, it was not easy to conceptualize something like the 'Maharashtra Dharma', though the Punjabi language and Gurumukhi script played a significant role.

All these factors were important for the transformation of Sikhism from peaceful sectarian teaching to the ideology of a mass militant movement. This process was connected with the name of the tenth guru Gobind Singh (1660–1708) who became the head of the community, while still a youth after his father, Guru Tegh Bahadur was beheaded in Delhi in 1675 on Aurangzeb's orders. Gobind Singh was well-educated; he had good knowledge of Hindi, Punjabi, Persian and Sanskrit, for at that time the sons of the Sikh gurus used to be educated like princes in languages, martial arts and other fields of knowledge. Gobind established his headquarters not at Amritsar, but in the small forts of Anandpur and Paonta, which soon became mighty fortresses, and from here were dealt many severe blows to the Mughal armies.

Guru Gobind authored some interesting and talented works collected into the *Dasam Granth*, or the Book of the Tenth (Guru). Of special interest here is the poem 'Bacittar Natak' or the 'Variegated Drama'. In this poem Guru Gobind delineates his biography in two spheres—mythological and real. Bringing the history of his family upto the sons of Rama, Gobind stressed his inseparable ties with Indian classical tradition, but in the VI Canto the story does an unexpected volte-face. The author reveals how in his previous birth he was an ascetic and practised yoga in the Himalayas. Here God ordered him to renounce asceticism, return to the world and take up arms in the struggle for the establishment of the true faith, and for the ruin of tyranny. The yogi was hesitant, so God told him: 'I created men, but they made Gods out of stone. I created rishis, sadhus, Muhammad, Rama ..., but no one could find me, each established his own religion ... I've created thee to establish my religion and to restrain the world from senseless acts.' So the Guru came into the world as Tegh Bahadur's son. The story goes further and gives a realistic description of the anti-Mughal struggle of the Sikhs. The yogi episode is the centre of the poem, serving like a bridge between tradition and reality, and giving a divine sanction to the anti-Mughal struggle. It also emphasizes that real devotion to God not in asceticism but in active struggle. Like any other work of medieval Indian literature, the '*Bacittar Natak*' opens with an invocation, not to God or king, but to the sword.[77]

In his activities against the Mughals, Guru Gobind tried to find support from the rulers of the small principalities which were in the nearby Himalayan region. But the rajas refused to help the Sikhs who were for them nothing but a plebeian throng. All hopes cherished by Guru Gobind for the rajas' knightly valour and love for freedom were ruined, and the Guru addressed them in angry words: 'You have abandoned worship of the True God and addressed your worship to Gods, Goddesses, rivers, trees, etc. Through ignorance you do not know how to govern your territories, through insolence and vice you never regard the interests of your subjects. ... In your quarrels regarding caste and lineage you have not adhered even to the ancient four divisions of Hinduism, but made hundreds of subcastes ... Your morals are so perverted that from fear and desire to please your Muslim rulers you give them your daughters. ...'[78] This angry homily seems to denote not only Gobind's disillusionment, but to some extent his transformation into a popular leader of the insurgent Sikhs.

Guru Gobind was a follower of Kabir's democratic views and always spoke of Kabir with great respect.[79] But in the atmosphere of armed struggle only criticism of social evils and deep love for God were not enough. Guru Gobind undertook a thorough reform of the Sikh community and ideology. Like Ramdas, he rejected the idea of humility and submissiveness, which was inherited by Sikhism from the *nirgun bhaktas*. A real Sikh, according to him, was not a peaceful householder but a warrior whose *bhakti* was devotion and struggle. 'I will not look silently on violence and oppression which rule supreme in the world'. ... 'I will not go into ascetic meditation and close my eyes to the world.' At another place he says: 'May food for the hungry be in one hand and a sword against the tyrants in the other'.[80]

As we have already discussed, the Sikh camp was filled by the downtrodden people from different parts of northern and central India, so it was not easy to formulate something like the

'Maharashtra Dharma'. The development of the reforms undertaken by Gobind took a somewhat odd direction.

These reforms had two main aims: democratization of the community and consolidation of the Sikhs to make them ready for the anti-Mughal struggle. To solve the first task, Guru Gobind utilized the long-smouldering anger of the ordinary Sikhs against the *masands* who behaved like feudal lords. According to Sikh sources, the Guru asked some actors to perform a play about the misdeeds of the *masands* and to show it to a large gathering of Sikhs. The performance touched the necessary chord, and the excited public attacked the *masands*, which made it possible for the Guru to raise his voice against this institution. But this was not enough, and Guru Gobind abolished the post of the guru and ordered the total power of the community to be vested in the whole community of Sikhs—the *khalsa*. He said that he himself was only a military leader of the Sikhs and not a divine guru: 'All who call me the Supreme Being shall fall into the pit of hell. Recognize me as God's servant only.' The Sikh chroniclers recorded an episode when the Guru publicly bowed to the temple, which was a violation of the Sikh regulation. He insisted that he be punished for this offence in a manner the ordinary Sikhs were to be punished. Afterwards he said that this was done to show himself as an equal to others in the community and as 'God's servant only'.[81]

But the main step towards reform was taken by him during the famous Baisakhi festival of 1699. There the Sikh leader displayed his political skill, inventiveness and deep knowledge of mass psychology. During a large gathering of the Sikhs he asked if there were some volunteers who would offer their lives in sacrifice. The Sikhs were shocked, as human sacrifices were never heard of among them. At last there was one volunteer, and the Guru brought him to a tent and shortly afterwards came out with his sword drenched with blood. He asked for volunteers once more; four more Sikhs volunteered to sacrifice their lives and shared the same fate. Panic-stricken, the people ran away. But suddenly the Guru opened the tent and the five volunteers appeared alive and well, wearing new clothes and turbans; a dead goat was also seen, the blood of which was on Gobind's sword. These 'five beloved', as the Guru called them, were the first to receive a new initiation from the Guru by being sprinkled with water shaken off a dagger and they themselves performed this ceremony on their leader. The meaning of this ceremony, so brilliantly staged by the Guru, was the following: to show that sacrifice and obedience were necessary in the struggle against the Mughals and a warlike spirit and self-respect were attributes that the Sikh masses of craftsmen, traders and peasants had to cultivate in themselves.

Since that day every Sikh had to pass through this initiation ceremony. New symbols were also introduced to distinguish the Sikhs from all others: a comb, a bracelet, a dagger, special forms of headdress and clothing; and every Sikh acquired the knightly name or title—'Singh', hitherto a prerogative of some Rajput feudals. This also gave to the Sikhs, self-respect and courage. Guru Gobind said: 'Let all embrace one creed and obliterate difference of religion. Let the four Hindu castes having different rules abandon them all and become brothers. Let no one deem himself superior to another; let men of the four castes receive my baptism and eat from one dish.' This was a great sacrilege for not only the *brahmans*, but also for some members of this community who were not ready to go so far.[82]

What was the meaning of this 'theocratical democracy', as some scholars call it?[83] Reisner explains Gobind's reforms through the necessities of war and emphasizes the anti-feudal character of the Sikh movement.[84] This estimate seems correct, but more will be said about the characteristics of the Sikh movement later in the chapter. Before that we offer some other observations.

First, as it has been pointed out already, the Sikh community has a long history of armed struggle. So Guru Gobind's reforms were something like a 'revolution within a revolution', an effort to withdraw power from the rich and elevated elite of the community and give more power to the rank-and-file Sikhs. The ordinary Sikhs' dissatisfaction with the *masands* and the elite became the impulse for Gobind's reforms. Thus the social aspect of reforms was clearer in the Sikh movement than in that of the Marathas.

Second, since no idea like 'Maharashtra Dharma' was applicable, the main factor behind the consolidation of Sikhs was religion. But this consolidation would hardly have been possible if all traditional forms of *nirgun bhakti* were utilized by the Sikhs, for these traditional forms of *bhakti* supposed that a person should support new ideas without breaking with traditional forms of social life. A break with some of the moral, ethical, doctrinal, philosophical and social traditions of Hinduism was necessary. According to this logic, if the Sikhs had to be united militarily they had to cease being Hindus.

Many thinkers of *nirgun bhakti* labelled themselves as neither Hindus nor Muslims or Hindus and Muslims at the same time. Sikhism shared the idea and laid even more stress on the worship of the Absolute God. Nevertheless, the followers of Guru Nanak were seen by their contemporaries as a Hindu sect and even Guru Tegh Bahadur was traditionally praised as a martyr defending the Hindus. Guru Gobind's reforms, for the first time, made a distinction between the Sikhs and followers of other religions, though this distinction at Gobind's time never supposed hostility. With this purpose the Guru introduced his innovations in dress, the keeping of long hair, etc. At the same time he criticized some Hindu traditions and ceremonies: 'If God is known as "ayoni", then how was Rama borne by Kaushalya? If God is called The Image of Truth (*satyasvarup*) and Peacemaker (*bair-virodhi*) why then did he drive Arjuna's chariot? ... All religions are false. They worship gods and goddesses and know not God ... Listen, yogis, you wander (here and there), occupied by greed and forgetful of sadhana. Why do you worship stones? Oh fools, why do you mount not horses and elephants, but the donkey of maya? ... (The yogis) oil their eyes and pretend to shed tears for love of God.'[85] A true Sikh, the Guru added, had to renounce belief in spirits and omens, worshipping of holy places and temples.[86] Here we see a blend of a rationalistic criticism of some unreasonable traditions and a negation of one religion for the sake of the other.

The reforms attempted by Guru Gobind helped him to build a well-organized and consolidated army whose moral spirit and dedication were high, so that even defeat by the Mughal army and the bloodbath that followed it failed to discourage them. Guru Gobind himself, defeated, shocked by the loss of his four sons and elderly mother, had the courage to address to the victorious Aurangzeb his famous letter in Persian, 'Zafar Nama'. This letter is an example of an unbroken spirit and outstanding moral force. It was as if Guru Gobind threw a gauntlet in Aurangzeb's face; he emphasized that the struggle of the Sikhs was a part of all people's resistance; he accused Aurangzeb of disbelief in God and Prophet, and of crimes against his own faith; 'With God's assistance I hope to shower blows on you, so that on this holy land no trace of the den of sin remain. From the south [Maharashtra] you have returned empty-handed, in Mewar the Rajputs taught you a lesson, and now you have your eyes on the Punjab, but I will inflame the soil under your feet. ...'[87]

After Guru Gobind was assassinated in 1708, the Sikhs were led by Banda Bahadur, under whose leadership the war continued upto 1715, and the Sikh armies became a real menace for Delhi. After Banda was defeated and executed, the struggle went on, and when the Mughal rule over Punjab ceased to exist, the Sikhs bravely resisted the Afghan invasion.[88] This was a proof of the validity and strength of Gobind's reforms and their influence on the Sikh community and movement.

But it would be a mistake to forget that the transformation of Sikhism from a peaceful sect into a separate religion and ideology of armed struggle was an internally contradictory process. On the one hand, as we have already mentioned, without Gobind's innovations the movement could not have become so consolidated and militant. But on the other hand, the transformation of Sikhism created a gap between the Sikhs and their would-be allies among the non-Sikhs. Sikh literature, especially after Guru Gobind, clearly fixed the process of the community's alienation or separation from other religious communities. Thus the ethical codes or *rahit-namas,* which appeared in large numbers, made it obligatory for the Sikhs to marry their daughters to Sikhs only, to employ only fellow Sikhs as cooks. A tolerant and friendly attitude to all other religions was also proclaimed in the *rahit-namas,* but the Sikhs were forbidden to buy meat from the Muslims and to cohabit with Muslim women.[89] These regulations are understandable in the atmosphere of anti-Mughal war, but one has to note here that some kind of caste exclusiveness and distance from non-Sikhs also made its way into Sikhism. After Guru Gobind's death an anti-Muslim feeling grew in both Sikh ideology and politics, which could not but alienate the Muslim traders, craftsmen and peasants.[90]

Thus we have attempted a brief review of the evolution of the religious reformist schools of thought. Over the centuries they passed on from rise to decay, changed their organizational forms and ideology. One of the most significant stages of the evolution of *bhakti* was its transformation to the ideology of the militant anti-Mughal struggle. Just as it is impossible to point out the exact inception of *bhakti* in India, it is likewise impossible to point to the final stage in the history of its development. The history of *bhakti* did not end with the end of the middle ages, and the same has to be said about Sufism also. Their influence on other schools of thought, religion, culture, mass consciousness, arts and literature was visible in the different epochs that followed the medieval period. There is an interesting instance of Bahtavar from Hathras, who in 1802, wrote a philosophical poem titled 'Sunesar', which was published in Hindi and Russian by I. D. Serebryakov. Bahtavar was a follower of *sunyavad*, a trend of naive materialism, but his social views and attitude to religion coincided with the views of the radical *bhaktas* and *sufis*. Some of his verses look like quotations from Kabir:

Blood is the same, brain is the same
Of a Brahman and of a Shudra.
One carries on religious rites from the dawn,
Another drags on his miserable existence, devoid of any rights.
So many tirthas are in the world, but all of them are in your heart.
And when you understand this, you are the place of them all.[91]

Religious and social-ethical principles, formulated by the *bhakti* and *sufi* saints, are even today an inseparable part of the Indian culture and mind. It is through Tulsidas' Ramayana and Surdas' 'Sursagar' that these became a part of the national culture. It is through *sufi* poetry that the north Indian, albeit a Hindu, forms his aesthetic principles and views. Similar examples can be found from all parts of India. The heroic legacy of Ramdas and Guru Gobind inspired the Indian people during the anti-colonial struggle, and remains a source of national pride and patriotic feelings. The history of *bhakti*, *sufism*, and Sikhism in India continues, and likewise its research has to be continued by the joint efforts of historians, philologists, philosophers, specialists in religion and sociology.

ARE ANY HISTORICAL PARALLELS POSSIBLE?

The question regarding the possibility of some schools of thought in the Orient being compared to the Renaissance and Reformation is sometimes discussed by historians. Different opinions exist on this matter and Indologists are now taking part in this debate. But we have to keep in mind, that this question can arise only if we assume that parallels can exist between historical processes which had innumerable variations in different countries. There is nothing wrong in comparing different medieval or feudal societies and their history of ideas, but similar methodological criteria should be applied to all societies equally.

To undertake such a comparison, we have to work out some methodological criteria, otherwise our research will face a danger of 'apriori applying the correlation of material, social and spiritual elements of one society (more fully researched) to the corresponding relations and elements of the other',[92] as Pavlov has justly warned.

In order to avoid this error, we have to bear in mind that the same principles, ideas and slogans may have had totally different meanings in different civilizational and historical conditions. For instance, the idea to return to the pure source of religion meant for the European Reformation, an appeal to come back to the equality and social norms of the early Christian communities.[93] Hinduism had no such historic background and hence Tulsidas' stress on the purity of tradition had the opposite meaning, i.e. the preservation of the caste system. There may be many such examples.

Ashrafyan discusses the differences between *bhakti* and the 'cultural-historic phenomena of the European Renaissance and Reformation which, as it is well-known, marked the crisis of feudalism and were trail-blazers of the future bourgeois revolutions'.[94] In our opinion, the question whether there was in India a European-type of Reformation is incorrect and based on ahistorical assumptions. The historical conditions of the two civilizations were very different. Moreover, even within Europe there were various processes of Reformation in different countries and so no uniform definition of Reformation can be used as a model. Any comparison will fail if only one society is used as a model and others are compared to it.

However, the material now available for research shows that despite all doctrinal, religious, ethical, and other differences between the Indian and European civilizations, some similarities did exist between the European Reformation and the religious reform movements in India. Among these similarities should be mentioned the principle of the priority of a believer's inner devotion over external rituals and formal worship. Just as for the radical *bhaktas* all pilgrimages, sacrifices, rites were a 'trumpery' and god's images were mere stones, so did the literature of the Reformation in Europe offer a critique of those, who, as Erasmus of Rotterdam put it, 'take ceremony for religion ... and strangely neglect real devotion.'[95] While educated people like Erasmus mocked the 'fools and blockheads' who 'worship the icons more devoutly than the saints depicted on them',[96] radical Reformation practised iconoclasm and called upon its followers to destroy, as the Hussites in Czechia demanded, 'false churches, altars, icons, jewelled adornments of the icons.'[97]

This was a protest against the lavishness and pomp of the Catholic church which was accused by the Reformation of 'forgetting the Apostles' poverty' and was nurtured chiefly by the bourgeois circles. Secondly, both European and Indian performers were united in the belief that God needed true and sincere devotion, and not a professional clergy. The leaders of the Reformation and, Kabir, would have held the same opinion in this aversion to, 'carry on your shoulders these thousands and thousands of priests, a tribe lazy and in most cases useless',[98] as Ulrich von Hutten, the great German reformer and thinker of the sixteenth century said.

Those who followed the teachings of the European Reformation and castigated the gluttony, avarice and idleness of the priests, would have agreed with the Kashmiri *sufi,* Nur ud-din Rishi:

The rishis of the past were real rishis.
Clad in the rags and loved the bhang leaves.
Aspired for nothing but a little barley.
Renounced and meditated in forests.
See the new rishis of today ...
Craving only for their bellies,
Not caring to remember God.
If such are rishis, who are thieves then?[99]

As early as the thirteenth century, Gerardo Sagarelli, head of the Italian sect of the 'Apostle brothers' and spiritual teacher of the famous Dolcino, leader of the popular uprising, stated that 'prelates were sinful' and said that 'Christ could be worshipped in the woods, even better than in the church.'[100] The Hussite preachers also followed this idea, offered prayers outside the church and rejected all the mysteries of a religious cult. The German sect of 'God's friends', some of whose ideas were shared by Muntzer, proclaimed that a real devotee needed no ascetic austerities, since he could remember God and worship him at any time during his every day life.[101] This idea seems very close to Kabir's thought.[102]

Another common feature of Indian and European medieval thought was the contrast between a true devotee's virtuous life and the vices of the hypocrites who followed formal religion. 'So many people light their candles in front of Virgin Mary's image. But few of them aspire to be like her in purity, humility and divine love. And this is the only devotion that can please the Divine', said Erasmus. These words would be supported by the *bhaktas* and *sufis*. For they also saw humility and purity as the main source and criteria of saintliness.[103]

The God of the Reformation, the God of the *bhaktas* and the God of the *sufis* had different names, but all of these deities were supposed by the reformers to understand 'the language of the heart' and needed neither temples, nor canonic languages, nor sacred texts. Much like Thomas Muntzer who contrasted the 'parchment Bible to the real Holy Book written in human hearts by the living finger of God', Kabir, Nanak and many other *bhaktas* and *sufis* like Baba Farid criticized those who 'searched for God in the books'.[104] It is noteworthy that both in India and in Europe the radical (plebeian) wings of the reformists were characterized by scorn for all forms of bookish knowledge, as well as any kind of non-mystical knowledge. As the Hussites said, 'One who studies free arts or acquires some degree in them, is a "good for nothing" man and a pagan.'[105] Nevertheless, it is well-known that the ideas of the religious reformist schools were also followed by many learned people like Ulrich von Hutten, Erasmus, Abu-l Fazl and Prannath.

The reformist religious thinkers in both Europe and India called upon people to worship God in the spoken language, and not in Arabic, Sanskrit or Latin which were understood only by a few. This appeal for the spoken languages to be used in worship also brings the Reformation close to *bhakti*, Sikhism, and some *sufis*. Here we must also point out a difference: for medieval Europe the Reformation meant a priority of the Bible, translated into vernacular languages, over the later holy traditions, theology, etc. 'True Christians should not follow anything written or said by learned men, they should keep only to what is said in the canonical Bible', said the Hussites. Zwingli, the famous reformer from Germany was of the same opinion.[106] Though it seemed that the *bhaktas* had the same attitudes towards their numerous vernacular versions of Ramayana, Mahabharata and Gita, in fact works like 'Ramacharitamanasa' or 'Sursagar' were not translations, but renditions of holy books, with large portions being original works, not available in the classical texts. One only has to compare Valmiki's and Tulsi's versions to see this clearly.

Among the followers of the *bhakti* saints, the sacred books of Hinduism were available to a small section of people, not only because of the language, but because of the traditional prohibition against low castes having access to them. The *bhakti* texts tried to provide their followers with their own holy literature. Many bhakti preachers denied the authority of the Vedas.[107] Martin Luther's translation of the Bible was however a verbatim version aimed at taking people close to the source of their religion. These differences were based on the individual peculiarities of religion and civilization of the European countries and India.

Another common feature was that both Indian and western reformers had as a social ideal a modest, hardworking and godfearing labourer or trader. For the sake of comparison we shall here quote the regulations of the sect of *sadhs*. This sect was founded in mid-seventeenth century and followed the principles of Kabir and the early Sikhs. Their principles were as follows:

(1) Acknowledge but one God who has made you and can destroy you; to him is all worship due, not to Earth, stone, metal, wood, etc. (2) Be modest and humble, avoid intercourse with those of different faiths. (3) Never lie, steal, distinguish your own from another's property, be content with what you possess. Let not your eyes rest on improper objects, nor on dances or shows. (4) Listen not to the devil's discourse, nor to tales, gossip, calumny, music, singing, except hymns. (5) Never covet anything, take not of another (man). God is the giver of everything, so trust him. (6) When asked what you are, declare yourself a *sadh,* speak not of caste. (7) Wear white, use no pigment, collyrium, *mehndi,* nor marks of caste, chaplet or rosaries. (8) Never drink intoxicants,

never chew betel, nor use perfumes, and tobacco; bow not your head in the presence of idol or man. (9) Take no life, nor do violence, nor seize anything by force. (10) Assume not the mendicant's garb, nor solicit alms, have no dread of necromancy. (11) Let a man have one wife, let a woman not eat a man's leavings, let her be obedient to man. (12) Let not a *sadh* be superstitious.[108] If some specific Indian features are neglected, many of these regulations would be similar to the Puritans or Calvinists.

Both Indian and European reformers of the middle ages cherished some ideas of 'God's kingdom on Earth'. This Utopian ideal in each case, since their civilizations and cultures were different. But both in 'Christ's kingdom' of the Hussites and in *Ramrajya* or the 'City of No Sorrows', poverty, oppressions, disease and violence were supposed to cease forever, and the power of God had to be established. Their God was one whose voice 'comes first from the multitude, the common people' as the German reformists preached[109] or, in the words of Surdas, 'who cares not whether you are a beggar or a raja'.

The idea of the equality of people in the eyes of God, which was in both Indian and European reformist schools of thought, transformed into the idea of people being equal among themselves. But it has to be noted that in India this process was more complicated. The religious reformers in India could not find in the Hindu tradition or religious dogmas some positive ideals similar in meaning to the early Christian communities, which became the main ideal and slogan for the European Reformation. That is why Indian thought had to pass through a more difficult stage of development to arrive at these ideas of equality of men. For the Hussites or for Muntzer the main aim was to make the gentry equal to the peasants, the privileged men of the cities equal to the plebeians,[110] and this was quite natural and understandable, since the knight and the serf, the trader and the poor workman were already equal according to the dogmas of Christianity. They stood together, shoulder to shoulder, in the churches, and performed the same rituals. Inevitably then the radical thinkers of the Reformation suggested and demanded that the social equality proclaimed by the Christian religion and followed by the early Christians, should be established in real life.[111] Hindu culture was less favourable towards the development of egalitarian ideas. It had first to come to the idea that 'God cares not whether you are a beggar or a raja', to doubt the holy principle of ritual purity, to mock the idea of 'pollution' and to state that saintliness and purity are not in one's caste, but in one's thoughts, heart and deeds. No wonder then that egalitarian ideas and their socio-economic ramifications were not so clear in India as compared to the Hussites, Muntzer or the British levellers. Even Kabir, Raidas/Ravidas and Nanak denounced social inequality and caste discrimination more in a moral and ethical sense. The development of egalitarian ideas in India and in the West occurred in different sociocultural conditions, hence were differently spelt out. In any case one has to remember the words of Engels that all these ideals of 'God's kingdom' could be nothing but a fantasy and the first attempt at implementing them had to inevitably return the movement to the framework of the historical development of the epoch.[112] This is what happened in India with the communities and brotherhoods of the *bhaktas* and the radical *sufis,* the *khalsa* of the Sikhs; this is what happened in Europe to the Tabor of the Hussites, the famous Munster Commune of 1534–35 in Germany.

We have discussed some important principles and ideas which were common to the Indian and European religious reformers of the middle age. We have also discussed some variations between the two which were due to the differences in civilizations, religions and social systems. But are these sufficient grounds for a comparison between the Reformist schools of Indian religious thought and the European reformation, which blazed the trail for the anti-feudal revolutions in Europe?

This question is quite natural and is the reason why one also has to compare the social characteristics of the reformist schools of thought in both medieval India and Europe and also compare the stages of their development.

As far as India is concerned, we have already mentioned that *bhakti,* Sufism, Sikhism or other sects and communities of this type were each a very complicated and heterogeneous complex of ideas. Each of them embraced different, sometimes polar views because they were a reflection of the sociocultural heterogeneity of those who found in these ideologies an answer to their concerns and hopes. In each of them one may select a radical wing which reflected the ideas of the urban craftsmen and workmen, poor traders and peasants, but for a long time the radical wings coexisted with more moderate ones. Some thinkers and schools of *bhakti* and Sufism did not refer to any social problems or their critique. Mira Bai, the Radha Vallabha sect and others are a few such examples,[113] though they played a great role in the development of Indian culture. For many poets and thinkers, the ideas of *bhakti* or *sufism* were directly connected with defending the traditional social order and values, including caste inequality. Thus no reformist trend in medieval India can belong exclusively to 'urban', 'peasant' or other definite category.

But was not the European reformation so heterogeneous and variegated in the same way? In their desire to bring the Church to the basics of early Christianity, people of different social standing and views were united. Yet, not all of them thought like the Hussites or Muntzer. The social and cultural differentiation between Reformation participants was vividly described by Engels in his work on the 'Peasants' War' in Germany, and the same can be said about the Reformation in other countries. Reformation in Europe seems to be a process more complicated than being only the struggle of the developing bourgeoisie against the feudal state and the Catholic Church.

Interestingly, the development of the religious reformist trends in Indian and European thought occurred in somewhat similar organizational forms. Both in India and in western European countries everything started from the numerous sects, communities, brotherhoods and orders which followed the ideas of reformed or 'purified' religion. It was at this stage that the European 'heretical' sects like the Anabaptists, the Lollards, and the Apostolic Brothers seem to have similarities with the *sufi* orders, *bhakti* sects, and early Sikhs. All of them preferred inner worship to the outward formal religion, preached the idea of the soul's direct contact with God without any professional clergy, held in scorn those who 'search for God in the books' and criticized luxury and monastic seclusion, greed, lust, pomp and ambition. Both preached the ethical norms of humility, meekness, submissiveness and modesty.

In both cases the culmination came when the peaceful sects were transformed into bearers of the militant ideas of liberation. In India and in Europe this struggle was seen as a holy duty, as God's will. 'It is crystal clear that God has hired me as a labourer for a penny a day, and I sharpen my sickle to cut the spikes. My voice will announce to highest truth', said Muntzer, and this sounds like Guru Gobind's statement on his divine mission in the "Bacittar Natak".[114]

The peaceful ideology of the European reformers too developed into the militant ideas of the Hussites in the beginning of the sixteenth century, and led to revolutions in the Netherlands and in England. We shall make here some comparisons between this process and the evolution of *bhakti* into the militant ideology of the Marathas and Sikhs.

The Soviet Indologist, Reisner, has described the Maratha movement as a freedom movement, and that of the Sikhs as a peasants' war. (Abd us-Samad, who led the Mughal armies against the Sikhs, was equated by Reisner to Truchzes, who suppressed the peasants' war in Germany.)[115] Alayev considers the Maratha movement as ethnic and that of the Sikhs as religious-communal and separatist, for which there is testimony like the 'religious and sectarian character of the ideology, recruitment and organization which brought about the feeling of the Sikhs' spiritual superiority over other people', and their distancing from the non-Sikh population.[116]

The Maratha movement was a struggle for freedom in which religious reformist ideas played an important role, but failed to become the main factor, for Marathi *bhakti* joined hands with the patriotic ideas of 'Maharashtra Dharma'. Since the liberation war was fought for restoring *dharma*, *bhakti* itself merged with the traditional ideology. The Maratha movement has some similarities with the history of other countries, like the Reconquista in Spain, the Caucasian peoples' struggle against Iran and Turkey and the anti-British uprisings in Ireland.

As far as the Sikh movement is concerned, it is more difficult to define its character. The peasants were the main fighting force in the movement, as were craftsmen and traders. Indeed in the regions occupied by the Sikh army, local Rajput feudals were driven away and their lands appropriated. But is this enough to consider the Sikh movement as a peasant war?

Looking through the literature of the Sikh movement we find that purely agrarian demands are conspicuous by their absence. Of course, nobody should expect to find in India something like

Watt Tyler's Smithfield Programme or the programme of the German peasants. This is quite natural since in India the word 'peasant' embraces a wide range of socio-economic groups. The majority of the Sikh agriculturists who fought under the banner of Guru Gobind and Banda—were members of the socially elevated strata of the rural communities. They were landholding peasants who, though they were exploited by the Mughal state and its taxation system, enjoyed at the same time social rights and were themselves masters of the tenants and low-caste 'community servants'.[117] These peasants had nothing in common with the feudally dependent peasants and serfs of Europe, were personally free, proud and militant. They declined to pay rent to the Mughal state, to feed the Mughal horses with their corn, or pay the humiliating *jizya;* they wanted to establish their own state where they could occupy the place of the Mughal *jagirdars.* The craftsmen and traders who fought in the army with the Sikhs also wanted to have their own 'City of No Sorrows', where, as Guru Gobind promised, all ruinous cesses and tributes would be abolished; fair interest rates would be established, and law and order would prevail.[118] All this was compatible with the egalitarian principles of Sikhism and patriotic ideas of the liberation war and was the basis for the movement, which cannot thus be seen as a peasants' war. As far as Alalyev's suggestion is concerned, the definition of 'religious-communal and separatist' seems an anachronism of the twentieth century and can be applied to any medieval and modern liberation movement, where religious reform played an important role.

In this connection we suggest a comparison of the Sikh movement with the Hussites' war in Bohemia or Czechia. Despite all civilizational and cultural differences both movements were a combination of the liberation war, social conflict and religious reformation. Both the Sikh and the Hussite movements starred as peaceful sects preaching the ideas of their founders. For the Sikhs it was Guru Nanak, for the Hussites Jan Hus and Jeronym Prazsky, the latter being the disciples of the famous British reformer of the Church, John Wycliffe (1330–84). While the Sikhs had peaceful and even friendly relations with the Mughal power initially, the Hussites were from the very beginning persecuted by the Catholic Church. In the year 1415 Jan Hus and Jeronym Prazsky were burnt at the stake, and the infuriated Hussites rose in rebellion.

Unlike the Catholic Church, Hinduism never had a strong organization or strict religious system of dogmas and was, therefore, tolerant of the numerous sects. The beginning of Sikh history almost coincided with Mughal invasion, and during the period of empire-building, the Mughals paid little heed to the Sikhs but tolerated them afterwards.

The Hussite preachers wanted to return the clergy to 'Apostolic poverty' and to confiscate Church lands and the monasteries. Nanak criticized the *brahmans* and the *mullahs* more on moral grounds. Yet, both schools wanted the clergy to be treated on par with the other members of the community, they demanded the use of vernacular languages at worship and a denial of idol-worship. The Hussite preachers neglected churches and preached their ideas in open places; they refused to worship icons, images, saints and holy water, rejected pilgrimages and celibacy, heard confessions in public. Likewise the Sikh gurus criticized 'stone-worship', rituals, pilgrimages, asceticism and ridiculed 'purity' of the high-caste men. Both the Hussites and Sikhs considered it necessary to hold joint feasts and community eating where all members ate together.[119]

The transition to a militant movement also had some similar features. In both cases it was a liberation war: in one case against the Mughals, in the other against the German feudals.[120] 'The religious and sectarian character of the ideology, recruitment and organization' were the same for both, the Sikhs and the Hussites. In our view, modern historiography now has accumulated enough data for the historians, especially Marxists, to stop 'making excuses' for the religious and sectarian character of the medieval movements and schools of thought. These movements and ideas had no other way to develop given their historical context. Mystical exaltation, visions, trances and the feelings of self-sacrifice and fanaticism—all these features were typical of the social liberators of the period. As far as 'spiritual superiority over the aliens' is concerned, this feeling was widespread among the Hussite masses even more than the Sikhs. Despite all their militancy, the Sikhs shared some common features of Indian culture, including the ideas of communal amity that were preached by all the Gurus. The Hussites on the other hand, believed in the 'Last Day of Judgement' when only their followers would survive while all others would perish.

We may compare the armed struggle of the Sikhs and the Hussites through an analysis of their characteristic features. Both movements were heterogeneous, socially and culturally, and were divided into two wings each. One was more radical, the other more moderate (the Calixtines or the Utraquists of the Hussite movement and the so-called 'pure' or *tat* Sikhs who did not recognize Gobind's reformation of the community). But after Gobind's reforms, the radical wing assumed power and changed the character of the movement with the destruction of the *masands*. In the Hussite movement, from the very beginning of the armed struggle, the radicals and the moderates acted independently. It is noteworthy that in both cases the leadership of the radical wings fell to patriotic-minded and talented people, who belonged to the social elite: Guru Gobind and Jan Zizka of the Hussites. Their military talents and organizational abilities played a great role in the development of these movements but at the same time prevented them from further radicalization. It is known that Jan Zizka mercilessly suppressed the ultra-radical wing of the movement—the Adamites who wanted equal property rights and spoke against all state organization.[121] We have no similar data on the Sikhs, but it cannot be doubted that Guru Gobind would have done the same with any radical group.

It is noteworthy that the ideas of equitable property distribution were much more widespread in the European Reformation movements than in their Indian counterparts. In the Hussite capital Tabor, wooden barrels were placed where those who came to join the movement had to deposit their belongings, but, as Engels observed, it was only a military measure.[122] The ideas of equal property or some forms of rigid egalitarianism were typical for many leaders of the European Reformation like the levellers and diggers of England, Muntzer and the Anabaptists. The most significant example of an attempt to put into practice these ideas was the Munster Commune of 1534–35. In India many saints preached renunciation of all worldly wealth and glorified poverty, but they never demanded this of the whole of society. When the author of 'Sunesar' advised people to 'destroy the mistake of "yours" and "mine"', it was more an appeal for generosity.[123] The absence of strong egalitarian ideas and appeals for equal property should not be seen as a weakness in Indian reformist thought. These ideas were naturally alien to the craftsmen, traders or peasants and would have been the demand of the lowest strata of society, the paupers and the rural poor.

Both Sikhs and Hussites established 'free zones' where they tried to at least partially put into effect their social and ethical ideas. But in both cases the results were quite opposite to the ones desired. The Hussites called upon peasants and traders to stop paying taxes and tithes to the feudal lords but at the same time they collected taxes from people for their own treasury. Their capital city of Tabor, as well as other cities which came under their control gradually became typical medieval cities with guilds.[124] Likewise the 'state of Khalsa' projected by the Sikhs was just a replica of the Mughal state.

In this connection it is not out of place to discuss whether the very notion of 'anti-feudal struggle' is applicable to all forms of social struggle and social movements of the middle ages. We should clarify whether the struggle of the peasants, craftsmen and other oppressed people against the feudal lords was always anti-feudal in the sense of it being directed against feudalism.

Historically we know of many an uprising of the people against feudalism and also for the preservation of some traditional, patriarchal institutions and 'liberties' of primitive tribes and communities. For example, the rebellions of Mu'qanna and Babeq in the Arab Khalifate and Valdences in Western Europe were efforts, as Engels points out, to somehow block the historical process.[125] Such movements were typical in early feudalism and their labelling as anti-feudal has to be qualified by the fact that they aimed at the conservation of some archaic pre-feudal structure. In a fully developed feudal structure movements generally aimed at abolishing serfdom, unifying the country, overcoming feudal disintegration and increasing the tempo of development. In some cases, the movements of later feudalism blazed the trail for bourgeois revolutions.

From this point of view both the Sikh and Hussite movements can be seen as belonging to the second stage. Their paths were, as Pavlov writes, directed 'against the dark side of their own stage of feudalism'.[126] Both the stages occurred in feudal states which had failed to solve the problems of ethnic and political disintegration (for India this task was not achievable at this stage, but a strong tendency towards it did exist). Neither the Hussite, nor the Sikh movement reached these goals due to reasons peculiar to each country. After the defeat of the Hussites, their movement returned to peaceful sectarian forms (e.g. 'the Czech brothers' community of Peter Chelchicky). The Czech-Hungarian Unia (merger) was defeated by the Turks in 1526, after which the Czech lands came under the jurisdiction of the Habsburgh Empire and it became impossible to establish an independent state upto 1918. In India the Sikhs, despite many a defeat never gave up their armed struggle and they played a role in the fall of the Mughal empire. A Sikh state was founded at the beginning of the nineteenth century only to disintegrate later and be conqured by the British.

Returning once more to the Reformation, our analysis has made it possible to state that the religious reformist movements in India and Western Europe had some common basic features. Some *bhakti* communities and Sikhism were typologically close to the European Reformation, but at the same time it has to be borne in mind that Kabir and Muntzer, Gobind and Cromwell represented different temporal stages and civilizational colours of the same process. The bourgeois reformation of the Indian religions began only in the nineteenth century, but the reformist movements of the middle ages became its crucial source of ideas and principles.

4

In Quest of the Way Out

Our study has reached a period of Indian history which is recorded in the historical memory of the people as a fateful and tragic one. The disintegration of the Mughal empire had become irreversible by the time of Aurangzeb who made some desperate efforts to stop it. But neither the bigotry of the emperor, nor his military might, nor the cruel suppression of the *kafirs* and unorthodox Muslims were of any avail, and shortly after Aurangzeb's death the mightiest empire of the Orient remained only in the nostalgic reminiscences of the old Mughal aristocracy. The independent states which emerged from the ruins of the empire started bloody wars among themselves. Neither the invasions of Nadir Shah and the Afghan rulers, nor the colonial expansion of European powers brought about unity among Indian rulers. Having initially come to India as peaceful traders, the Europeans became a military power and political force which increasingly interfered with governance of the Indian states. The main aim of the European companies was not just profit, but greater colonial possessions in India. The military rivalry between the European powers for domination in India ended with the victory of the British which, as Marx observed, became a power both military and territorial.[1] The process of the colonial transformation of India began.

The main events, actors and results of this historical drama are well known to scholars and readers. Our interest will be centred not on events, but on the way they were reflected in the sphere of ideas and on what the Indians thought of this fateful epoch.

THE TRAGIC AGE

All scholars agree that the eighteenth century was a tragic age for India. But apart from this emotional estimate there exist two scholarly approaches to this period in the history of India. One approach can be called traditional, since it is a long-established one. The main idea of this estimate is as follows: with the fall of the Mughal empire, the Indian society entered a stage of deep crisis and disintegration which affected all spheres of life. Bloody wars, feudal anarchy, ruin of the cities, impoverishment and starvation of the peasants, decay of arts and crafts, moral degradation became rampant. According to Sarkar, 'the retrogression of medieval Indian civilization under Aurangzeb is noticeable not only in the fine arts ..., but still more in the low intellectual type of the new generation'.[2] To Raghuvanshi, the 'breakup of the Mughal monarchy released forces of political disintegration which destroyed the creative and co-operative spirit of man. They caused deterioration in every phase of national life'.[3]

Some scholars criticize this approach as one-sided and Delhi-centric. They argue that the gloomy and sinister pictures of decay are given only by the Mughal chronicles, which reflected the sorrows of the Delhi nobility after the loss of absolute power. The disintegration of the empire was also accompanied by a development of arts, literature, languages and polity in the independent states. Thus Muzaffar Alam gives a convincing description of the economic development of Awadh and the Punjab in the first half of the eighteenth century and hence rejects the 'uncritical acception of the British descriptions and Persian chroniclers' estimate'.[4] According to Panikkar, from the ruin of the Mughal empire a new political, economic and cultural life emerged and, 'the pre-colonial political anarchy, intellectual stagnation and cultural backwardness when contrasted to the "progress" under British benevolence were to some an explanation and to others a justification for the conquest of India'.[5]

Indeed, when one reads the Mughal chronicles and the literature of the eighteenth century, especially north Indian literature, the picture that is conjured up is of a society whose best days were already behind it, leaving only wars, blood, ruin and desolation. The Urdu and Persian poetry of the period uses the rhetorical image of an abandoned garden once full of flowers but now desolate and dried up by the merciless sun.

No flowers, only thorns are visible,
Green trees have withered,
Pillars of dust rise on the flower-beds,
Like hands lifted in despair

This was written by Nazir Akbarabadi, a great Urdu poet of the epoch. In his poem 'Shahr-e ashob' he gave a shocking description of the ruined and desolate Agra, once a flourishing Mughal capital, but in Nazir's days, a city of impoverished and starving people who lamented their fate and prayed for a quick death as the only way out.[6]

We may also turn to the brilliant *qalam* of Muhammad Rafi Sauda. He was a poet and a satirist, and in his immensely popular pamphlets he says,

The ministers of the empire have been summoned for consultation. See how they consult for the welfare of the state. The Imperial Paymaster is thinking up some scheme to stay at home doing nothing and still draw his pay, while the Chief Minister has his eyes on the silver knobs of the royal tent and is calculating how much they will fetch in the market. They are all of them strangers to any sense of shame. They spend time in gambling and only come when summoned. ... Yet each of them in his own estimate is a veritable paragon. If war comes they creep out of their fortresses just long enough to draw up an army which, you may depend on it, will turn and run from every battle, soldiers who quake with fear even when they see the barber take out his razor to shave them, horsemen who fall out of their beds at night even at the dream of a horse rearing under them.

But even this celebrated satirist's castigating words choke in his throat, and he bursts out in the genuine pain of a true patriot:

How can I describe the desolation of Delhi? There is no house from where the jackal's cry cannot be heard. ... Its citizens do not possess even the essential cooking pots, and vermin crawl in the places where in former days men used to welcome the coming of spring with music and rejoicing. The lovely buildings which once made the famished man forget his hunger are in ruins now. ... The villages are deserted, the trees themselves are gone and wells are full of corpses. Jahanabad, you never deserved this terrible fate, you who were once vibrant with life and love and hope like the heart of a young lover, you for whom men afloat upon the ocean of the world once set their course as to the promised shore, you from whose dust men came to gather pearls.'

The literature of the eighteenth century which flourished at a time when the whole of India waged wars and all states fought among themselves, had to introduce changes even in some traditional feudal ethics. Traditionally war was a virtue for a feudal ruler, his aspiration for more lands and glory was praised.[8] But amidst the sinister realities of the eighteenth century the author of *Insha-e Herkern* wrote that for the benefit of the society 'kings of empire (should be) content with their portions (and) establish between one another the bonds of sincerity and unity, so that people of God may build a mansion of rest ... and merchants may peacefully trade and make people glad with the rarities of each place'.[9] Unfortunately, in the atmosphere of the eightneenth century India this was but a dream.

Even in these conditions however, progress was inherent. In our opinion, those Indian scholars who suggest that the fall of the imperial centre meant the uplift of the provinces and regions are justified.[10] Indeed, these were hard times for Delhi and Agra. But do not the sources testify to the progress and flourishing of Lucknow, Pune, Srirangapatnam, etc.? Despite wars and desolation trade was carried on and local markets flourished in many places.[11] This century is sometimes seen as the one where fanaticism and obscurantism ruled supreme, but it is also a fact that Sawai Jai Singh, his famous observatories and research in astronomy belonged to this century. He was the first Indian to use telescopes for astronomical observations. The eighteenth century has also left us a lot of treatises on medicine, mathematics, chemistry and other practical sciences and technologies.[12] The eighteenh-century Indian historiography (both in Persian and in regional languages) developed a number of novel and interesting approaches that deserve further research.

Religious reformist schools of thought continued their activity in all religious communities. Brotherhoods and *panths* of the *bhaktas* and *sufi* orders enjoyed popularity. For instance, among the *bhakti* saints of the period we may note such names as Prannath and Charandas (1703–80). The latter was a *nirgun bhakti* follower and called upon the devotees 'not to be entangled in the Vedas and

Puranas', admitted all people, including women and 'untouchables' into his community where common feasts were organized for all members and guests.[13] Charandas belonged to the tradition of Kabir, but other schools of *bhakti* and *sufi* orders flourished at that period.

Despite all odds, the development of literature and the arts continued. Some traditional forms and genres indeed withered away but were replaced by new ones. The decay of Mughal miniature painting was followed by the development of regional schools like Kangra, Pahari, etc. The development of literature in India at this time was marked by many complicated processes. They should not be seen only as features of decadence and panegyrics to the kings and immorality, as some scholars suggest. It is too narrow a frame for the diversity and polyphony of eighteenth century literary works, which include the scathing satire of Sauda, the tragic and noble lyrics of Mir, the wise and democratic verses by Vemana and the heroic poetry of the liberation movements. There were also the pamphlets and letters of Shah Valiullah Dehlavi, the eloquent prose of the Gujarati writer Premanand, the diaries of Ananda Ranga Pillai; all these laid the foundation for the development of prose. The century was crowned by a jewel in the form of Nazir Akbarabadi. This poor teacher from Agra was a great poet who not only lamented the plight of the people of Agra, but depicted the beauty and majesty of common life. Against the background of the tragic events of the eighteenth century his famous *Admi Nama* or 'The Book of Man' stood out splendidly:

In this world a Shah is a man,
And a wretched pauper is equally a man ...
A man offers his prayers (in a mosque)
While a man steals his shoes.
A man sacrifices his life for a man,
And a man kills a man with a sword ...
A man can be like a priceless ruby,
And a man can be more nasty than filth.
One who is black like the bottom of a frying pan is a man,
And one who is white like silver is also a man.
Oh Nazir, a man is the best of all,
And the worst of all is also a man.[14]

The reality of eighteenth century India was as complicated and interwoven with good and evil as 'a man' in Nazir's poem. It is obvious that the fall of the empire was not a starting point for any revolutionary change in the society. But does this mean that, in the words of Antonova, 'the disintegration of the Mughal empire was only one of a number of cyclical events, which were so frequent in Indian history and were by no means a factor of some socio-economic changes in the society'? This estimate was preceded by Antonova's analysis of the whole kaleidoscope of emerging and crashing empires in India.[15]

If we adopt such a viewpoint it will mean that after the empire crashed the Indian society was, for the whole of the eighteenth century, waiting for the new masters and that it failed to notice their advent. But if this were really so, why did the process of colonial empire-building last so long? And more importantly, if the great empire crashed into a conglomerate of states and each part was just a small copy of the Mughal state, why did some states become easy prey for the British while others resisted bravely and even tried to introduce some reforms? And last but not the least, if in the eighteenth century the Europeans found the Indian society primitive, then why did Indian thought produce its first enlightened and bourgeois reformers, its first national press and national movements at the beginning of the nineteenth century? Whence came these people, who were capable of understanding new ideas? We can hardly explain all this as a beneficial influence of the 'British Raj', for even in 1853, Marx observed that the constructive efforts of the British in India were hardly visible from the heap of ruins.[16]

To have a greater understanding of the problem, let us try to compare the disintegration of the Mughal empire with similar processes in the Delhi sultanate. At first glance, both empires had much in common during their integration and disintegration processes. Indeed, the Mughals possessed a greater territory as compared to the Sultanate, but the Mughals had a more developed and efficient administrative machinery, were more powerful militarily and were able to create a whole 'style of life', which is even now known as 'Mughlai'. Despite all this, centrifugal tendencies overpowered it.

But on analysing the two disintegration processes, we see some important differences. The fall of the Mughal empire was to a large extent a result of the great popular movements, into which anti-Mughal slogans were interwoven with the religious reformation. Nothing of this kind happened in the Delhi sultanate. Of course, there were popular movements during the sultanate also, and many famous *sufi* and *bhakti* communities existed but these communities and their ideologies bear no comparison with the Sikhism of Guru Gobind or the ideas of Ramdas. Firoze Shah Tughlaq destroyed some 'dirty-headed sects' for the sake of the purity of Islam. His adversaries were peaceful preachers who met secretly and sang hymns in the bazaars.[17] Unlike the Delhi Sultans, Aurangzeb had to fight not just for the sake of Islam but for the sake of the empire for which the mighty armies of Shivaji and the Sikhs were a deadly menace.

Secondly, unlike parts of the Delhi Sultanate, the seceding states of the Mughal empire were large and powerful, populated by ethnically and culturally consolidated peoples (this was especially so for Avadh, Bengal, Hyderabad, Mysore, Carnatic, Punjab, though there are reservations about the Maratha state). Also the disintegration process in the Mughal empire took place in a society ethnically, culturally, socially and economically more mature than the Delhi sultanate. Thus the two disintegration process were basically different and the crash of the Mughal state was not just 'an ordinary cyclic event'. But what was it then?

We have already stated that the Mughal empire emerged at a period when integration processes within the Indian society were too weak to be effective. The crash of the Delhi sultanate and the mighty empires of the South was painful, bloody and cruel, but an inevitable process. The seceding states were also engaged in rivalry, but the period between the two empires was by no means a dark age. Relatively small states like the Gujarati sultanate, Jaunpur and the Rajput principalities had suitable basis for the development and consolidation of economy, trade, market and cultural identity. It can be supposed that later on, as it happened in Europe or Russia, the borders of the smaller states became too narrow for the market economy and a strong centripetal tendency followed, at least for some of the more developed and ethnically close regions. This path of development cannot now be clearly emphasized because of the assumptions of the readers that feudal disintegration was an evil for which Russia and India paid a heavy price. But despite this, the historical experience of many countries shows that to reject disintegration and to strive for unity, a feudal society had to live through a disintegration under which all the necessary premises for unity can emerge.

Mughal invasion had interrupted this process of development of Indian society at the important stage of feudal disunity. In world history as well as in the history of the Orient there exist several examples of similar situations, i.e. a more developed feudal society was a neighbour to a less developed or tribal society. The latter society began to live through the crisis of tribal relations and the early phase of feudalism which was usually very militant and ever desirous of acquiring more lands (this happened many times with the Germans, the Franks, the Slavs, and so on). And so a new empire-builder fell upon a prosperous neighbour who had already lived through the early feudal stage but was not able to overcome feudal disunity. In such a state the more developed society was an easy prey for any invader (as were Russia, Hungary, Poland for the Mongols). A tribal, semi-tribal or early feudal society thus gained ascendency over a more developed country, which was subjugated and kept under control by military might. Such an empire might have achieved a high stage of cultural and economic development, but sooner or later it would disintegrate, since the socio-economic, cultural, political and ethnic processes of the feudal disunity period were not halted by the invader. India was not ready to be a united state before the Mughals arrived, so the centrifugal forces acquired strength and power despite the invasion.

Unlike Russia, India lived through the process described above several times in its history. If we bear in mind the invasions of Huns, Rajputs and so on, no matter whether the empire-builder was an Indian or an outsider, we see that similar situations occurred in the pre-Muslim period also. The main reason for this was that each time the invasion forcibly halted the natural process of socio-economic and political development. So that the stage of feudal disunity was not allowed to continue naturally and to work objectively for the basis of future unity. After a passage of time centrifugal forces resumed their activity to bring the society back to the situation that it was in before the invasion. Though, of course, each time such a return took place at a higher stage of socio-economic, political, ethnic and cultural development.

The disintegration of the Delhi sultanate was generated by the objective reality of the local markets, languages, cultures, their consolidation and development. But Mughal society was much more mature economically, culturally and politically. One of the most important testimonies to this was the tendency to build a strong centralized state which signified the approach to more developed forms of feudalism. Since this process was incapable of being successful in a multi-ethnic state like India (during feudalism), the attempt to do so, undertaken by Akbar, failed. But this attempt also gave a boost to the further development of Indian society. This evolution, however, took several trajectories and forms and became the main basis for the mighty anti-Mughal movements.

The fall of the Mughal empire was a result of an objective disintegration process which was necessary at this stage for Indian society to develop further. It was not a mechanical repetition of what happened with the Delhi sultanate. Neither was it a beginning of the crisis of feudalism. Indian feudalism had at that time far from exhausted its potential, and the fall of the empire might have had an accelerating effect. But, as Antonova rightly observes, 'the colonial expansion of the European powers made the disintegration a tragic event for India'.[18]

Sometimes the whole of the eighteenth century in India is measured by the yardstick of colonial invasion. If such an approach is adopted, India appears to be the heroine of some medieval romance. She is seen as conquered, abducted, fought for, but without any reaction on her part. The Mughals were gone, and the sleeping princess waited for another strong hero, now in the red dress of the British soldier. Such a traditional view fails to take into consideration the processes and developments in the independent states, as well as the reaction of Indian thought to the sinister events of the age. What the Indians thought about the situation in their country and what they considered as necessary to improve their situation, is a very important topic for the history of ideas, and this will be the main theme of this chapter.

'TO SAVE AND REBUILD THE EMPIRE'

The fall of the Mughal empire altered not only the state but the very way of Indian life. This process was especially painful for the Mughal aristocracy, which instead of being the 'lords of the time' found itself in the gloomy position of the people whose good days were over. Ordinary people also felt pain and shock at the disruption of the stability of the society. Quite naturally these people saw the only way out of the crisis in returning to the bygone days of the empire. The times which were previously called the 'Dark Age' were now seen as ideal. This longing for the 'golden era' of the past is a feature of all periods of history and all civilizations. The ideas of the re-establishment of the empire were strongly and convincingly put forth by Shah Waliullah Dehlavi (1703–62). This well-known thinker was a hereditary scholar of theology and the head of the famous Rahimiya *madrasa* in Delhi. As a religious reformer he was profoundly concerned with the country's fate. His patriotism was not a contemplative one, but active and forceful.

Looking at the main reasons for the crisis of the empire, he felt that they were the mundane ones of socio-economic disproportions and imbalances in Mughal society. He stated that many people like *ulema,* warriors, poets and nobles appropriated public wealth and gave nothing back for the benefit of society, while the workers and traders suffered oppressions and hence became hostile to the state. The result, according to Waliullah, was social disorder and moral degradation of those whose duty was to take care of the country's security. This fact was used by the enemies, among whom he listed the Sikhs, the Marathas and the Rajputs, for their own ends.[19]

Not limiting himself merely to critical analysis, Waliullah approached the king and aristocracy of the empire, as well as mighty independent chiefs with concrete plans for the re-establishment of the Mughal empire. This programme included the following points: (1) To immediately pacify the rebellious *Jats* who were at the time dangerous for the empire. (2) To enlarge significantly the royal domain of the *Khalisa* lands, 'for the empire is weakened when the crown lands are curtailed and the treasury empties'. (3) To grant lands only to the highest *umara* of the empire, while other officers should receive salaries in cash, since they are economically weak, they fail to keep their *jagirs* under control and the lands are lost to the *ijaradar's* possession. (4) To remove from royal service all those who had defiled themselves with disloyalty and treason, to confiscate their ranks and *jagirs.* (5) To strengthen the army, to appoint as commanders only those who are generous, brave, and loyal to the Shah. Salaries paid to the army should be regulated. (6) Leasing and farming out crown lands should be prohibited. (7) To appoint as judges and government officials only honest, incorruptible and religious men. (8) To strengthen Islam. (9) 'The king of Islam and his *umara* should not waste their time in luxury and enjoyment; it behoves them to repent and never commit such sins in future.'[20]

This programme is one of the most interesting documents of the epoch. According to Waliullah, rebirth of the empire was possible only if efforts were made in all directions, socio-economic, political and moral. This very complex approach testified to Waliullah's rationalism. But if we analyse his suggestions now, it will be clear that Waliullah's main ideals and means of salvation were those that had been carried out in the past. Strong royal power, controlling the main part of the lands, abolition of the feudal grants system and transformation of feudal landholders into the salaried officials—these were all a return to some of Akbar's ideas on reforms. All the measures proposed by the Delhi thinker had the aim of improving the economic situation and establishing the strength and might of the Mughal empire, and relieving the tax burden on the peasants, craftsmen and traders.

Does it mean that Waliullah planned to rebuild the empire on Akbar's principles? We could have answered positively but for one important aspect: while proposing the implementation of the socio-economic reforms of Akbar, Waliullah renounced his religious policy. The empire he wanted to build was to be a Muslim state where all non-Muslims could only hope for tolerance. Moreover, Waliullah regarded the *Jats*, the Marathas and the Sikhs as rebels and as enemies of Islam.

For the sake of justice one should note that Waliullah had never been a bigot. He as a rationalist, critically assessing mundane and religious problems. He insisted that every Muslim should have a right to *ijtihad* or independent judgement on all religious dogmas. Like the 'enlightened philosophers' of Akbar's court he criticized blind faith and thoughtless pursuit of all traditions.[21] Moreover, he was bold enough to state that religion itself should change as the realities of life had changed. Waliullah was an ardent supporter of the practical sciences and research; he considered it the greatest gift to be 'vested with the robes of invention'.[22] Waliullah wrote a Persian translation of the Quran, while his son Abdul Aziz translated this into Urdu—the language of the Delhi bazaars and secular literature. Waliullah is rightly seen as a predecessor of the great Muslim reformers of the nineteenth century, who contributed so much to the modernization of Islamic thought.[23]

Waliullah was close to the freethinkers of Akbar's age, but failed to understand the ideas of Hindu-Muslim cultural interaction and he claimed to have distinguished between 'true' and 'false' religions. While not an enemy of the Hindus, he considered that the moral rebirth of society should be based on Islam only and the non-Muslims should be only a submissive community of *kafirs*. One of the main features of the crisis was, for Waliullah, that 'all remaining power was with the Hindus, since the majority of officials are Hindus. All luxury is now in their homes, while the Muslims have a cloud of grief and poverty over their heads.'[24] For the rebirth of the empire, according to Waliullah, one had to return everything to the proper place of the pre-Akbar state model and this was an effort to combine Akbar's reforms with pre-Akbar (if not Aurangzeb's) religious policy.

When Waliullah realized that neither the Mughal king nor the grandees of the empire were in haste to gird their loins for the uplift of the empire, he made a rather dubious attempt himself. He invited the Afghan king Ahmad Shah Durrani to come with his armies to India. He wrote, 'To save the cause, a mighty king is needed who possesses greatness and military strength. There is no way out. The great king has to invade India, to ruin the Maratha domination and to save the Muslims from the clutches of the infidels.' Afghan invasion was to become a war against the *kafirs* for the establishment of Islamic power. In the same letter he wrote: 'May God forgive Nadir Shah who was victorious over the Muslims and touched not the *jats* and the Marathas. After Nadir

Shah the enemies gained strength while in the camp of Islam confusion rules supreme. If, God forbid, the infidels remain in the same position and Muslims be weak, no sight will remain of Islam.'[25]

There was nothing unpatriotic in this view for if it was impossible to rebuild the Mughal empire by Indian princes a new Babur was needed. The whole construction of the 'return to the past' had a logical justification. It has to be borne in mind that Afghanistan was, for a significant period of time, a part of the empire, so its ruler was not a foreigner for Waliullah. For the Delhi thinker, the Muslim rulers of Afghanistan and even Iran were more his compatriots than the *Jats* and Marathas. Here Indian thought as represented by Waliullah can be compared with Abu-1 Fazl who said that his love for his country co-existed with an equal feeling of spiritual closeness to all the cultures and communities of India.

It has to be noted that the hope for a new Babur warmed, at this time, not only Waliullah's heart. In a collection of letters of the Nawab of Broach compiled by Kishore Das, secretary to the Nawab, there is a letter to Ahmad Shah Durrani. In this letter, the Nawab says, 'people of Hindustan are fed up with the oppression of the infidels', and the Afghan ruler was begged to 'restore the lost fortune of India and the prestige of the Timurid dynasty'.[26] It would be unjust to Waliullah to say that he was ignorant of the consequences of the proposed medicine for the diseased Mughal empire. He was fully aware of the real cost of the invasion. In a letter to Najib ud-Dawlah, the Nawab of Rohilkhand, he wrote, 'lamentations of the oppressed are heard everywhere, so if your army enters Delhi, measures should be taken to avoid giving any offence to the Muslims and zimmis.'[27]

Waliullah's plan was then to save the empire. The Delhi scholar was destined to see it implemented when the Afghan armies of Ahmad Shah Durrani invaded India and looted Delhi, after their victory over the Marathas in Panipat in 1761. This did not, however, give him any joy as Ahmad Shah and the Indian *umara* did not care about India or the prestige of the Timurid dynasty. They looted what was left after the invasion of Nadir Shah and others and hurried back to avoid the danger of internal rebellion.

ATTEMPT AT A BREAKTHROUGH

When in the first half of the eighteenth century Waliullah spoke of the enemies of the empire, he meant the Marathas, the Rajputs, the Sikhs and other rebels. But later in the century emerged one more menace which threatened not only the Mughal empire and its remnants, but the whole of India. This was the European, and more importantly British colonial expansion. After the fateful battle of Plassey, Bengal, the gem of the Mughal crown, came fully under British control, to be followed by Orissa, Awadh, Varanasi, etc. At the same time the British won the seven-year war in the South (1756–63) and became masters of rich and populous land. While expanding their colonial empire, the British inevitably clashed with the independent states who were successors to the Mughal empire.

Athar Ali has divided the successor states into two main categories. One category was the 'succession states' and was characterized by similarities to the Mughal empire and employed the Mughal administrative machinery. This category included states like Hyderabad, Bengal, and Awadh. The second category, according to the scholar, included the Maratha confederacy, the Sikh state, etc., and though they 'used some Mughal elements, had different political backgrounds'. Outside these two was Mysore with its 'serious attempt at modernism'.[28]

Such a classification seems interesting and justified. No newly independent state could avoid Mughal influence and even Shivaji, lifelong enemy of the Mughals, ordered the compilation of a special dictionary of Sanskrit and Persian administrative terms, for under the guise of Sanskrit and Maratha terminology Mughal institutions were actually working.[29]

The 'succession states' were those which emerged according to the traditional scheme of feudal separatism: finding the centre weak, the Mughal viceroys of Awadh, Hyderabad and Bengal proclaimed themselves independent rulers like their counterparts in the Delhi sultanate. The Sikh and the Maratha states, however, owed their independence to the mighty anti-Mughal struggles under the banners of religious reformation. In our opinion, this testifies to the fact that the Mughal empire was an attempt to cement together people and regions who were ethnically, economically and politically different, and when the empire crashed, these differences became even more vivid. Perhaps this can also explain why the Indian states reacted so differently to European colonial expansion.

While analysing the events of the eighteenth century, especially the second half, we may view Athar Ali's scheme from a new angle. A large number of 'succession states' became an easy prey for the European powers; with the exception of Siraj ud-Daulah and Mir Kasim, none of the rulers of these states even tried to resist the British invasion. An Indian proverb advises, 'If you live in a river, make no feud with the crocodile', and the river, according to them, already belonged to the English. This process was somewhat like the establishment of the feudal empires of the past when independent sovereigns declared themselves as vassals of a victor to receive security and power privileges from the new master. Some Indian princes of the eighteenth century found in the person of the British Resident, a good administrator who freed them from administrative problems, while the red-robed battalions provided protection from aggressive neighbours and from one's own people.

Other states not only resisted the colonial invasion but tried to introduce some serious reforms. The examples are Maharashtra, Punjab and, of course, Mysore.

We shall make some observations on the character of the reforms in these states, excluding Punjab where all these events took place in the nineteenth century. What has been called an attempt at a breakthrough was this effort to introduce some more or less serious reforms in view of the British colonial expansion, which itself acted as a great stimulus.

Different states of eighteenth century India reacted differently to the military supremacy of the English. The 'succession states' were passive and it is in these states that some European adventurers trained army regiments and the local *sipahis*. In many cases such regiments were used only to enhance the princes' prestige during military parades. The rulers of Hyderabad, Carnatic and Awadh preferred another type of 'modernization': power was given over to the British residents, protection to the British battalion, taxes to the Company, in return for traditional luxury, large pensions and the arrogance of power. According to subsidiary treaties, the Indian princes had to allocate some revenue resources and money for the maintenance of the 'protecting' British forces. The impoverished population rebelled and this made the British strengthen their power 'for the sake of law and order' and in many cases to establish their total authority over the state under the pretext of its 'bad administration' and the people's well-being.[30]

The Maratha confederacy was a different case. After the death of Shivaji, this independent state lived through many ordeals like the Mughal invasions, wars against the Afghans and the disaster at Panipat. In spite of all this, the Marathas continued to be a leading political force in India throughout the eighteenth century.

The Maratha state at that time included Maharashtra, Indore, Gwalior, Nagpur and Baroda. The rulers of the member states acknowledged the *Peshwa*'s authority, but only to a certain extent.

The Maratha confederacy was nothing but an amorphous combination of independent parts. Instead of the regular army which had made Shivaji victorious, a traditional feudal system was adopted, where the soldiers obeyed not the state but an individual *sardar,* and the *sardar* obeyed only his own interests.[31] Reisner was right to observe, that one reason for such a transformation was the feudalization of the rural elite. In Shivaji's times this process was in its initial phase and served as a catalyst for the liberation movement.[32] But in the eighteenth century former rural chiefs were 'no doubt, small but independent chiefs of the country, sharers of the kingdom. They always want to be strong, to get more land, fortify places, rob the travellers, make peace with foreign invaders'.[33]

These are the words of Ramachandra Pant Amatya, who held high official posts under Shivaji and his heirs. In the year 1716 he wrote a book titled *Ajnapatra* which contained the author's views on the Maratha statehood and administration. The ideals of Shivaji had already vanished in the first quarter of the eighteenth century, and Ramachandra advocated a strong centralized state called *svaraj.* (This word came into special use during the anti-Mughal struggle and played a significant role in the anti-colonial movement.) In order to overcome centrifugal tendencies, Ramachandra suggested that the *watandars* be kept 'between, conciliation and punishment and never allowed to fortify their dwellings.' He also suggested that old land grants be left untouched but no new ones made. All those working for the government were to be paid in cash; the

traditional land grants to temples and divines were to be given to
the worthy only, not to 'fakirs and yogis who practice sorcery and
wander about'. All government officials and army personnel were
to receive their salary from the government exclusively, not from
other persons; this was a closer appeal to return to Shivaji's
regulation on the matter. Ramachandra Pant gave great attention
to the merchants because he saw them as 'ornaments of the
kingdom' and called upon the king to protect them and to establish
favourable conditions for their business.[34]

In the text of *Ajnapatra* we see a mixture of some progressive
ideas of statehood and an attempt to preserve tradition. This
contradiction was a feature of the Maratha state. Progress required
new approaches, but the ideals of 'Maharashtra Dharma' were to
be preserved. This attitude to tradition was dictated by the realities
of the anti-Mughal war.

During the whole of the second half of the eighteenth century
the Maratha confederacy waged wars against the British only from
1776–79 and from 1780–82. After that the Marathas became allies
of the British against Mysore. It would be unfair to say that the
Maratha rulers were ignorant of British military superiority. Some
serious reforms were undertaken in Maharashtra to establish a
regular army, to restructure and train the infantry in the European
style. Huge factories were established by the state to supply the
regular army with munitions and arms, serious attempts were made
to establish a strong navy.[35] These steps were significant but
unfortunately, they were the only ones towards Maratha
modernization, as society remained unchanged.

The Maratha confederacy however, did have talented statesmen.
There was Nana Farnavis, who was the real ruler of the confederacy
and power behind the Peshwa. But this talented statesman never
attempted any serious reform since he was totally dependent on
the *sardars*. Nana Farnavis preferred the alliance of the British
rather than wage war against them. Against the armies of the
Nizam, for instance, the newly organized Maratha army had an
advantage, but when in the first quarter of the nineteenth century
the British turned their arms against their former allies, it became
clear that the 'modernization' of the Maratha state was nothing but
an architectural decoration on a traditional building. The Maratha
state, pretended to be the main successor of Mughal dominance

but was based on traditional Hindu values. Here we have to stress 'traditional', not 'Hindu', for the state of Hyderabad also shared this attitude but on an Islamic basis.

Quite a different path was selected by Mysore where the Wodeyar dynasty was overthrown by a Muslim army chief, Haidar Ali. This man, who started his military career with the low rank of *naik*, succeeded in giving an efficient administration and expanding the country's territory. Under Haidar Ali and his son Tipu Sultan, Mysore turned into the mightiest power of southern India from being an insignificant principality. Conflict between Hyderabad and the Marathas was inevitable, but very soon the Mysore rulers realized that their main enemy were the English.

These events are well known to our readers, so our attention instead will be centred on the modernization of Mysore from the point of view of the history of ideas and the state.

Like other Indian states, Mysore started its reforms with the army with the purpose of matching the Marathas, Hyderabad and, of course, the English. The reorganization of the army attempted by Haidar Ali and furthered by Tipu Sultan created a regular army which had the best fighting qualities in the India of those days. This army had uniforms, manuals, clear-cut organization and strict discipline. In the preface to the manual it was clearly said that the authors took into consideration the military superiority of the English and thought it necessary to learn from them with the sole object of putting an end to this superiority. The Mysore army had many distinctions as compared to the other Indian armies of that period: all men received salaries strictly from the state; the infantry was four times larger than the cavalry; there was a clearly established segmentation of the army into divisions, regiments, companies, etc.; detailed rules were established for promotion and the strict hierarchy of ranks was obligatory for all, even the bravest and the noblest. The Mysore treasury was rich enough to pay good salaries to the army, to supply the wounded and the families of dead soldiers with pensions, to maintain hospitals and even schools for the soldiers.[36]

Further on, the very logic of the struggle against the English made it necessary to establish a strong navy, which consisted of 72 armed ships, built under the supervision of European officers. There is evidence that Tipu Sultan planned to establish a naval school where Mysore sailors would learn from European navigational experience.

In Mysore, the restructuring of the army was more complete than anywhere else. But the peculiarity of Mysore was that unlike other states military reform became a part of more wide-ranging reforms in the socio-economic and administrative spheres. Firstly, Haidar Ali and Tipu fulfilled what Akbar had failed to do: they abolished the *jagirdari* system and privileges of the local Hindu feudals, the *palayakkars*, rents and taxes were collected not by *jagirdars* but by salaried officers of the state. Land belonged to the peasants, the rural community was preserved, but waste lands were to be confiscated by the state. The state barred the peasants from leaving their lands. This makes Alayev observe that Tipu made the Mysore peasants something akin to 'state serfs',[37] though no evidence exists for such a statement. Peasants were personally free and under the new system had to deal with the state exclusively, but the state was a strict master and had no traditional patriarchal institutions to obey. Corruption of the state officials was also an evil which the Mysore administration was unable to check.

Significant changes were made in the administrative systems too. Instead of a loose, amorphous structure which had no strict distinction between military and civil, judicial and religious institutions, there was in Mysore a clear-cut system of the departments, each having a staff of officers who had to solve problems by vote. For the first time in India, military and civil administration were separated in Mysore: each province had a military governor (*faujdar*) and a civil governor (*asaf*) as well as a tax collector (*amil*) who had distinct functions.[38]

Great attention was paid to trade. Foreign merchants were granted protection, and the Mysore navy protected the Chinese merchants ships from piracy. Trade factories were established in Pegu, Jeddah, Muscat and other places, people were encouraged to invest their savings in the state economy in return for a good interest. Well-to-do peasants and craftsmen were offered taxation rebates to make them more prosperous economically. State factories employed European engineers under whose supervision high quality firearms, uniform, paper, mirrors and even watches were produced.[39]

These reforms as well as reasonable economic policies enabled Mysore to resist the British invasion bravely and forcefully; no

Indian prince of any period was so hated by the English as Haidar
Ali and Tipu Sultan. A great many books were written to prove
that the rulers of Mysore were cruel tyrants, religious fanatics and
enemies of progress. But even the British officers who fought
against Mysore had to observe that the 'country (was) well
cultivated, had industrious inhabitants, cities newly founded,
commerce extended, towns increased. The peasants of his (Tipu's)
dominions are protected, their labours encouraged and rewarded.'
Even in the year 1793, when Mysore was defeated by the allied
forces and Tipu had to give away one-third of his territory along
with a huge contribution and to send his two sons as hostages to
Madras, it took only two or three years to restore the economy
and to strengthen the army, so that Lord Dundas wrote in
apprehension: 'Tipu enjoys perfect tranquility. Our allies around
him are exhausted, while he is improving his revenues, recruiting
armies.'[40] All this testifies not only to the effectiveness of the policies
of Haidar and Tipu but also to significant support of these policies
by the population. The peasants and craftsmen of Mysore put on
the tiger coloured uniforms and fought heroically in the Mysore
army, surprising even their enemies with their courage and loyalty.
Even when in the year 1799, Srirangapatnam was stormed and
Tipu Sultan preferred death to the wretched destiny of a British
vassal, the resistance continued. A Marathi officer of the Mysore
army, by name Dhundaji Waug collected the remnants of the
army and a large number of peasants and established a 'liberated
area' around the fortress of Shimoga.[41]

Analysing the 'modernization' of Mysore, we may state that
these reforms had much in common with the ones initiated by
Akbar, especially in creating a strong centralized state. In many
spheres the rulers of Mysore went even further than Akbar, and
it would not be an overstatement to observe that but for military
defeat Mysore might have developed into a strong, centralized
absolutist state.

According to orthodox Marxist scholars, absolute monarchy
was a balance of forces between the newly developed capitalist
class and the feudal class, exhausted but still strong to control a
country. By this yardstick absolutism was just the threshold of the
capitalist revolution. If such a definition be adopted, our observation
on Mysore is wrong. But historical experience proves that if the

above mentioned rule was valid for some countries like Sweden, France and pre-revolutionary England, it was different for Russia, Prussia and Spain. These countries in the eighteenth century were quite far from capitalist revolutions, but absolutist forms of state emerged there. We do not have enough data to examine Mysore state as an absolute monarchy of the Russian or Prussian type. But whatever data is available makes us presume that among all the Indian states of the eighteenth century, Mysore took the most significant steps towards absolutism, in the sense of development towards the later stage of feudalism. Some undertakings of Tipu Sultan which were traditionally seen as good-for-nothing whims of the 'Mysore tyrant' should be reconsidered in the light of the above mentioned observations. For instance, Tipu was reproached for changing the calendar, but in reality it was an attempt to create a unified calendar for the ethnically and religiously diverse population (significantly, a local Hindu calendar was selected).[42]

Interestingly, Mysore 'modernization' had much in common with the reforms introduced by Peter the Great in Russia in the first quarter of the eighteenth century. The transformation of the traditional feudal army into the regular western-type one, the clear distinction between civil, military and judicial administration, the building of a modern navy, adoption of western technologies, industrial and trade development, and the bureaucratization of the state machinery (it has to be noted here that bureaucracy played a progressive role in the absolutist states as it took the state machinery away from feudal elements) are some of the similarities.[43] Another common feature was that in both countries modernization took place in the extreme conditions of war which threatened the very existence of the state, and was carried on by violent and sometimes cruel methods. The great Russian poet Pushkin said that Peter's reforms were written by a whip; the same can be said of the reforms in Mysore.

These common features should be noted for further comparative research; but their differences should not be ignored. These distinctions were inevitable since the two countries belonged to different cultural traditions and civilizations. The main difference was, indeed, in the very outcome of the reforms. Peter the Great succeeded in making Russia a strong absolutist state and removing obstacles for further development. Mysore was defeated by the British.

Analysing this defeat, Antonova and some orthodox Marxist scholars observed that 'the decisive victory of capitalist England over feudal Mysore was unavoidable',[44] though this very capitalist England had been defeated several times by the feudal Afghans. We should look for an explanation not in some theoretical constructions but in the peculiarities of Mysore and India.

Reforms in Mysore were to a significant extent supported by peasants, craftsmen and traders (unconnected with the British companies). But these social groups were too weak politically. In the highest strata of society the situation was different. Abolition of *jagirs* and privileges of the *palayakkars* made the majority of feudal circles hostile to Haidar and Tipu. The whole history of the Anglo-Mysore wars was a history of treason. Mysore feudals who hated the very idea of becoming salaried officers of the state openly cooperated with the English, surrendered mighty fortresses and punished officers loyal to Tipu. It was enough for an English general to promise a restoration of *jagir* to a high-ranking Mysore official like Mir Sadiq and full cooperation was guaranteed to the British army. It does not mean that the nobles of Mysore were all prone to treason: the reforms in Mysore had no social basis among the ruling classes. Such a basis for reform existed in Peter's Russia: it was the petty gentry which was ethnically unified, patriotic and sure that Peter would relieve them from the pitiable condition of being the wretched subordinates of big landlords (the *boyars*). This gentry actively supported Peter and was in command of the new regular army.[45]

In Mysore the ruling social groups belonged to different religions and ethnicities; some of them did not consider Mysore their motherland and were ready to serve any master who would restore their *jagirs* and privileges. The feudals were also offended by the plebeian origin of Haidar and Tipu and by their attitudes to the old aristocracy. 'The Amirs and Khans of old times, whom the late Nawab had lured to his service from all cities and countries were now (in Tipu's times) cast down rank and power. And low-bred vulgar young men were appointed. As the confidence of the Sultan was chiefly placed in the artillery and muskets, the brave men who excelled in handling sword and spear lost heart.'[46] These words by the Mysore historian Kirmani might have been supported by the Russian landed aristocrats, the main enemies of Peter and his reforms. But unlike Peter, Haidar Ali and his son had no other social group from which to recruit officers, ministers and commanders.

The situation in Mysore was different from the religious point of view also. Haidar Ali, a Muslim, came into power in a country where Hindus were in a majority. Moreover, after the Hindu dynasty of Wodeyars was overthrown, the British authors spared no efforts to show up Haidar Ali and especially Tipu as Muslim bigots and enemies of the Hindus. They also pointed to the Mysore rulers' uncompromising struggle against the *palayakkars* and Tipu's confiscation of the landholdings of the temples (the latter measure was dictated by the necessity to pay a contribution to the British).[47] Kirmani also tried to describe Tipu as a fanatical Muslim.[48] But the real facts were different. Both Haidar and Tipu were wise enough to realize that no support from the Hindu population was possible without a balanced religious policy. In Mysore all communities lived in peace, and if one looks at the ruins of Srirangapatnam, the replicas of the mosques will be seen side by side with the replicas of the temples and churches. Among the higher officials of the state, Hindus were represented in large numbers and Tipu with his habitual love of good order specially ordained that during oath-taking and traditional feasts no religious discrimination or offence against the traditions of any community would be tolerated. In the manual of the Mysore army, among the qualifications necessary for promotion, religion or caste were not mentioned.[49] Tipu's correspondence with the Swami of Sringeri is well-known. The Mysore king reverently addressed him as *Jagatguru* and quoted Sanskrit *slokas* to seek his blessings. He also addressed a letter to the Archbishop of Goa with a request for some Christian priests to be sent for the Mysore Christians.[50] Tipu's sincere curiosity and aspiration to learn from the West also show him as no bigot. Nor do the beautiful paintings of battles which decorate Tipu's summer residence Darya Daulat Bagh testify to a Muslim fanaticism on the part of the Mysore ruler.

Nevertheless, while in their socio-economic and administrative reforms Haidar Alt and Tipu followed the footsteps of Akbar, their religious policy never reached Akbar's level. One can agree with Hasan Khan that religion was for Tipu nothing but an instrument to be used when needed.[51] Haidar and Tipu carried on their struggle under the banner of Islam and failed to adopt anything like the ideas of *sulhe-kul* which might have helped a great deal to consolidate society. Tipu's passionate appeals for *jihad* were made against the British and their allies like the Peshwa (the Muslim rulers of Hyderabad were also branded by Tipu as infidels).[52] We may sum it up by saying that in Mysore socio-economic, military and administrative reforms were not supported by changes in religious policy which remained at the stage of pre-Akbar tolerance.

Analysing the failure of Mysore's attempt at the breakthrough, we suggest that in the fateful year of 1799 Mysore was defeated not only by capitalist England, but also by the feudal, anti-Mysore union of the British, the Peshwa and the Nizam, though the British were a minority in this alliance. The main reason for this coalition's success, so cleverly utilized by the British, was the hatred of the feudal rulers of the South for a powerful neighbour. The Marathas and the Nizam were ready to forget all old conflicts for the sake of enriching themselves with the lands and wealth of Mysore.

After the break-up of the alliance with the French in 1783, Tipu looked for new allies. His passionate appeals to the rulers of India, Nepal, Turkey, Iran were not heard. Till his last moment he hoped that the Marathas and the Nizam would understand that by allying themselves with the British they had signed a death sentence for themselves and for the freedom of India. In an interesting document, discovered in Russia by Antonova, a French observer David Cossigny, brother of the well-known French governor, wrote: 'It is easy to realize that however powerful the English in India might be now, their power is always in danger since it is much weaker than the allied forces of the Marathas, the Nizam and Tipu Sultan, if such an alliance be possible.'[53]

Unfortunately, old feudal prejudices prevented such an alliance. When the French governor of Pondicherry tried to suggest an alliance with Tipu to the Nizam, he received this reply from the ruler of Hyderabad: 'You are not ignorant of my being the immediate representative of the Great King (the Mughal–E.V.) and this villain is only a vassal of mine. Should I degrade myself by courting my vassal?'[54] Tipu's plebeian origin also hindered any alliance as he was scorned by the Maratha and Hyderabad rulers even in official documents as 'the son of naik'.[55]

The statesmen of the epoch were by and large unable to think of a united India. Mysore was a foreign country, *pardes* for Hyderabad, for the Marathas, for the famine-stricken Bengali peasants who joined the colonial armies to escape starvation and stormed Srirangapatnam under the British flag. The British utilized very successfully the differences between the Indian states which were at that time on different levels of sociopolitical, ethnic and cultural development. And it was quite natural that 18 years after the fall of Mysore, the Maratha confederacy was also vanquished by the British.

TOWARDS ANOTHER SHORE

Our analysis of Indian thought in the eighteenth century would be incomplete if we ignore the importance of the contact of Indian culture with European technology, social and political ideas, religion and culture. This process began shortly after the Portuguese anchored their ships in India and carried out their designs despite the heavy odds and dramatic events of the period.

It has to be noted that generally Indian culture has never been characterized as closed and secluded. Despite all the efforts of the bigoted keepers of ancient traditions, India was always open to the world. In ancient times India had trade and cultural links with Egypt, Mesopotamia, Iran, Greece, Rome, and countries of South-East Asia. And in medieval times the Arab countries, Iran, Turkey, Central Asia, China, parts of Africa carried out an active exchange in merchandise, ideas, views and cultural traditions. An educated Indian of the middle ages never supposed his country to be the only one in the world. Scientific treatises of the day quoted from Euclides and Ptolemy, Plato and Aristotle, Ar-Rushd and Farabi, Ibn Sina, Biruni and Ulugh Beg. The poetry by Khayyam, Rudaqi, Nizami and other great names of Persian literature was very popular, among people of all religions. In order to praise a picture or a sculpture an Indian would have equated it to the 'creations of the artists of Chin or Rum', which supposed, albeit from hearsay, some knowledge about the existence of these countries. When

Bhushan Tripathi, a court poet of Shivaji, praised the Maratha hero, he said that Shivaji's bravery and generosity 'is famous in the world like the Russians' physical strength, the Khurasanis' swords, the Britishers' political mastery, the Chinese eloquence, the Hindu's courage, the artfulness of the Arabs, the Turks' pride, the Persians' lust and the Frenchmen's slyness'.[56] Here the poet discloses the stereotypes of his time but also shows some knowledge of the outside world.

Naturally, the attitude of the Indians towards the European newcomers depended on many factors, first and foremost on the 'firangis' behaviour. When the Europeans came as peaceful merchants or missionaries who taught the Indians to worship 'Hazrat Isa and Bibi Mariam', or Jesus and Virgin Mary, the attitude was calm, friendly and curious. But when they came with weapons in their hands or, like the Portuguese, made Indians familiar with the Inquisition's *auto-da-fé*, they were met with understandable wrath and hostility. Thus a work from Kerala by one Zayn al-Din (sixteenth century) described the Portuguese as bloody invaders, robbers and killers of peaceful people.[57]

The sixteenth and the eighteenth centuries were periods when the educated elite of Indian society became familiar with the different achievements of European culture. Many western travellers of the period noted how curious the Indians were to know more about Europe, and this curiosity was in most cases friendly.[58] Among the aristocrats and rich merchants European mirrors, looking glasses, laces, and wines became fashionable; some even preferred a coach to the traditional palanquin. Great popularity was also enjoyed by European paintings. As far back as the beginning of the seventeenth century Sir Thomas Roe, the British envoy to Jahangir, reported to his government in a letter that the '... presents you sent are extremely despised by all who see them. ... Here nothing is esteemed but of the best quality and sort: good cloths and pictures come out from Italy overland, so they laugh at us for such as we bring and, doubtless, they understand them as well as we.' Sir Thomas himself was unable to distinguish a painting by a British master, presented to Jahangir, from an Indian-made copy of the same work.[59] In the miniature paintings Christian motifs became fashionable, and some painters began to use European technique.

Sincere interest was exhibited by the Indians in the technical achievements of Europe. Royal *karkhanas* employed 'firangi' engineers and specialists. The result was a serious attempt to adopt new technologies in arms manufacturing, glass making and shipbuilding.[60]

The attitude towards the activities of the Christian missionaries too was friendly. Among the downtrodden people of all communities there were many who were desirous of adopting the new faith. For the educated people, Christianity was just one more way to worship God, as lawful and true as any other.

Curiosity and sincere interest in anything that is new and in the wisdom and ideas of other peoples was a feature of the 'enlightened philosophers' of Akbar's court. Abu-l Fazl said of himself: '... my mind had no rest and my heart felt itself drawn to the sages of Mongolia, and to the hermits of Lebanon; I longed for interviews with the lamas of Tibet or with the padris of Portugal, and I would gladly sit with the priests of the Parsis and the learned of the Zendavesta.'[61] But of especial interest is a letter written by Abu-l Fazl on behalf of Akbar in 1582. This 'Letter to the Learned of the West' was published in full by Nizami. An extract is quoted here:

...It has been said by the wise that whoever borrows knowledge from the other countries and enlightens himself by the light of the other peoples' wisdom, penetrates all mysteries. In this mundane world which is but a reflection of the celestial world, there is nothing more elevated than love and there is nobody unworthy of friendship. The Almighty himself has established this with love and care, so that each heart, illuminated by sympathy, may be purified of the darkness of ignorance. And should not the kings whose virtues are the foundation for universal goodness, establish among themselves bonds of friendship and cooperation, so that the peoples, for God's glory, may enter into good and worthy relations among themselves? Especially desirable is this with the countries where the spiritual excellence of the Christian religion has manifested itself as a shining light and the duties of justice and protection are fulfilled by the mighty kings ...

Due to the resistance of the authorities and the people's own arrogance society is stopped behind the curtain of ignorance; this situation has to be improved... As the majority of men of this epoch are slaves of blind following (*taqlid*) of all the behests of the forefathers, a faith flourishes among the people which is devoid of the searching spirit—the best among the creations of reason. Consequently, nowadays communication between wise men of different faiths, high-spirited and eloquent, is very desirable. Because of the language differences it would be praiseworthy to have the main Christian ideas and postulates rendered into elegant Persian for the sake of happiness and bliss, so that the holy books like the Torah, the Gospel, the Psalms of David be translated into Arabic or Persian. If these books along with translations and commentaries be sent to us, it will serve to establish divine laws and build a mansion of concord as well as the dominion of enlightenment which helps to elevate pure faith, friendship and virtue. We hope for further intercourse.[62]

Akbar needed a Persian translation of the Gospel for the same purposes as he needed a Persian version of the Mahabharata—as one more weapon against blind faith and religious bigotry. Abu-l Fazl and his learned friends discussed with the Christian missionaries not only religion but other matters of interest, for instance, the discovery of America. For Danishmand Khan, a noble at Aurangzeb's court, Bernier translated into Persian works by Descartes, Harrey, and Gassendi, great rationalists and naturalists of the West. Jai Singh Sawai studied with the help of the Jesuits the astronomical tables and treatises by Flamstede and Tiho Brahe.[63]

Here we have to point out that cultural contacts were at this period two-way and equal. The Indians and the Europeans studied and learned much from each other. Both sides had religious prejudices, and a fanatical rejection of whatever was outside tradition. Nevertheless this process of interaction continued. Thus the French traveller Tavernier overcame traditional prejudices to state that 'although these idolaters are completely blind to a knowledge of the true God, this does not prevent them from leading in many respects, according to nature, moral lives'.[64] Khafi Khan, the Mughal chronicler, felt aversion to the Europeans for their attempts to convert orphaned children to Christianity, but he confessed that he used to visit the churches and 'conversed with their learned men'.[65] Prejudiced, narrow-minded bigotry had to retreat and surrender to the normal human feelings of curiosity and interest in the achievements of other people. No doubt, this process touched only a small minority of the educated elite, nobles and merchants, but then the number of Russian people who were able to have a peep into the 'window of Europe', opened by Peter the Great was not much larger. Of much greater importance for us is the fact that prior to the open colonial expansion of the eighteenth century all cultural contacts with Europe were carried on equally and bilaterally. Educated Indians studied western innovations with curiosity but without suspicion and fear. At the same time the educated europeans came to an understanding that they were dealing not with 'savages' or 'pagans', but with an ancient and great civilization. Indology as a field of research came into being not only from the necessity of learning more about the new subjects of the British empire and governing them effectively, but also because of the genuine interest of learned Europeans in the achievements of India. While the missionaries expounded to the Indian public some fundamentals of Christianity, Europe was discovering the spiritual and religious treasures of India. While the European engineers and gunners worked in the royal *karkhanas* of Delhi and Agra, the great English scientist Robert Hooke studied the Indian methods of manufacturing the highest quality steel (wootz) and the French chemist Courdoux specially came to study the methods of dyeing cloth.[66]

Indian thinkers quite clearly understood at that time the real political aims of the 'firangis'. Very observant was Ramachandra Pant Amatya in whose *Ajnapatra* we read:

Portuguese, English, Dutch and French merchants, also Danes, and other hat-wearing merchants carry on trade. But they are not like other merchants, for their masters are ruling kings. Under their orders and control these people come to trade in the provinces. How can it be that the rulers have no greed for territories? The hat wearers have all intentions to enter, increase their territories and establish their religion. In some places they have succeeded. Moreover, this race is very obstinate. When a place comes into their hands they will not give it up even on peril of their life. They should be therefore restricted in their coming and going for trade. Never give them a place for factories near the sea, only deep inland, within control of neighbouring towns, for their strength lies in the navy. ... It is enough if they come and go and don't trouble us; we need not trouble them.'[67]

Such a suspicious attitude became more widespread in Indian society as colonial expansion grew. This expansion came to be a deadly blow for the cultural links between India and Europe. This was natural, for any cultural contact is successful only if it goes on freely and equally without humiliation or force. The tragic realities of the eighteenth century fostered the development of conservatism, obscurantism and a tendency to cultural separatism and seclusion, for if one's traditional culture and way of life is in danger, one stands in its defence forgetting all criticisms and disappointments previously experienced. Thus the 'firangis' began to be seen as a hostile and dangerous force and all contacts with them as a violation of holy traditions. This attitude was recorded by many travellers of the eighteenth and nineteenth centuries, and to them we are obliged for the numerous stories of fanatical and conservative Indians.[68]

Still, hatred for the 'hat-wearers' never prevented Haidar Ali and Tipu Sultan from adopting European methods of army organization and training, and from being sincerely interested in the technological and scientific achievements of Europe. Thus in a letter to the Governor of Pondicherry Tipu enquired about the newly invented method of measuring the body temperature of a sick man by a thermometer. In the same letter the ruler of Mysore mistakes the name of this instrument for barometer, which indicates that he had some knowledge of the latter also. In the huge palace library of Mysore a number of European books were available.[69]

Shah Abdul Aziz, the son and spiritual heir of Waliullah was sworn enemy to the English. He proclaimed all territories acquired by them as *dar ul-harb* or hostile territory, and considered it a sin for a Muslim to serve the British. But at the same time he considered it desirable to learn English for acquiring knowledge of the technical and scientific achievements of Europe.[70]

It was the eighteenth century which brought some very important features to the process of cultural contacts. Apart from technical, scientific and religious matters some Indian thinkers began looking attentively at the sociopolitical spheres of European culture, and came to the conclusion that some sociopolitical foundations of western life were just and progressive and might be adopted by Indians.

As European goods and influence increased in India, so did the number of Indians who decided to link themselves with the new and fortunate masters. Trade agents, interpreters, secretaries, dealers—these people had ways and motives to serve the British. Among the Indian personnel employed in the European factories there were many who had consciously adopted some aspects of the western way of life and preferred to live under the protection of the 'firangis' which was understandable in the given situation of crisis and constant war. Among these people was the family of Ananda Ranga Pillai. This Tamil merchant was a trade agent of Dupleix, the Governor of Pondicherry. The whole family of Ananda Ranga faithfully served the French administrators; a cousin of Ananda even went to France, had interviews with the king and the Duke of Orleans and was awarded the Order of St. Michael. In his memoirs, Ananda Ranga praised the law and order, effective administration and generous character of Dupleix and other Frenchmen. At the same time Ananda Ranga never insisted that his countrymen should copy the European way of life. He displayed a sense of humour when depicting converted Hindus building a wall inside the Church to avoid low-caste and high-caste Christians from sitting together.[71]

A sincere admirer of the 'hat-wearing British' was Ghulam Husain Salim, the author of the *Riyaz us-salatin* or 'History of Bengal', written between 1786 and 1788. He praised the new masters of Bengal as great inventors and just rulers, excellent administrators and protectors of the weak and the oppressed. He also glorified them for their non-interference in the religion and traditions of the Muslims.[72]

At this time quite a number of Indian writers began praising the British with the same zeal as they praised the Mughal emperors or the independent rulers. However not all those Indians who chose to link their destinies with the British were unpatriotic or slavish career-seekers. For some of them, at least, the English were representatives of some just and progressive sociopolitical ideas.

One example of this way of thinking was Mirza Abu Talib from Lucknow. The present writer has the privilege to be the first to familiarize Soviet readers with this thinker's views in an article. Mirza Abu Talib was born in Lucknow in the year 1752 in a family of a government officer who fell out of favour with the Nawab and had to migrate to Calcutta with his family. After the death of his father, Abu Talib returned to Lucknow and held the important post of an *amil* or revenue officer in Etawah. But in the year 1787 he resigned from this post as a protest against corruption and oppression in the revenue administration of Awadh. He returned to Calcutta, where he was received by Lord Cornwallis who promised him assistance and employment though none was granted. The family struggled on in poverty, till a friend of Abu Talib, who was a captain, invited him to join his ship for a journey to Europe. Thus Abu Talib found himself in Ireland and then in England where he tried to establish an Oriental college. Though the Orient was in fashion with London high society and Abu Talib was enthusiastically received by many including the royal family, there was no interest for his project. Empty-handed, he set out for home visiting France, Italy, Turkey and Iraq on the way. On his return to India in the year 1803, he was appointed a collector in Bundelkhand where he died in 1806.[73]

Abu Talib wrote a book on his journey to Europe, which is the first hitherto known source of this kind written by an Indian. But before we discuss this book we should turn to his Awadh chronicle or the *Tafzihul-ghalifin,* written during his service in Awadh.

The form of *Tafzihul-ghalifin* is the traditional chronicle, but the contents and ideas are totally different. Its castigating criticism of the Nawab's policies and the whole feudal establishment of the Awadh of Asafuddaulah has no match in the history of Indian literature. Social criticism was frequent in medieval literature, but it was one thing to denounce some abstract kings and nobles or to depict them in forms like Ravana, Kansa, etc., and quite another thing to write about a ruling king: 'All things are carefully and fondly cared for by the Nawab save men.'[74] The book abounds in descriptions of the Nawab's profligacy, bad administration, careless attitude to the needs and fate of his people. Criticism was aimed also at the corrupt and heartless nobles, officers and army commanders. Abu Talib minced no words to describe the lavish profligacy of the Lucknow nobles who wasted exorbitant sums on festivals and enjoyment, and stressed that the only source of this profligacy was bribery and swindling. The author also depicted the corruption of officialdom and decay of the army. The construction of the Imambaras and other wonderful buildings of Lucknow, which are even today the pride of this city, had a dark side for the writer, for the common people of the city became victims of the 'Nawab's building mania'. They were driven away from their houses without any compensation, and the state monopoly of bricks deprived them even of the material for building tombs.[75]

Denouncing the rulers of Awadh, Abu Talib expressed sincere sympathy for the common people. He wrote about the impoverishment of the peasants and humiliation of a respected master chintz-printer. 'Strangely, notwithstanding the Nawab's tyranny over his people is enormous waste, the Wazir expects that people will yield him allegiance on account of the names and claims of his ancestors.'[76] Whatever was strange for Abu Talib was normal for many generations of the people. For Abu-l Fazl a real noble was one who was noble in deed, not in mere pedigree.[77] This same opinion was expressed by many *bhakti* and *sufi* saints. But Abu Talib went even further and refused to respect even a good king, which was a deep-rooted tradition in India and elsewhere. 'Suppose a man of angelic goodness be found, how can he reform the medley of soldiers, subjects, officials who have been for years demoralized and grown into evil habits?'[78]

The book reflects the author's painful concern about the destiny of his country and people. 'There is no knowing how God's people will obtain relief from the oppressors. There is release in separation from them, but as it involves desertion of their native land in great number, it is impracticable; and as to rebellion, though it would effect deliverance, it is not practicable for the apathy of the public, their habitual reconciliation with the customs of India. ...'[79]

The solution that was suggested by Abu Talib is shocking to a patriot: to establish English control over Awadh. An 'Englishman knowing India (should) be appointed to the administration; the vazir's expenses limited, he should have no voice in revenue and military affairs, English officers should train the troops. To get rid of all old collectors, etc., as they are puffed up with pride and prodigality. Middle class and poor men must be brought forward and appointed to offices.'[80]

Thus Abu Talib saw the way out in deep sociopolitical reforms. Of especial interest here is his idea to dismiss the old administrators and to employ middle class and poor men. But according to him, all this was possible only if control of the state would be in English hands.

Abu Talib was well aware of the dubious character of this idea. So to explain and support it with the necessary arguments he used the form of dialogue, so frequent in world literature. The central place in the book belongs to the conversation of the author with a certain friend, a high-placed court noble. Abu Talib described to his companion the pitiable plight of the people and the crisis of the state, stressing, that in this situation Awadh might become a prey to any invader, especially when rumours were afloat of the new Afghan invasion. Abu Talib's companion agreed, but when Abu Talib said that only British control over Awadh would be the salvation, he disagreed: 'Possible, but there is a proverb about people flying away from one great calamity and falling into a still greater one. The English, as soon as they get a footing, will make the condition of people here like those in Bengal.' This was a serious argument, but Abu Talib opposed it in the following way: 'In the condition in which the people are now it is difficult to imagine worse treatment. Though the prosperity of some persons who are now masters and rob thousands of others would wane, the prosperity of those thousands would result, and in case of war the lives and honour of people will be safe.'[81]

In short, according to Abu Talib 'things could not be worse than now', and even the British with their ruinous policies in Bengal should be a better choice for the people of Awadh than the Nawab. Here we see a representative of the views of those Indians who saw in British rule a way out of the crisis. Such an approach seems logical against the background of Indian historical experience. History indicates that during the whole of the medieval period feudal anarchy was overthrown by adventurous invaders who would act as a strong hand in uniting the fighting principalities and bring about long cherished peace.

If we compare Abu Talib's views with that of Waliullah we see some common features. Both thinkers hoped that some benevolent force would come from outside and save the country, both considered that sociopolitical reforms necessary. But the commonality ends here. For Waliullah the Afghan invasion was to restore the Mughal empire and Muslim power. Abu Talib lived in the second half of the century, when the public cherished no illusions about the rebirth of the empire, but his religion was a private affair and had nothing to do with his sociopolitical views. While Waliullah wanted the Afghans 'to save the Muslims from the infidel clutches', Abu Talib hoped that the British control over Awadh would save all people, Hindus and Muslims, from tyranny and starvation. It has to be noted here, that Abu Talib thought in terms of Awadh only, not for the whole of India.

With these hopes and views the Lucknow writer went to Britain. His travel book is of immense significance as it gives an Indian's impression of the West and its culture. The Indian who arrived at the shores of Britain was not an 'Oriental barbarian', but a well-educated intellectual aspiring for greater knowledge.

Abu Talib wrote his book with a concrete purpose in mind: to inform his compatriots about life in Europe and to awaken in them a curiosity and passion for learning. Among the western achievements, which roused Abu Talib's admiration, were technical innovations like the steamer, the mechanical spindle 'jenny', and the printing press which he considered a marvellous device for the enlightenment of the people. In Oxford, he admired the study of anatomy, their observatories and theatrical innovations. His appreciation of drama and opera testifies to the absence of religious prejudices.

Abu Talib was all praise for the British parliamentary system, the tradition of clubs, and for the newspapers which even carried cartoons of ministers and high officials. Abu Talib's democratic views, sympathy with the workers and sense of justice always remained his guiding principles. His attitudes were pragmatic and objective. Praising the industrial genius of the British, he never forgot to observe that the 'jenny' produced coarse thread and that building material was of inferior quality as compared to that in India. While emphasizing that parliamentary democracy and the laws of England were a guarantee for the equality of the people, Abu Talib made an unexpected observation that 'this equality is more in appearance than in reality for the difference between the comforts of the rich and the poor is greater in England than in India'.[82] For him, the poverty of the Irish peasants was a shocking experience and he said that the Indian peasants, whose life he knew, were rich compared to them. England was not a 'City of No Sorrows' for him and of the English judicial system he said, 'The judge often overawes the jury and dictates what they are to do. I was disgusted to observe in these courts that law overruled equity and well-meaning honest man was frequently made the dupe of an artful knave.'[83] Abu Talib wanted his countrymen to learn from the British, but only the good and useful things. That is why he protested against the establishment of the British judicial system in India.

Here then is the evidence for the necessity of a balanced approach to any comparison between East and West. If we put on one side the luxury of the Nawabs, the starvation of the peasants, the obscurantism of the *brahmans* and the *mullahs* and the fanatic sacrifices of the Jagannath devotees (so frequently and lucidly described by the European travellers), we also have to show, for the sake of justice, the sinister 'work-houses' and the problems created by the British factories of the Industrial Revolution, the protest of the Church against smallpox vaccination introduced by Jenner (on the pretext that smallpox was God's punishment for the sins of men), the cruelty of the slave trade and colonial wars where whole tribes were destroyed.

Abu Talib serves as a good example of a balanced approach even for the scholars of today. This travel book is an interesting example of cultural contact where the Indian representative displayed more tact, openness and tolerance than did his western hosts. As a successor to the enlightened philosophers of medieval India, he castigated the British for their contempt towards the customs of other countries: 'I was frequently attacked on the apparent unreasonableness of Muhammaddan customs ... from my knowledge of the English character I considered it a folly to argue the point philosophically, so I parried the subject. When they ridiculed the ceremonies of the pilgrims in Mecca, I asked them why they supported the ceremony of baptism ... for the salvation of a child who could not be sensible of what it was all about.' When his English hosts ridiculed the Oriental tradition of eating with one's hands, Abu Talib politely reminded them that all the bakers of London used their feet for kneading dough.[84] In this way Abu Talib justified not only his traditions and religion, but something more: the ideas, worked out by generations of Indian freethinkers and humanists who always acknowledged the rights and dignity of 'other worshippers of God'. It was appropriate then that while describing the practices of Masonic gatherings, he praised their tradition to 'never interfere with any man's religion and consider each other as brothers'.[85]

The travel book by Abu Talib encourages us to further research in other spheres, for instance, the attitudes and thoughts of Indian intellectuals of that period on the events and ideas of the French Revolution. Some knowledge of this event was available in India from the French traders and officers who served in the Indian armies and Wellesley feared them as 'determined jacobines'. [86] In the year 1795, the British resident in Hyderabad wrote a letter to the Peshwa informing him of a

'certain group of people in France who call themselves philosophers and champions of human rights, but who are against the divine right of kings. They propose a new political philosophy and a creed denying the existence of God and their aim is to revolutionize the existing social order and if opportunity affords itself, they upset the rulers, nobles and elite whom they regard as tyrants ... They preach to the masses that the rich have usurped their wealth. Thus duped, the masses despoil the rich and revolt against the rulers and nobles.' [87]

Tipu Sultan also was well informed about the events in France; French officers in Srirangapatnam even had their own Jacobine club, and the ruled of Mysore hoped that the Republican government would be a better alternative than the existing one. In 1801 Abu Talib left England and arrived in the France of Napoleon. He seems to be the first Indian who reported the story of the French Revolution and wrote a biography of Napoleon. Abu Talib had an insufficient knowledge of the country and language, but felt nevertheless that revolution took place because of the king's tyranny over his people. Once again he shows his faithfulness to the ideas expressed in the *Tafzihul-ghalifin*. His biography of Napoleon was short but vivid; the great man of France had impressed the Indian traveller as a man of low origin who made a brilliant career. [88] It also corresponded with Abu Talib's ideas that the middle and lower class of people were more efficient to run the state than were the nobles.

It would be no exaggeration to suggest that Abu Talib's book was one of the first works of the Indian enlightenment. The writer avoided didacticism, his main aim was to awaken the spirit of learning and innovation in his compatriots, to make them adopt the useful experiences of other countries. While being loyal to his own country and never idealizing the West, Talib considered the social order and laws there more just and progressive than those of feudal India and for this reason he supported the British invasion of India as the best out of two evils—these ideas allied Abu Talib to the thinkers of the Indian enlightment of the nineteenth century. The desired progress was connected with the foreign invaders, and this made Abu Talib's position questionable, not unpatriotic. He loved India and for its own benefit wanted it to be a British possession. This contradiction was overcome only by the national liberation movement.

5

Instead of a Conclusion

Any research work is supposed, by a long-standing tradition, to have a concluding paragraph or chapter where the main ideas of the author are summed up. This tradition has to be respected, but ours is a special case, for if we follow the general rule for the present study, it may signify that the research of the problem is to a considerable extent concluded and the topic exhausted.

In the book presented hereby for the reader's judgement, efforts have been directed not so much to answering all questions but to stimulating discussion on the problems related to the history of ideas in medieval India.

The source material now available shows that medieval India was not a static society without any conflicts of ideas or withdrawn from mundane problems, fully absorbed in transcendental musings. Medieval Indians lived an active spiritual life which was by a thousand ties connected to the real problems of society. The Indian thought of the medieval period was as contradictory, variegated and diversified as India itself. Here we shall try to chalk out some directions of the development of the Indian thought in the period under review.

Crucial changes were going on in the sixteenth and seventeenth centuries in the attitude of the Indian mind towards the social problems of the time. Thus an objective and powerful tendency to create a strong centralized state gave rise to new political ideas and made it necessary to reconsider some traditional views on the role and significance of state power. A factor that was of great significance was the cultural and religious contact between Hinduism and Islam which had a bearing on every sphere of life. This interaction, though itself a complicated process, had a stimulating effect on the development of literature, arts, philosophy, religious thought, science and technology, but in the sphere of ideas its most important result was the theory of *sulhe-kul* and the appeal for the 'merger of the oceans' which in practice meant an attempt to establish the ideas of communal amity and peace, equal rightfulness of all religions, refusal to distinguish the 'true believers' from infidels. The numerous religious reformist schools of the middle ages, pertaining to Hinduism, Islam and other religious communities, produced a variety of mystical practices, socio-ethical principles and cultural traditions. But in this kaleidoscope only those trends which were bold enough to reconsider many dogmas of the official religions manifested themselves. One of the significant features of these religious reformist schools of thought was the flexibility and elasticity of their ideas and principles, their ability to adapt themselves to the changing sociopolitical and ethnic situation. This ability of self-development and creative reconsideration of orthodoxies manifested itself in new religious and political ideologies like Sikhism and the anti-Mughal movements.

Even during the tragic eighteenth century with its atmosphere of sociocultural and political crisis, the fall of the Mughal empire, the rivalry of its heirs and the colonial expansion of European powers, the spiritual life and the intellectual quests of Indian society did not abate. Indian thinkers searched for a way out of the crisis, reassessed critically the past and present of their country and looked for new perspectives. At that time Indian thought could propose only three ways to counter the crisis: to rebuild the Mughal empire, to resist internal feuds and colonial invasion and at the same time to introduce some modernization in the military, economic, social and political systems of the independent states and, third, to accept British colonial rule as a painful and torturous, but necessary treatment for the ailing society.

Indian thought of the medieval period developed according to natural law whereby new ideas establish themselves by some form of struggle against the old obsolete ones. The tolerance of the Indians helped the country with its kaleidoscope of religions,

ethnicities and traditions to survive. We may borrow
Dr Lamshukov's term and classify the Indian society as 'elastic',
but this elasticity had its limits which were dangerous to violate.

Like the other parts of the world, medieval India too experienced
some bitter and violent forms of the conflict of ideas. On one side
there was religious bigotry and communal animosity, on the other,
the ideas of *sulhe-kul*, then again there was strict observance of
centuries-old tradition and unchallenged authority of the ancient
sages against attempts at rationalist freethinking; the reverential
attitude to the laws of *varnashrama* was contradicted by others
who felt that 'only a fool is proud of his caste'. In this struggle of
ideas India produced many examples of courage, fortitude and
moral strength, and it would only be justified to include some
Indian names among thinkers, scholars and spiritual leaders of the
world history of the middle ages.

The mainspring of the development of Indian thought during
this period was the development, albeit slow and inconsistent, of
humanistic ideas. The humanism of medieval India was not like
that of Italy, France, England or Germany because those civilizations
were historically different, and if we admit that these differences
do not negate the unified character of human culture, we can
make a clear assessment.

The thinkers of medieval India did not have to search for
ancient manuscripts and study ancient languages, for unlike Europe,
India never suffered a break with its ancient past. The western
public of the early Renaissance discovered for itself the treasures
of Greek and Roman arts, literature and sciences which had been
previously damned or distorted by bigoted monks. In India, on
the contrary, the authority of ancient sages was never challenged.
In Europe, the humanists looked back to antiquity to find in the
ideals of ancient Greece and Rome a weapon against medieval
dogmas. In India searching for answers to modern questions in
ancient books was itself a dogma, against which the best minds
protested. Similarly Indian humanists had no necessity to withstand
what the Christian Church called 'mortification of the flesh', for,
unlike Christianity, Hinduism considered *kama* and *artha* as lawful
aims of human life and saw nothing sinful in them. Islam also
allowed its followers, except *derveshes*, to experience all the joys
of normal life. So Indian poets and writers, from very ancient days

knew and described the beauty of a human body as well as all forms and kinds of love.

If we believe that despite all civilizational differences there were some common laws of historical development and the result was what is now called 'general human values' of every epoch, we may suppose that one of these common laws of human history was the following: in every significant stage of socio-economic and political development the notion and image of 'Man' changed. The medieval idea of 'Man' differs from the modern; but even within the medieval period this notion of 'Man' also changed, and these changes signified, perhaps, some important processes in the social development of the period. These processes are sometimes not so visible in economic spheres where we search for 'precapitalist elements', as in the sphere of ideas. A thorough research on this process is still to be undertaken but some observations should be made here.

It is well known that in every medieval society, 'Man' was perceived not as an indiviual, but as a member of some community, caste, religion, estate and India was no exception to this. For modern society a man is interesting in his specific features of character and behaviour, in his being different from other people. For medieval society the criteria of judgement was the opposite: a man was assessed according to his being like other members of his community or estate. In Europe a man was defined only as a knight or trader, priest or a layman, a peasant or a serf, a Christian or a 'pagan'.[1] In India also a man was seen as a member of a caste, a Hindu or a Muslim, a Sikh or a Parsi, etc. Medieval Indians and medieval Europeans held the same opinion that a brave knight or a brave Rajput raja was noble, valiant and generous by the very fact of his caste or estate. It is not accidental that in the chivalrous romances of European literature and similar literary works of medieval India, the hero and his adversary were equally brave and noble, since they belonged to the 'noble' social group. Likewise a merchant had to be clever and industrious, a priest— generous and pious, etc. All the characters in the literary works of medieval writers were static and unchanging: if a man's nature wholly depended on his birth in a certain social group, if he was fully determined by his social position his individual traits could be very well predicted. In *Shahnama*, Rustam's son was able to catch wild horses by their tails since babyhood, and the great Firdausi saw nothing impossible in this, for the boy was, by his birth, a hero and a son of Rustam. Negative examples were also frequent but these negative examples were needed to specify that to deviate from the caste and estate norms of behaviour was sinful and disgusting. The Indian tradition was much more flexible in this matter, for in many medieval works, a noble and generous *chandala* would be depicted as either a *brahman* or even a deity, serving out some penance. Despite the criticism of foolish *brahmans* and *mullahs* in Indian literature of the middle ages, despite the generous description of *chandalas* like Shabari, the main principle that it adhered to was that a man was as good or bad, as he was loyal to his caste *dharma*. Caste and community were supposed to determine not only a man's morals and behaviour, but his abilities, even physical features. Heroes and heroines of many a literary work had to live in disguise, but they were easily recognized, for 'such a beauty cannot be of a low caste'. A *brahman* was clean by his very nature, a *chandala* was not by the same, and such an approach is not a total anachronism even in the India of today.

Against this background the new ideas of some saints and thinkers of medieval India are noteworthy. The way to God and to salvation, proposed by them, was connected neither with canonical knowledge, nor with caste purity, nor with access to sacred books. Changes were introduced by the saints in many a traditional criteria of purity, saintliness, virtue. These values of human nature, according to the *bhakti* and *sufi* saints, were not dependent on one's caste, community and lineage. A *brahman* was respected only because of his being born one but Kabir was bold enough to say: 'You are good from outside, but within you is rubbish', while Raidas/Ravidas, who was scorned as an 'unclean *chamar*' was considered a holy man by Kabir.[2] According to these saints, a kind, generous, pious man was dear to God because of his qualities and not because he was a member of some caste or community.

Some *bhaktas* and *sufis* even criticized caste inequality. As we have already noticed, this social criticism seemed weaker than that of the radical Reformation of the west. The Indian reformers could not support their views by means of an ancient tradition as could the west with its early Christian communities and their egalitarian principles. So in the Indian cultural and civilizational atmosphere even a mild (by European standards) criticism of caste purity and hierarchy was of greater significance than the heroism of the Hussites, Muntzer and other radical reformers of medieval Europe.

The new approach to assess man in medieval India was directly linked with the fact that religious reformist schools and preachers considered that the path to God required neither philosophical research, nor rituals, nor sacred text but moral purity and a deep love for God. The opportunity to make a free choice of a *bhakti marga* or other ways of worship was significant. The *bhakti* and *sufi* literature disclosed the richest variety of human feelings and emotions where everything was acceptable from the ecstatic love of Mira Bai to the naive kindness of Shabari. In this literature two viewpoints coexisted and naturally blended into one another. One viewpoint was that of mundane human feelings, another was divine and mystical love. There is no exaggeration in the remark made by Sazanova about the clear-cut Renaissance features in the works of Surdas, whose Yashoda, according to the scholar, had many features in common with the Madonnas of the Italian Renaissance. The similarity here was in the author's aspiration to humanize the mystical feeling of divine love and to raise ordinary feeling of maternal love to the celestial height of divine *bhakti*.[3]

We can here suggest that the religious reformist movements of the middle ages were connected with the historical process of the development of individualism, as well as with the growing interest in human qualities and individual emotions. It was not surprising that during the later middle ages the traditional literary genres of hagiography (saints' life) changed into real biography, depicting not only legendary wonders but the real life and individual character of a person. *Ardhakathanaka* by Banarasi Das, autobiographical chapters in Abu-l Fazl's works, autobiographies by Bedil, Shah Waliullah, etc. are good examples. Many poets and thinkers of ancient and medieval India are known to us only from legends and sometimes it is impossible to determine the authenticity of their lives and activities. The later medieval literary works were by and large dated and in many cases the authors informed the readers about themselves. Also, it was in this period that the idealized images of people in painting gave way to real portraits (see the well known miniature paintings of Akbar, Aurangzeb, Shivaji, etc.). Significant also was the interest of the Indian artists in the realistic techniques of European painters.

The main achievement of the religious reformers was a changed attitude to 'Man'. They tried to shift the criteria of the assessment of a person from caste and lineage to individual emotions, feelings and moral conduct. The notions of religiosity, saintliness and purity also underwent a change. A true *sufi* or *bhakta* had an intimate contact with God and this enabled him to disclose the whole treasury of his individual feelings, moods and emotions; sometimes passionate love, painful separation, at other times Yashoda's maternal love, the *gopi's* jealousy, and sometimes a gentle rebuke to Krishna for his whims and *lila*.

Each devotee was given an opportunity to have an individually chosen preceptor and an individual path of salvation. To choose a preceptor his personal virtues were to be taken into account, not his caste or creed. Some modern scholars see an individual path of salvation as inferior to the aspirations of European radical thought which sought to change not the individual self, but society as a whole. In our opinion, both approaches were equally valid for the cultures and civilizations of the world. Moreover, these paths were not mutually exclusive—sometimes a peaceful *bhakta* would become a militant freedom fighter. Likewise the European Reformation never limited itself to active social protest and sometimes chose the way of peaceful mysticism.

Changes in the traditional outlook and approach towards 'Man', his character, criteria of assessment and social role were a result of the development of the majority of medieval civilizations. As far as the reformation of social and caste attitudes to 'Man' are concerned, India made several important efforts, though they were not so radical and effective, as they were in Europe during the last phase of feudalism. But the religious thinkers in medieval India were able to develop a theory which was a significant step forward from the ancient Indian tradition of tolerance.

Even the best minds of late medieval Europe failed to spread their humanistic ideas to non-Christians. The thinkers of the Renaissance tried to Christianize the Greek and Roman sages of the past, for according to the Europeans of the period, it was impossible to be a genius like Plato or Aristotle and to be a non-

Christian. The European attitude to non-Christians was either hostile, or at best, compassionate: these 'poor creatures' who actually represented civilizations more ancient and more developed than the European ones, were to be sympathized with and, of course, shown the 'right path' to God, if not by the carrot, then by the stick. This was in total contrast to the perception of Indian thinkers for whom the very idea of the 'right' and 'wrong' paths to God was absurd: they accepted only right or wrong people. What is important is that these ideas were developed, albeit differently, by either semi-literate people like Kabir or by the intellectual elite. Indian religious reformers and freethinking intellectuals struggled uncompromisingly against religious fanatics and bigoted theologians, but their aim was not religion itself, but traditional values and approaches to God and man. They tried to make religion more humane and free from obscurantism and fanaticism, flexible and in tune with the realities of the time. The interaction of the two great cultural oceans on Indian soil produced people who were able to discard communal prejudices and see a living, human being in any 'other worshipper of God'.

This then seems to be the most precious and significant contribution of medieval India to world culture, more important, than the introduction of zero and invention of the chintz-making technique. India has every right to be proud of this, but, unfortunately, this great achievement is not fully appreciated by the successors of medieval Indians. The lofty ideas of *sulhe-kul* and 'merger of the oceans' were unable to triumph fully, and the same can be said about the ideas of Renaissance or Enlightenment in Europe. But the very fact that medieval India could produce these noble principles speaks volumes for the strength and depth of the humanistic tendencies present in medieval Indian thought.

It does not mean that at the end of the middle ages, India experienced 'that very' Renaissance, which is sometimes wrongly seen as the only necessary component of the crisis of feudalism and advent of capitalism.[4] It is sufficient to compare Italy and England to see that the Italy which produced the greatest stars of Renaissance culture lagged behind in economic and political development while England, which was peripheral from the point of view of Renaissance culture, made a socio-economic breakthrough. This serves as a good example to prove that links between socio-economic, political, cultural and ideological spheres undeniably exist, but they should not be seen as direct and linear. This will be nothing but a vulgarization of both Marxism and historical realities.

Thus a study of Indian thought in the context of the world history of ideas reveals some common features in the development of ideas in medieval India and Europe. If we compare the general direction of development, we may note the following: common to both was a tendency to assess the feelings and moral qualities of individuals not as inborn characteristics of a caste or an estate, but as individual qualities; a tendency to humanize and individualize religious worship and to elevate mundane feelings to spirituality. They shared the rejection of the traditional criteria of piety, purity and morality. While tracing these common concerns of the two civilizations, one must not negate the wide differences in economy, polity, ethnicity, religion and culture.

The history of European thought of the later medieval and early modern times is very well known. The humanistic tendencies of the Renaissance suffered a defeat in the new epoch, which proved to be quite different from the ideals of the humanists, and significantly Thomas More established his utopia on a faraway island, and not in his home country, like the Italians did. The Reformation passed through great bloodshed and succeeded in spreading an ideology which was necessary for the new mode of production. Then came the age of enlightenment which was a total triumph over the medieval world vision. As we trace this history we may see that each age is simultaneously marked by new developments and a continuity of tradition. The history of Indian thought needs a similar approach so that all the trends and tendencies of the colonial and modern epoch can be shown as having roots in medieval society.

While scholars who research on the history of Europe or China have already overcome the stereotype of the 'dark middle ages' and are aware that all the tendencies and trends of modern thought and culture could not have existed without a medieval basis, for many Indologists all the reformist schools of the nineteenth century, all attempts to modernize the Indian religions and minds are the fruits only of the British influence. According to this viewpoint, only weakness, conservatism and 'feudal remnants' linked the nineteenth century thinkers to the middle ages. Indian scholars cannot avoid the habitual scorn for the 'feudal remnants', but, this scorn often goes hand in hand with the romantic idealization of the past. For other scholars, especially for the Marxists, a somewhat simplified idea of social progress means that all vestiges of the medieval epoch in modern thought, all traditions of the past are totally reactionary.

However, the material utilized in this book leads to a different viewpoint. As far back as the late sixties and seventies some Soviet scholars like E. Komarov, and later B. Rybakov, were bold enough to suppose that, despite the significance of British influence, many trends in India's reformist and nationalist thought of the nineteenth and even twentieth centuries had their premises in medieval India.[5] This position can be corroborated by an elementary logic: in any cultural contact the role of both sides is equally significant, the transferred experience is as important, as the readiness of the recipient society to adopt the new ideas.

The development of the modernist and reformist schools of thought in nineteenth century India would not have been possible if medieval Indian civilization had failed to produce people who were capable of critically reconsidering a sacred dogma, or looking at their world from the viewpoint of reason. For example, an Indian may have studied English and served the British administration for the sake of money, security or career. But he would not have been able to comprehend and assess the useful and progressive features of western education, but for the tradition of medieval religious reformers and freethinkers.

Sometimes it appears that there existed a huge gap between the thinkers of the middle ages and those of modern or colonial times. But in reality this gap between the 'not yet' and the 'already' was very narrow both in time and space. Raja Rammohan Roy was just twenty years younger than Mirza Abu Talib and they might have met somewhere in Calcutta. One of the first Muslim scholars and modernists, Abdul Rahim Dahri, who was considered a predecessor of the celebrated Sir Sayid Ahmad, the founder of Aligarh University, was a student of Waliullah's son in the Rahimiya *madrasa*.[6]

The religious reformist schools and movements with their criticism of traditional and empty forms of worship, and their attempts to decanonize and humanize religion, formed a bridge, however narrow, over which the thought and culture of India moved from the middle ages into the nineteenth century and further.

Progressive trends of medieval Indian thought were never fully victorious, but they succeeded in producing a tradition of their own, in producing people who could discard some obsolete ideas and move forward, at the same time preserving all that was useful in their legacy. There would have been no Raja Rammohan Roy, Sir Syed, Jotiba Phule, no Tilak or Gandhiji if there had been no Kabir and Surdas, no Abu-l Fazl and Akbar, no Waliullah or Abu Talib, to list just a few names.

Such people were small in number, and so could not have adequately represented an epoch as complex as this. Indeed, not so many people in India thought like Abu-l Fazl or Dara Shukoh and Kabir is too 'leftist' even for modern India. But should we adopt a quantitative method for the history of ideas? We use labels as 'the Age of the Renaissance', 'the Age of Enlightenment', but do we seriously believe that all Europeans thought like Leonardo da Vinci, Erasmus or Voltaire?

The progressive thinkers of medieval India could never expect that their ideas would be agreeable to the masses. Moreover, they often suffered defeats at the hands of orthodox traditionalists. Nevertheless their ideas proved so vital that they were able to bring about transformation and development that lasted for centuries.

No scholar will deny the role of tradition in contemporary Indian society, but not all of them take into consideration that tradition was heterogeneous and contradictory within itself. India has indeed a tradition of caste inequality, but does it not have a tradition of struggle against this social problem? India has a tradition of religious bigotry and communal discord, but does it not have a tradition of communal amity and *sulhe-kul*?

The legacy of the past is still felt in India, and many social problems of the twentieth century have much in common with the problems on which medieval thinkers pondered. The problems of modern India have, no doubt, modern reasons, but the core of a social conflict has some similarities with what happened in the middle ages. For instance, one can refer to the model of a state and principles of governance in modern India. On the one hand, in modern India there are powerful communal and political forces which advocate the establishment of a Hindu state, a Muslim state, a Sikh state, etc. where the representatives of other communities would expect only tolerance. Does this not appear to be a return to the pre-Akbar state model? This approach is contradicted by a complex of ideas, now known as secularism, which advocates equal validity of all religions and a secular character for the state. This tendency is clearly the legacy of the 'enlightened' philosophers, *bhakti*, and *sufi* saints, and it is only natural that the secularist forces in India quite often appeal to the legacy of the medieval thinkers, for the lofty ideas of communal amity and secularism are an inseparable part of the Indian tradition. Thus in India, to be a traditionalist should not necessarily signify as being a bigot or a communalist.

Indeed, the legacy of medieval India is being utilized differently by different political and cultural forces of our times. The name of Shivaji was an inspiration for Tilak in his fight for freedom and can now be used by a certain political force whose aims are quite different from that of Tilak. The name of Guru Gobind may be used either by those who advocate communal amity or by those who spread exactly opposite ideas. Appeal to the historical and cultural tradition is natural and unavoidable for a country like India. But very important is the fact that this tradition itself is very heterogeneous and contradictory. The ideas that are now being utilized by communal and conservative forces had been rejected and resisted by the best minds of India centuries ago. Centuries lie between Kabir's criticism of caste inequality and Gandhiji's struggle for the upliftment of the *harijans*, centuries lie between the 'enlightened philosophers' and the secularists of modern days. This long period of time is not only a border between the middle ages and modernity, but also unites the thinkers, who are far from each other in history but are close in spirit.

The legacy of medieval thought lives on in the contemporary India. It still forms, albeit unconsciously, a part of the thought processes of people, their moral and aesthetic values. The ideas from medieval thought participate in political, cultural and ideological conflicts and sometimes coexist peacefully with modern civilization. The medieval cultural legacy plays an indispensable role in the process of modern India and makes India at the same time an inseparable part of humanity.

Notes and References

CHAPTER I

1. See Ashrafyan, K.Z., *Feudalism in India*, Moscow, 1978, pp. 158–203 (Russian); Pavlov, V.I., 'Stadial–Formation Characteristics of the Oriental Societies in Pre–Modern Times'–A Part of the Collective Work by Ye. M. Zhukov, M.A. Barg, Ye. B. Cheryak and V.I. Pavlov, *Theoretical Problems of the World Historical Process*, Moscow 1979, pp. 198–214, 247–55 (Russian); Srivastava, M.P., *Policies of the Great Mughals*, Allahabad, 1987; Nizami, Kh. A., *The Delhi Sultanate and the Mughal Empire: Genesis and Salient Features*–IC, 1981, vol. 55, nos 3–4, p. 169. See also Hermann Kulke (ed.), *The State in India 1000–1700*, Delhi, 1997 (paperback edition, first published in 1995) for both the contents and well-compiled bibliography.

2. Vigasin, A.A., Samozvantsev, A.M., 'Arthasastra', *Problems of Social Structure and Law*, Moscow, 1984, pp. 145–9 (Russian).

3. Quoted from 'Mahabharata', XII, 24.17 by G.M. Bongard–Levin and G.F. Ilyin, *Ancient India*, Moscow, 1985, p. 562.

4. Sukra, *Sukranitisara*, Bombay, 1921, p. 6 (text in Sankrit and Hindi translation). Some controversy still exists about this source; scholars attribute it either to the early medieval period (but what to do with artillery described there?) or even to the XIX century, as Lallanji Gopal supposed. In our view, an early work might have been annexed by some later portions. Anyhow, it reflected a certain level of the ideas of the state. Mr Lallanji Gopal's suggestion (vide his 'Sukraniti, a Nineteenth Century Text' in *BSOAS*, XXV, pp. 224–556) that some places and ideas in *Sukraniti* sound modern and agree with the political and administrative system of British India, may be counterposed by an argument that the British administrators utilized some traditional postulates of the Indian polity to make their rule efficient in India.

5. Somadeva's 'Vetalapanchavimsati', in *Kathasaritsagara*, Tr. By C.U. Tawney, Bombay, 1956, p. 23.

6. Udgaonkar, P., *The Political Institutions and Administration in Northern India During Medieaval Times*, Delhi, 1969, pp. 52f. Bayly, C.A., *Origins of Nationality in South Asia: Patriotism and Ethical Government in the Making of Modern India*, Delhi, 1998, p. 12. In Medieval Orissa the king was proclaimed God's viceroy. See Kulke, Hermann, 'Royal Temple Policy and the Structure of Medieval Hindu Kingdoms' in A. Eschmann, H. Kulke, and G.C. Tripathi (eds), *The Cult of Jagannath and the Regional Tradition of Orissa*, Delhi, 1978; von Steitencon, Hr, 'Early Temples of Jagannatha in Orissa: the Formative Phase' in ibid.

7. I have consulted the Russian translation of this part of *Kathasaritsagara* by I.D. Serebryakov, Moscow, 1982, p. 318.

8. *Sukraniti*, p. 6.

9. Ibid., p. 3

10. Ibid., P. 4.

11. Ghoshal, U.N., 'A Comparison Between Ancient Indian and Medieaval European Theories of Divine Right and the Nature of Kingship,' *IHQ*, 1955, vol. XXI, no. 3, pp. 264–6.

12. Ghoshal, U.N., *A History of Indian Political Ideas. The Ancient Period and Period of Transition to the Middle Ages*, Oxford, 1959, p. 536.

13. Chaudhury, R., *Mithila in Age of Vidyapati*, Varanasi, 1976, p. 43.

14. Bongard–Levin, G.M. and Ilyin, G.F., *Ancient India*, p. 563.

15. Satyanarayana, K., A *Study in the History and Culture of the Andhras*, Delhi, 1983, vol. II, p. 291.

16. Ibid., p. 106; Sastri, N., Venkataramanayya, M. (ed.,tr.), *Further Sources of Vijayanagara History*, Madras, 1946, vol. III, p. 164.

17. The evidence to the kings patronizing arts is numerous; practically, the whole of Ballala's *Bhojaprabandha* (English Translation, New Haven, 1950) speaks of the king paying poets lakhs per syllable. Donating money and lands to the seats of learning as well as supporting the afflicted was also considered the royal duty (*See* Satyanarayana, vol. II, pp. 106 ff).

18. Vidyapati Thakur, *Kirtilata*, Jhansi, 1962, pp. 19f (Maithili Text and Hindi rendering).

19. R.S. Sharma, 'The Kali Age: A period of Social Crisis', in D.N. Jha (ed.), *The Feudal Order: State, Society and Ideology in Early Medieval India*, Delhi, 2000.

20. Mahalingam, T.V., *South Indian Polity*, Madras, 1967, p. 23.

21. Sukraniti, p. 7; Chaudhary, R., *Mithila*, p. 43.

22. Nikiforov, V.N., *The Orient and World History*, Moscow, 1975, pp. 81–93 (Russian).

23. Inden, R., *Imagining India*, Cambridge, MA and Oxford, UK, 1992, p. 3. The same subject is discussed in Teltscher, Kate, *India Inscribed: European and British writings on India 1600–1800*, Delhi, 1995, p. 26.

24. For more detail, see Metcalf, Thomas R., *Ideologies of the Raj*, New Cambridge History of India series, Cambridge, 1995, pp. 6–15.

25. Chaudhary, R., *Mithila*, p. 45.

26. *Sukraniti*, p. 21; Satyanarayana, K., *A Study of the History and Culture of the Andhras*, p. 107.

27. Satyanarayana, K., *A Study of the History and Culture of the Andhras*, p. 107.

28. *The Private Diary of Ananda Ranga Pillai*, Madras, 1904, vol. II, pp. 42–7.

29. Chaudhary, R., *Mithila*, p. 48; Mahalingam, T.V., *South Indian Polity*, pp. 18f.

30. Rama's Later History or *Uttara Rama Charita*. An Ancient Hindi Play by Bhavabhuti. Tr. By S.K. Belvalkar, Harvard, 1915, vol.1, pp. 1–102.

31. Somadeva's *Vetalapanchavimsati*, pp. 129–33.

32. I have consulted the Russian translation of this romance from the Norman French by N. Rykova, Moscow, 1980, p. 59.

33. *The Saxon Mirror*. Russian Translation by L. Dembo, Moscow, 1985, p. 15. See also about this treatise: Mundy, J.H., *Europe in the Middle Ages*, New York, 1973, pp. 9. 100, 262, 233, 371.

34. Gurevich, A., *Categories* p. 182.

35. *The Saxon Mirror*, p. 16

36. In medieval Europe also people of the low social status were not advised to read the Scripture as it was considered sacrilegious to expose the holy texts to the profanes; most people had to learn prayers by rote or at best to read breviaries or collections of prayers. Only monks and priests were allowed to read the holy book, but no severe regulations existed in this matter, unlike India.

37. Vigasin, A.A., Samozvantsev, A.M., 'Arthasastra', pp. 216–22. *See also*: Kangle, R.P., *The Kauthilya Arthasastra*, vol. III. A Study, Bombay, 1964, pp. 62–4.

38. *Sukraniti*, p. 132.

39. Gurevich, A., *Categories*, p. 196.

40. For an interesting example of the Andhra oilmen claiming *kshatriya* status see Kanaka Durga, P.S. 'Identity and Symbol of Sustenance: Explorations in Social Mobility of Medieval South India', JESHO, 2001, vol. 44, pt 2.

41. Stuzhina, E.P., *The Chinese Crafts in the XVIth–XVIIth Centuries*, Moscow, 1970, pp. 43–6 (Russian).

42. Dikshit, S., *Local Self-Government in Medieval Karnataka*, Dharwar, 1964, pp. 141–69; Velayudhan, K.P., *Trade Guilds and the Character of State in Early South India–Proceedings of Indian History Congress*, 39th session (1978), pp. 200–7; Yarlagadda Tejaswini, 'Social Groups and Economic Change: 7th–13th Centuries' in Aloka Parasher Sen (ed.), *Social and Economic History of Early Deccan: Some Interpretations*, Delhi, 1993, pp. 169–78.

43. Watters, T., *On Yuan Chwang's Travels in India (629–45)*, London, 1904–5, vol. I, p. 176.

44. Samozvantsev, A.M. and Vigasin, A.A., *Arthasastra*, pp. 145–54; Hesterman, J.C., *The Inner Conflict of Tradition: Essays in Indian Ritual, Kingship and Society*, Delhi, 1985, p. 18; Inden, R., *Imagining India*, pp. 162–212, for a comprehensive review of the discussions about the character of medieval Indian states see Kulke, H., 'Introduction: The Study of the State in Pre-Modern India' in Hermann Kulke (ed.), *The State in India 1000–1700*, pp. 1–47.

45. Vigasin, A. A., Samozvantsev, A.M., 'Arthasastra', pp. 145–7 (*Arthasastra*, VI. 1.8.)

46. Askari, S.H., 'Material of Historical Value in Ijaz–I Khusravi,' *MI*, 1971, vol. I, p. 6.

47. Habib, M., Salim Khan, A. (tr.) *The Political Theory of Delhi Sultanate*, Allahabad, n.d. pp. 2f.

48. Ibid., pp. 5, 40.

49. *Futuhat–i Firuz Shahi*, Aligarh, 1954, p. 11(Persian).

50. Askari, S.H., *Material*, p. 11.

51. *Political Theory*, p. 38; *Futuhat–i Firuz Shahi*, p. 10.

52. Discussed in more detail by André Wink, *Al-Hind: The Making of the Indo–Muslim World, Vol.II, The Slave Kings and the Islamic*

Conquest, 11th –13th Centuries, Delhi, 1999, pp. 242, 265–8, 294, cf.

53. *Political Theory,* p. 38–40.

54. Chattopadhyaya Brajadulal, *Representing the Other? Sanskrit Sources and the Muslims,* Delhi, 1998, pp. 45, 71–86.

55. Abu-l Fazi Allami, *Ain-i Akbari,* tr. by H. Blochmann, vol. I, Delhi, 1977, p. 3; Habib, Irfan, 'A Political Theory for the Mughal Empire,' *PIHC,* Proccedings, 59th session, 1998, pp. 333–5.

56. Habib, Irfan, ' A Political Theory for the Mughal Empire,' p. 333.

57. Abu-l Fazl Allami, *Ain-i Akbari,* tr. by H. Blochmann, vol I. p.3.

58. Rizvi, S.A.A., *Muslim Revivalist Movements in Northern India in the Sixteenth and Seventeenth Centuries,* Agra, 1965, p. 223.

59. Ibid., pp. 195–6. For an evaluation of the *mahzar* see: Streusand, Douglas E., *The Formation of the Mughal Empire,* Delhi, 1999 (OUP paperback edition), pp. 114–19.

60. Antonova, K.A., *Essays on the Social Relations and Political System of Mughal India of Akbar's Times (1556–1605),* Moscow, 1952, pp. 248–50 (Russian).

61. Ibid., pp. 185–8; Abu–l Fazl Allami, *Ain–i Akbari,* vol. I, p. lxxiii.

62. Nizami, Kh. A., *Akbar and Religion,* Delhi, 1989, pp. 373–80; Haidar Mansura, *Mukatabat-i Allami Insha–i Abu–l Fazl, Letters of the Emperor Akbar in English Translation, Edited with Commentary, Perspective and Notes,* Daftar I, Delhi, 1998, p. 96.

63. Richards, John F., *The Mughal Empire,* The New Cambridge History of India, Cambridge and Delhi, 2000, pp. 40–1.

64. Ibid., p. 4.

65. Ashrafayan, C.Z., *Medieval Indian City, XIIIth to mid XVIIth Centuries,* Moscow, 1983, p.66 (Russian).

66. Abu–l Fazl Allami, *Ain–i Akbari,* vol. I. p. 4.

67. Ibid., pp 247–59; Abu–l Fazl Allami, *Ain–i Akbari,* vol II.I, tr. by H.S. Jarret, Delhi, 1978, pp. 43–6, 64, 68–72.

68. This play depicts an uprising of the peasants who killed their feudal lord to avenge his cruel and tyrannous behaviour, especially to girls and women of the village. All peasants were tortured by the police but refused to disclose the name of the real killer, a youth whose bride was kidnapped and dishonoured by the lord; even under torture the peasants kept saying that the oppressor was killed by the whole village. The king took their side and established justice; the

playwright depicted the royal power as a stabilizing force and a protection against the tyranny of feudal lords.

69. Khan, A.R., *Chieftains in the Mughal Empire During the Reign of Akbar,* Simla, 1977, pp. 206–33.

70. Azimdjanova, S.A., *Babur's State in Qubal and India,* Moscow, 1977, pp. 3, 150 (an English article by this author was published in *Soviet Oriental Studies,* Calcutta, 1970, pp. 143–51. The theme is Babur's *divan* and its insight into political and cultural life of India).

71. Azimdjanova, S.A. *Babur's State,* pp. 99–105, 116–17, 124–5.

72. Ashrafyan, C. Z., *Medieval Indian City,* p. 193.

73. See, for instance, Ali, M. Athar, 'Towards an Interpretation of the Mughal Empire' in Hermann Kulke (ed.) *The State in India, 1000–1700,* Delhi (OUP paperback edition), 1997, pp. 203–77.

74. Some scholars see the Mughal empire under Akbar as a 'patrimonial –bureaucratic' state (see, for example, Blake, Stephen P., 'The Patrimonial Bureaucratic Empire of the Mughals, in ibid., pp. 278–304). I should here agree with those scholars who view this concept as a modernized version of the 'oriental depostism' model.

75. *Political Theory,* pp. 20, 97–8; Ali Muhammad Khan, *Khatima-e Mirati Ahmadi,* Baroda, 1930, pp. 135–7 (Persian).

76. Pavlov, V.I., *The Stadial Formation Characteristics,* p. 223.

77. *Complaint and Reform in England, 1436–1714,* New York, 1968, pp. 32–9.

78. Abu-l Fazl Allami, *Ain-i Akbari,* vol. II, pp. 54–5; Chikolini, L. S., 'Political and Legal Concepts of Janfrancesco Lottini', *Middle Ages,* Moscow, 1984–5, vol. 48, pp. 165–70.

79. Faruki, Z., *Aurangzeb and His Times,* Bombay, 1935, pp. 25–31; Sinha, H.N., The Development of Indian Polity, New York, 1963, pp. 443–59; Nizami, Kh. A., *The Delhi Sultanate,* pp. 171–5.

80. Nehru Jawaharlal, *The Discovery of India,* Delhi, 1981, p. 270.

81. Chopra, P.N., Some Experiments in Social Reform in Medieval India: *The Cultural Heritage of India,* Calcutta, 1969, vol.II, p. 627.

82. Mukund Lath Led., (ed., tr.), *Half a Tale, Ardhakathanaka,* Jaipur. 1981, p. 242 (Hindi).

83. Nizami, Kh. A., 'Naqshbandi Influence on Mughal Rulers and Politics', *IC,* 1965, vol. 39, no. 1, p. 47. For similar expectations from Akbar's Successor see: Muzaffar Alam and Sanjay Subrahmanyam, 'Witnessing Transition: Views on the End of the Akbari Dispensation', in *The Making of History, Essays Presented*

200 Ideas and Society

to *Irfan Habib,* ed. by K.N. Panikkar, Terence J. Byres, and Utsa
Patnaik, Delhi, 2000, p. 112.

84. Ali Muhammad Khan, *Mirat–I Ahmadi,* Baroda, 1931, vol. I, pp.
160–1.

85. Ibid., pp. 175–7.

86. *Sinha,* H.N., *The Development,* pp. 514f; Srivastava, M.P., *Policies
of the Great Mughals,* Allahabad, 1978, p. 91.

87. *Ruqaat–i Alamgiri or Letters of Aurangzeb,* tr. by J. Billimoria,
Delhi, 1972, p. 5, ff.; Ali Muhammad Khan, *Mirat–i Ahmadi,* vol.
I, pp. 260–3; Richards, J.F., *The Mughal Empire,* pp. 175–7.

88. Quoted by Sarkar, J., *History of Aurangzib,* Calcutta, 1919, vol. III,
pp. 325–9; for Raj Singh as author of this letter *see:* Sharma, G.N.,
Mewar and the Mughal Emperors, Agra, 1962, p. 211.

89. Sarkar, J., English Translation of *Tarikh–i Dilkasha,* Bombay, 1972,
p. 231.

90. *Ruqaat,* p. 158.

91. Ashrafyan, C.Z., *Feudalism,* p. 168.

92. Pavlov, V.I., *Stadial Formation Characteristics,* p. 229.

CHAPTER II

1. Comp.: Nehru, Jawaharlal, *Discovery of India,* Delhi, 1981, pp. 241,
265–9; Panikkar, K.M, *A Survey of Indian History,* Bombay, 1954,
p. 129.

2. Nehru, Jawaharlal, *Discovery,* p. 237.

3. Kutsenkov, A.A., *Evolution of the Indian Caste,* Moscow, 1983,
p. 67 (Russian).

4. Vidyapati, Thakur, *Kirtilata.* Jhansi, 1962, pp. 111, 115–19 (Maithili
and Hindi rendering).

5. See *Futuhat–i Firuzshahi,* Aligarh, 1954, pp. 9f (Persian); Habib, M.,
Khan, Salim A. (tr.), *Political Theory of the Delhi Sultanate,*
Allahabad, n.d., p. 46

6. Vidyapati, Thakur, *Kirtilata,* pp. 114f.

7. Sarkar, J., English Translation of *Tarikh–i Dilkasha,* Bombay, 1972,
pp. 1–2f; Kishore Das Munshi, *Majmua–e Danish,* Bombay, 1957,
pp. 2, 5. For an all-embracing study of the Persian language in the
Mughal empire and its influence upon the Hindus, see: Muzaffar
Alam, 'The Pursuit of Persian: Language in Mughal Politics', *Modern
Asian Studies,* 32, 2, (1998), pp. 325–42.

8. Such examples may be multiplied. A fifteenth century *brahman* poet Dinkar wrote Persian *naziras* (answers) to Amir Khusrau's ghazals; Jonaraja, the continuer of the *Rajatarangini* also wrote Persian verses. Numerous were Persian versions of Sanskrit classics like Zia ud–din Nahshabi's and an–Naari's versions of *Tuti Namah.* Vide also: Serebryakov, I.D., *Literatures of the Indian Peoples,* Moscow, 1985, p. 149 (Russian).

9. Sometimes it was not that easy to say whether an author was a Hindu or a Muslim. A vivid example is 'Madhavanal–Kamkandala', a sixteenth-century Hindi poem by Alam (see, by the present author, "Madhavanala-Kamakandala" by Alam: A Hindi Poem of Akbar's Epoch' *IHR,* vol. xx, nos 1–2, July 1993 & January 1994, pp. 66–77. Same can be said of the *sufi* romances by Mulla Daud, Manjhan, Usman, Jayasi, or the *bhakti* poetry by Rahim.

10. Mukundoram Chokroborti's *Chandimongol,* a sixteenth century Bengali poem, gives a graphic description of the city population community–wise (Russian translation by I. Tovstykh, Moscow, 1980, pp. 150–7). Parallel Hindu–Muslim social and professional strucure is shown very vividly here. *See also : Munhta Nainsi ri Likhi Marvad ra pargana ri Vigat,* Jodhpur, 1977, vols I, II, pp. 6, 65–6, 224, 361, 498; cf.

11. Pavlov, V.I., *Stadial Formation Characteristics,* p. 244.

12. Grewal, J.S., *Guru Nanak in History,* Chandigarh, 1969, pp. 160–3.

13. Ambastha, B., *Non-Persian Sources of Indian Medieval History,* Delhi, 1983, p. 22.

14. Naik, C.R., *Abdur–Rahim Khan Khanan and His Literary Circle,* Ahmedabad, 1966, pp. 228–31, 463–5.

15. 'Kabir Bijak: Pad, 20–2', Callewaert, Winand M. and Op de Beeck, Bart (eds), *Devotional Hindi Literature,* Delhi, 1991, Vol–I, p. 357.

16. Zelliot, Eleanor (tr.), 'A Medieval Encounter between Hindu and Muslim: Eknath's Drama–Poem, *Hindu–Turk Samvad'* in F. Clothey (ed.), *Images of Man, Religion and Historical Process in South Asia,* Madras, 1982, pp. 177–87.

17. Callewaert, W.M., (ed., tr.), *The Hindi Biography of Dadu Dayal,* Delhi, 1988, p. 38 (English tr.), 93 (Hindi orig.); Savitri Chandra Shobha, *Social Life and Concepts in Medieval Hindi Bhakti Poetry: A Sociocultural Study,* Delhi, 1983, p. 42.

18. Mc Leod (ed., tr.), *Textual Sources for the Study of Sikhism,* Manchester, 1984, pp. 63f; Ganda Singh, *Development of Sikh Thought upto the End of the XVIIIth Century. Ideas in History,* Delhi, 1968, p. 12.

19. Athar, Ali M., 'Sidelights into Ideological and Religious Attitudes in the Punjab During the XVIIth Century' *MI,* vol. II, pp.188–90.

20. *Jayasi Granthavali,* Allahabad, 1936, pp. 4f (Hindi); Dvivedi, P., *Hindi Premgatha,* p. 184 ; *Chandayan Daud Virachit Hindi Pratham Sufi Premkavya,* ed., Mataprasad Gupta, Agra, 1967, p.9.

21. Ishaq Khan, ' The Societal Dimensions of the Mystical Philosophy of Nur ud–din Rishi Kashmiri', *PIHC,* 1987, p. 259.

22. *Some Specimens of Satpanthi Literature.* Tr. by V. Hooda-Collectanea, Leiden, 1948, vol. I, pp. 125–35.

23. Callewaert, W.M., *The Hindi Biography,* pp. 48–53 (English), 98–105 (Hindi).

24. Badauni said that Mahabharta was 'absurd': 'Badauni Abd al Qadir', Akbar, Elliot and Dawson, *The History of India as Told by its Own Historians,* Calcutta, 1961, pp. 68–9.

25. Faruki, Z., *Aurangzeb and His Times,* Bombay, 1935, pp. 32f; Srivastava, M.P., *Policies of the Great Mughals,* Allahabad, 1978, p. 85.

26. *Political Theory,* pp. 46–8.

27. Abu–l Fazl Allami, *Akbar–Nama* Tr. by H. Blochmann, Delhi, 1979, vol. III, pp. 398–400.

28. Abu–l Fazl Allami, *Ain–i Akbari,* vol III, pp. 5f.

29. Dvivedi, G.P., *Hindi Premgatha Kavya Sangrah,* Allahabad, 1953, p. 184; Vanina, Eugenia, 'Madhavanala–Kamakandala by Alam', pp 74–5.

30. *Rationalist Tradition and Modernity,* India, Moscow, 1988 (Russian).

31. Abu–l Fazl Allami, *Ain–i Akbari,* vol. III, pp. 426f; *Akbar Nama,* vol. III, pp. 369f

32. Narang, S., *Transformation of Sikhism,* Delhi, 1960, p. 24.

33. Abu–l Fazl Allami, *Ain–i Akbari,* vol. I, p. 289.

34. Ibid, vol. III, p. 2

35. Ibid, pp. 29–49, cf.

36. Rizvi, S.A.A., 'Abu–l Fazl's Preface to the Persian Translation of the Mahabharata', *PIHC,* 1950, pp. 198–201.

37. Rizvi, S.A.A., *Religious and Intellectual History of the Muslims of Akbar's Reign With Special Reference to Abu–l Fazl,* Delhi, 1971, p.100

38. Abu–l Fazl Allami, *Ain–i Akbari,* vol. I, p. 209 (An extract from Badauni interpolated into the edition of *Ain–i Akbari*).

39. Jarric, S.J., *Akbar and the Jesuits,* London, 1926, p. 29.
40. Abu–l Fazl Allami, *Akbar Nama,* vol. III, p. 366.
41. Antonova, K.A., *Essays,* pp. 20f.
42. *The Dabistan or a School of Manners,* Tr. by D. Shea and A. Troyer, Paris, 1843, vol III, pp. 78–84.
43. Abu–l Fazl Allami, *Ain–i Akbari,* vol. I, p. 207; *Dabistan,* p. 78.
44. *Political Theory,* pp. 48f.
45. *Futuhat–i Firuzshahi,* p. 7; Ashrafyan, C.Z., *Medieval Indian City,* p. 134.
46. Pavlov, V.I., 256–9.
47. Gurevich, A., *Categories,* p. 22.
48. Abidi, S. 'Talib Amuli, His Life and Poetry', *IC,* 1967, vol. 41, p. 129.
49. Hadi Hasan, *Qasim–i Kahi. His Life, Times and Works,* Calcutta, 1967, p. 28.
50. Abu–l Fazl Allami, *Ain–i Akbari,* vol III, pp. 4f.
51. Ibid, vol. III, pp. 427f.
52. Nizami, Kh. A., *Akbar and Religion,* Delhi, 1989, p. 81.
53. Ibid., p. 60
54. Pavlov, VI, p. 268.
55. Rizvi, S.A.A., *Muslim Revivalist Movements in Northern India in Sixteenth and Seventeenth Centuries,* Agra, 1965, p. 167.
56. Rizvi, S.A.A., *Religious and Intellectual History,* p. 427.
57. Rizvi, S.A.A., *Muslim Revivalist Movements,* pp. 207–54.
58. Jarric, S.J., *Akbar and the Jesuits,* p.69; Badaoni, *Akbar,* p. 51.
59. Antonova, K.A., *Essays,* pp. 257–60; Polonskaya, L.R., *Muslim Trends in Social Thought of India and Pakistan,* Moscow, 1963, p. 72.
60. *Dabistan,* pp. 104f.
61. Srivastava, M.P., *Policies,* p. 90.
62. Rizvi, S.A.A., *Religions and Intellectual History,* p. 391; Streusand, Douglas E., *The Formation of the Mughal Empire,* Delhi (OUP paperback edition), 1999, pp. 148–51.
63. Siddiqui, M., 'Shah Muhibullah Illahabadi and the Liberal Tradition in Islam', *PIHC,* 1981, pp. 289–93.
64. Rizvi, S.A.A., *Muslim Revivalist Movements,* p. 337. Alam, Muzaffar, 'Assimilation from a Distance: Confrontation and Sufi Accomodation

in Awadh Society' in R. Champalakshmi and S. Gopal (eds), *Tradition, Dissent and Ideology: Essays in Honour of Romila Thapar,* Delhi, 1996. pp. 175–7.

65. *Dargarh Quli Khan, Muraqqa–e Delhi. The Mughal Capital in Muhammad Shah's Times.* Tr. by C.S. Sharma and S.M. Chenoy, Delhi, 1989, pp. 29–31.

66. Sen, S., *History of Bengali Literature,* Delhi, 1960, p. 87.

67. Munshi, K.M., *Gujarat and Its Literature from Early Times to 1852,* Bombay, 1952, p. 233; *Malukdasji ki Bani,* Allahabad, 1946, pp. 28, 37 (Hindi).

68. Vallabha's *Parasarama Charita.* Tr. by N. Wagle and A.R. Kulkarni, Bombay, 1976, pp. 5, 59; Joglekar, D., *Sri Samartha Ramdas,* Bombay, 1951, pp. 29f (Hindi).

69. Singh, M.P. ed., *Lal Krit Chatraprasad,* Delhi, 1973, pp. 96f (Hindi).

70. Sarkar, J., *History of Aurangzib,* Calcutta, 1919–24, vol III, pp. 325–9.

71. Muhammad Hashim Khafi Khan, *Muntahabu–l Lubab.* Tr. by J. Dawson, Calcutta, 1960, p. 52.

72. Kulkarni, A.R., 'Social Relations in the Maratha Country (Medieval Period)'. Presidential Address, 32nd Session of the *Indian History Congress,* Jabalpur, 1970, pp. 7–31 (Reprint).

73. Narang, S., *Transformation of Sikhism,* p. 24.

74. Singh, Gopal, *Guru Gobind Singh,* Delhi, 1968, p. 122.

75. Macauliffe, M.A., *The Sikh Religion,* Oxford, 1909, vols 5–6, pp. 203–6; Kohli, Surinder Singh, *The Life and Ideas of Guru Gobind Singh,* Delhi, 1986, pp. 8, 21.

76. Nara, Israr Singh, *Safarnama and Zafarnama,* Delhi, 1985, pp. 35–116; Kohli, Surinder Singh, *The Life and Ideas,* p.8.

77. *Bhushan Granthavali,* Allahabad, n.d., p.20 (Hindi); Divakar, K., *Bhonsla Rajdarbar ke Hindi Kavi,* Varanasi, 1969, p. 166 (Hindi).

78. Puri, J, Shangari, T., *Bulle Shah,* Amritsar, 1986, p. 463; Rama Krishna, L., *Punjabi Sufi Poets,* Delhi, 1973, p. 78.

79. Chaturvedi, P., *Sufi Kavya Sangrah,* Allahabad, 1967, pp. 235–9

80. Sen, S., *History,* p. 143.

81. Unfortunately, Bedil's works are still waiting for a researcher. Though his Kulliat are published, no interest is still drawn to this great personality by the Indian scholars. I have used a work by a Soviet scholar, I. Muminov, *Philosophical Views of Mirza Bedil,* Tashkent, 1957, p. 54 (Russian).

82. Dara Shukoh, *Sirr al-Akbar*, Tehran, n.d. pp. 4–6 (Perisian).

83. Hasrat, B., *Dara Shikuh, Life and Works*, Calcutta, 1953, pp. 265–9; Abu–l Fazl Allami, *Ain–i Akbari*, vol. III, p.2

84. Roslyakova, Ye. A., *On Religious and Philosophical Views of Dara Shukoh – South Asian Countries. History & Modernity*, Moscow, 1976, p. 44 (Russian).

85. Hasrat, B., p. 220; *Dara Shikuh, Majmua ul-Bahrain*. Tr. by Malfuz ul–Haq, Calcutta, 1982, p.38.

86. Quoted by Faruki, Z., *Aurangzeb and His Times*, p. 145.

87. Muhammad Hashim Khafi Khan, *Muntahab*, p. 4.

88. Ibid., p. 37.

89. Rai, Lakhpat, *Sarmad, His Life and Rubais*, Gorakhpur, 1978, pp. 15–53.

90. *Gujrat ke Santon ki Hindi Vani*, Ahmedabad, 1966, p. 116 (Hindi).

91. Chaturvedi, P., *Uttari Bharat ki Sant Parampara*, Prayag, 1951 (Hindi), Growse, F.S., *Mathura District Memoir*, Delhi, 1979, pp. 231–7.

92. Ibid, p.231; *Gujrat ke Santon ki Hindi Vani*, pp. 116, 120–1.

93. Jani, M., *Rajasthan evam Gujrat ke Madhyakalin Sant evam Bhakt Kavi*, Mathura, n.d., pp. 126–8, (Hindi).

94. Correa Affonso, J., *Letters from the Mughal Court*, Bombay, 1989, pp. 22–3, 34–59.

95. Jarric, S.J., *Akbar and the Jesuits*, pp. 29, 67, 68.

96. *Erasmus of Rotterdam and His Times*, Moscow, 1990, pp. 244–75 (Russian); *Documents on Renaissance and Reformation History*, D. Webster and Louis Green (eds), Stanmore, 1969, p.114.

CHAPTER III

1. Serebryany, S.D., *Some Aspects of 'Author' and 'Authorship' in the History of the Indian Literatures–Literature and Culture of Ancient and Medieval India*, Moscow, 1979, pp. 180–3 (Russian).

2. Antonova, K.A., *Essays*, pp. 173–202; Ashrafyan, C.Z., *Medieval City*, pp. 133–45.

3. Sharma, Krishna, *Bhakti and Bhakti Movement: A New Perspective*, Delhi, 1987, p. 28.

4. Nabi, M., 'The Conception of God as Understood by the Early Muslim Mystics of India', *IC*, 1956, vol. 39, no. 4, pp. 288–91; Nizami, Kh. A, *The Life and Times of Shaikh Farid ud–din Ganj–i Shakar*, Aligarh, 1955, p. 81.

5. Puri, J., Shangari, T., *Bulle Shah*, Amritsar, 1986, pp. 457–8.

6. *Mahikdasji ki bani*, p. 22.

7. Nizami, Kh. A., *The Life and Times*, pp. 45–55, cf.; Rizvi, S.A.A., *A History of Sufism in India*, Delhi, 1978, vol. I, pp. 128, 163, 191–225.

8. Nizami, Kh. A., *The Life and Times*, p. 100; Khan, Yusuf Hussain, 'Sufism in India', *IC*, 1956, vol. 3, pp. 252–7.

9. Dargah Quli Khan, *Muraqqa–e*, Delhi, p. 35.

10. Bilgrami, F.Z., 'Mullah Shah Kashmiri and the Mughal Rulers', *PIHC*, 1986, pp. 250f.

11. Ashrafyan, C.Z., *Feudalism in India*, pp. 193f.

12. Tsvetkov, Yu. V., *Surdas*, Moscow, 1979, pp. 38–41. Vide also: Mittal, P., *Ashtachap Parichay*, Mathura, 1949, p. 220 (Hindi).

13. Dvivedi, H., *Kabir*, Bombay, 1960, pp. 230, 273 (Hindi); 'Kabir Bijak: Pad, 97–5', Winand M. and Op de Beeck, Bart (eds), *Devotional Hindi Literature*, Delhi, 1991. vol. I, p. 368.

14. *The Dabistan*, vol. II, p. 189.

15. Dvivedi, H., *Kabir*, p. 262.

16. Athar Ali, M., 'Sidelights of the Ideological and Religious Attitudes in the Punjab During the XVIIth Century', *MI*, vol. II, p. 188.

17. *The Dabistan*, vol. II, pp. 188f.

18. Hans Sharsode, K., *Marathi Sahitya ka Itihas*, Allahabad, 1950, p. 74 (Hindi); *The Poems of Tukarama*, Tr. by N. Frazer and K.B. Marathe, Delhi 1981, p. 319, cf.

19. Dvivedi, H., *Kabir*, p. 262; 'Kabir Bijak: Pad, 40', Callewaert, Winand M. and Op de Beeck, Bart (eds), *Devotional Hindi Literature*, vol. I, p. 359.

20. Surdas, *Sursagar*, Mathura, 1970, pp. 519f. (Hindi).

21. 'Kabir Granthavali: Sakhi, 25–2', 'Kabir Bijak: Pad, 40', Callewaert, Winand M. and Op de Beeck, Bart (eds), *Devotional Hindi Literature*, vol. I, p. 297.

22. Singh, Gopal, *Guru Gobind*, Delhi, 1968, pp. 120f.

23. *Selections from the Sacred Writings of the Sikhs*, London, 1960, p. 116; Macauliffe, M.A., *The Sikh Religion, its Gurus, Sacred Writings and Authors*, vol. I, Oxford, 1909, p. 207.

24. Dvivedi, H., *Kabir*, p. 324; *The Poems of Tukarama*, p. 319; Macauliffe, M., *The Sikh Religion*, vol. I, pp. 229, 269.

25. *Devotional Songs of Narsi Maheta.* Tr. by Swami Mahadevananda, Delhi, 1985, p. 132; Ramdas, *Manche Slok,* Nagpur, 1953, pp. 157f (Hindi tr.).

26. *Selections,* p. 25; Macauliffe, M. 'Kabir Granthavali : Sakhi, 3–3', Callewaert, Winand M. and Op de Beeck, Bart (eds), Devotional Hindi Literature, Vol. I, p. 283.

27. Chatterji, A.N., 'Sri Chaintanya and His Sect', *PIHC,* 1980, pp. 289–91.

28. Tulsidas, *Kavitavali.* Tr. by R. Allchin, London, 1964, p. 168; Mohan Singh, *An Introduction to Punjabi Literature,* Amritsar, n.d., p. 87; Macauliffe, M., *The Sikh Religion,* vol. I, p. 356; *Selections, p.* 82.

29. *Selections,* p. 214.

30. *Gosvami Tulsidas Krit Sacitr Ramcaritmanas,* Samp. Syamsundar Das, Allahabad, n.d., p.1074. I have also used the Russian translation of 'Ramcharitmanas' by A.P. Barannikov, a work highly esteemed in India (Moscow, 1948).

31. *Ramcaritmanas,* Barannikov translation, p. 839; Surdas, *Sursagar,* Mathura, 1970, p. 176.

32. Ibid., pp. 996–1007, cf.

33. For the varying descriptions of *Ram-rajya* by Valmiki and the *Bhakti* poets see: Menon, A.G. and Schokker, G.H., 'The Conception of Rama-Rajya in South and North Indian Literature' in A.W. Van der Hoek, D.H.A. Kolff and M.S Oort (eds), *Ritual, State and History in South Asia: Essay in Honour of J.C. Heesterman,* London, New York, Köln, 1992, pp. 610–31.

34. Surdas, *Sursagar,* pp. 276–8.

35. Sazanova, N.M., 'The Ocean of Poetry' by Surdas, Moscow, 1973, p. 11 (Russian).

36. Surdas, *Sursagar,* p. 47.

37. 'Raidas, 36, 1–5, 1–3', Callewaert, Winand M. and Op de Beeck, Bart (eds), *Devotional* Hindi Literature, vol. I, pp. 433–4; Singh, P.G., Sant Ravidas, *Vicarak aur Kavi,* Jallandhar, 1977, p. 192.

38. Singh, K. Ch. *Akshay Ras, Gujrat ke Mahan Sant Kavi Akho ki Hindi Vani,* Baroda, 1963, p. 206 (Hindi).

39. Krishna Rao, M., *Purandara and Haridasa Movement,* Dharwar, 1966, p. 139; Rice, E., *Kanarese Literature,* Calcutta, 1921, p. 73; Das, R.K., 'Social Protest in Medieval Orrisa', *PIHC,* 1980, p. 344.

40. Dvivedi, H., *Kabir,* p. 246; 'Kabir Granthavali: Pad, 181–1', Callewaert, Winand M. and Op de Beeck, Bart (eds), *Devotional*

Hindi Literature, vol. I, p. 333; Machve, P., *Hindi aur Marathi Nirgun Sant Kavya*, Varanasi, 1962, p.189.

41. Macauliffe, M., *The Sikh Religion*, vol. I, p. 278; Gopal Singh, *Guru Gobind*, p. 122.

42. We agree here with the position of Dr Savitri Chandra Shobha (*Social Life and Concepts*, p.1) and Dr Krishna Sharma (*Bhakti and Bhakti Movement*, p.1).

43. Shobha, Savitri Chandra, *Social Life and Concepts*, p. 1.

44. Surdas, *Sursagar*, pp. 138–42.

45. Macauliffe, M., *The Sikh Religion*, vol. I, pp. 282, 286.

46. Panikkar, K.M., *A Survey of Indian History*, Bombay, 1954, p. 143; Krishna Rao, M. Purandara, p. 105; Joshi, T.D., *Social and Political Thought of Ramdas*, Bombay, 1970, pp. 5–9.

47. Chandra, Satish, 'Historical Background to the Rise of the Bhakti Movement in Northern India', reprinted in *Historiography, Religion and State in Medieval India*, Delhi, 1996, pp. 128–30; Das Gupta, Ashin, *Merchants of Maritime India, 1500–1800*, Brookfield, 1994; also, by the present author, 'Urban Industries of Medieval India: Some Aspects of Development', *Studies in History*, 1989, no. 5, 2, pp. 272–86.

48. For Sultan Ala ud–din Khalji's displeasure with the lordly lifestyle of rural headsmen see: Zia ud–Din Barani, 'Later Kings of Delhi or Tarikh–i Firoz Shahi', in H.M. Elliott and J. Dowson, *The History of India as Told by its Own Historians: The Muhammaddan Period* (reprint edition), Calcutta, 1958, pp. 102–03.

49. *The Poems of Tukarama*, p. 351; *Goswami Tulsidas krit sacitr Ramcaritmanas*, pp. 1074–8.

50. 'Raidas, 47', Callewaert, Winand M. and Op de Beeck, Bart (eds), *Devotional Hindi Literature*, vol. I, p. 436; Sharma, B. (ed), *Santguru Ravidas Vani*, Delhi, 1978, p. 90

51. Mazumdar, B.P., *Socio-Economic History of Northern India*, p. 109; Kanaka Durga, P.S., 'Identity and Symbols of Sustenance: Explorations in Social Mobility of Medieval South India', *JESHO*, 2001, vol. 44, pt 2.

52. Growse, F.S., *Mathura District Memoir*, Delhi, 1979, p. 236 (translation is made by the present author from the Hindi quotation of this verse. English version by F.S. Growse is slightly different).

53. Vidyapati Takur, *Kirtilata*, p. 86.

54. Ibid., pp. 14f.

55. Rizvi, S.A.A., *A History of Sufism in India*, Delhi, 1978 (2 vols) and other works by this author on different aspects of Sufism are quoted in this monograph many times.

56. Jani, M., op. cit., pp. 127f.

57. Kabirpanthis are a weavers' subcaste; raidasis are tanners' subcaste. They should be distinguished from the religious communities of Kabir and Raidas, though these two great *bhaktas* are worshipped and revered by the above mentioned subcastes.

58. Ashrafyan, C.Z., *Medieval City*, p. 140.

59. Mukund Lath (ed., tr.), Half a Tale: Ardhakathanaka, Jaipur, 1981, p. 230.

60. Ibid., pp. 214–17 (Meghavijaya's text was translated into English and annexed by Dr Mukund Lath to his edition of *Ardhakathanaka*).

61. Callewaert, W.M., *The Hindi Biography of Dadu Dayal*, Delhi, 1988, pp. 38, 63–4 (English), 92–3 (Hindi).

62. Sardar, G., *The Saint Poets of Maharashtra*, Bombay, 1969, p. 25.

63. Rich literature exists on the Marathi saints and *bhakti* poets. Their life stories, based on the eighteenth century works by Mahipati were translated and published by Justin E. Abbott (*The Poet Saints of Maharashtra* Series). Numerous English and Hindi translations are also available (by McNicol, Frazer, Marathe, etc.).

64. Reisner, I.M., *Popular Movements in India XVIIth and XVIIIth Centuries*, Moscow, 1962, pp. 118f (Russian).

65. Joshi, T.D., *Ramdas*, pp. 43–5, 56, 108–11.

66. Joglekar, D., *Sri Samartha Ramdas*, Bombay, 1951, pp. 29f (Hindi).

67. *The Poems of Tukarama*, p. 230.

68. Joshi, T.D., *Ramdas*, pp. 58, 79.

69. Ramdas, *Dasbodh*, Tr. by R. Sharma, Benares, 1956, pp. 20–5, 310–11 (Hindi).

70. Ramdas, *Manche Slok*, p. 27.

71. For the varying interpretations of 'Maharashtra *dharma*' see: Gordon, Stewart, *The Marathas 1600–1818*, The New Cambridge History of India, 1993, pp. 65–66; Glushkova, Irina, 'From Maharashtra Dharma to Maharashtrian Asmita: A Philogical Approach to Regional Ideology', paper presented at International Symposium of Regions, organized by Arizona State University and University of Pune, forthcoming in *Proceedings*, ed. by Anne Feldhaus and Rajendra Vora. For Shivaji's portrayal as the defender of Hinduism see:

Vallabha's Parasarama Carita, tr. by. N. Wagle and A.R. Kulkarni, Bombay, 1969, p. 61.

72. Ranade P.V., 'Feudal Content of Maharashtra Dharma', *IHR,* 1978–79, vol. V, nos. 1–2, pp. 46f.

73. Reisner, I.M., p. 182.

74. Ibid., pp. 189–94.

75. Narang, S., pp. 59, 71.

76. Kohli, Surindar Singh, *The Life and Ideas of Guru Gobind Singh,* Delhi, 1986, p. 74.

77. *Sri Dasam Guru Granth Sahibji,* Lucknow, 1973, vol. I, pp. 163–7 (Hindi); Macauliffe, M., *The Sikh Religion,* vol. VI, pp. 286–322.

78. Macauliffe, M., *The Sikh Religion,* vol. VI, pp. 100–1.

79. Ibid., p. 113.

80. Singh, Gopal, *Guru Gobind,* p. 124.

81. Kohli, Surindar Singh, pp. 55, 76.

82. Macauliffe, M.A., *The Sikh Religion,* vol. VI, pp. 93–100; Reisner, I.M., pp. 200–2.

83. Narang, S., op. cit. p. 80.

84. Reisner, I.M., op. cit., p. 202.

85. *Sri Dasam Guru Granth Sahibji,* vol. II, pp. 697–9.

86. Ibid., pp. 691f; Grewal, J.S., *Essays on Sikh History,* Amritsar, 1972, p. 79.

87. Singh, Mahip, *Guru Gobind Singh aur Unki Hindi Kavita,* Delhi, 1969, p. 122 (Hindi); Macauliffe, M., *The Sikh Religion,* vol. VI, pp. 203–06.

88. Reisner, I.M., pp. 2059–220.

89. Kohli, Surinder Singh, p. 102.

90. Dr Muzaffar Alam in his book *The Crisis of Empire in Mughal North India. Awadh and the Punjab 1707–1748* (Delhi, 1986) presented some evidence on this subject, but we can hardly agree with his suggestions that it was Guru Gobind who had deviated from Nanak's legacy of Hindu–Muslim accord. Dr Alam supposed that Guru Gobind's frequent usage of Hindu mythology and his disciples' mission to Benares testified to this deviation (p. 154). But these facts can be given a different interpretation—for instance, as most Sikhs were of a Hindu origin, it was quite natural to use Hindu traditions and mythology in Guru's preaching to them. He spoke many an angry word against the Mughal rule, but not against Muslim religion.

91. Bahtavar's *Sunesar,* Parallel Hindi Text and Russian tr. by I.D. Serebrykov, Moscow, 1976, pp. 100–6.

92. Pavlov, V.I., p. 256.

93. Engels, F., 'Peasant War in Germany', *Collected Works by Marx and Engles,* in Russian, vol. VII, p. 362.

94. Ashrafyan, C.Z., *Medieval City,* pp. 144f.

95. *Erasmus of Rotterdam and His Times,* Moscow, 1990, p. 155; see also *Documents in Renaissance and Reformation History,* ed. by D. Webster and Louis Green, Stanmore, 1969. p. 176.

96. *Erasmus of Rotterdam, Praise of Folly,* World Literature Library, vol. 33, Moscow, 1971, p. 166; Elton, G.R., *Renaissance and Reformation, 1300–1638,* London, 1969, pp. 29–34.

97. *Lavrenti from Brezova, Hussite Chronicle.* Translated into Russian by V. Sokolov, Moscow, 1962, pp. 103–5; Vide also: Kaminsky, H., *A History of The Hussite Revolution,* Berkeley, 1967, p. 338.

98. Von Hutten, Ulrich, *Dialogues,* World Literature Library, Vol. 33, Moscow, 1971. p. 527.

99. Qaiyum Rafiqi, A., 'Medieval Kashmiri Poet: Shaikh Nur ud–din Rishi', *PIHC,* 1987, p. 234.

100. Skazkin, S.D., *From the History of Socio–Political and Spiritual Life of Western Europe in the Middle Ages,* Moscow, 1981, pp. 95f (Russian).

101. Smirin, M.M., *The Popular Reformation of Thomas Muntzer and Peasants' War,* Moscow, 1955, p. 201; Ozment, S.E., *Mysticism and Dissent: Religious Ideology and Social Protest in the Sixteenth Century,* New Haven and London, 1973, pp. 56, 83–5.

102. Dvivedi, H., *Kabir,* p. 262.

103. *Erasmus of Rotterdam, Praise of Folly,* p. 166; Singh, p., *Sant Ravidas,* p. 43; *The Poems of Tukarama,* pp. 225–9; *Selections,* pp. 21, 77.

104. Ozment, S.E., *Mysticism and Dissent,* p. 95; Hillerbrandt, H.J., *The Reformation: A Narrative History Related by Contemporary Observers and Participants,* New York, 1964, pp. 223, 293; *Devotional Songs of Narsi Maheta,* p. 132; *Selections,* p. 66; Dvivedi, H., *Kabir,* pp. 300, 324.

105. *Lavrenti from Brezova,* p.112; Kaminsky, H., op. cit., p. 338.

106. *Lavrenti from Brezova,* p. 112.

107. Joshi, T.D., *Ramdas,* p. 8; 'Kabir Granthavali: Pad, 58–2, cf', Callewaert, Winand M. and Op de Beeck, Bart (eds), *Devotional Hindi Literature,* vol. I, p. 312, cf.

108. Wilson, H.H., *Essays and Lectures on the Religious Sects of the Hindus,* Delhi, 1976, vol. I, pp. 353–5.

109. Mullet, M.A., *Radical Religious Movements in Early Modern Europe,* London, 1980, p. 52.

110. Engels, F., Peasant War in Germany, p. 362.

111. Ibid., p. 362.

112. Ibid., p. 363.

113. Members of Radha Vallabha Sect (also known as Rasikas) were equally celebrated as poets and musicians. Greatest among them were Hit Harivansha and Haridas, teacher of the famous Tansen. Their role in the development of North Indian music is outstanding.

114. Smirin, M.M., op. cit., p. 268; Ozment, S.E., *Mysticism and Dissent,* pp. 79–80. Compare: Macauliffe, M.A., *The Sikh Religion,* vols. V–VI, pp. 297–9.

115. Reisner, I.M., p. 112, 178, 211.

116. Alayev, L.B., 'Popular Movements in the XVIIth–XVIIIth Centuries, India as Seen by the Soviet Indologists', *Popular Movements and Their Ideology in the Precapitalist Societies of Asia', Proceedings of a Seminar,* Moscow, 1985, pp. 3–4 (Russian).

117. These peculiar features of the rural community in India were analysed by many scholars whose opinions differed. Among the Soviet works on this subject Dr L.B. Alayev's works are noteworthy, especially his *Rural Community in Northern India. Main Stages of Evolution,* Moscow, 1981. He was also a participant of the *Cambridge Economic History of India.*

118. Singh, Mohan, *An Introduction to Punjabi Literature,* pp. 123–8.

119. Kaminsky, H., op. cit., pp. 338f, Macauliffe, M.A. *The Sikh Religion,* vol. I, pp. 206, 241, cf.

120. *Lavrenti from Brezova,* p. 50.

121. Lifshitz, G.M., *Reformation Movement in Czechia and Germany,* Minsk, 1978, pp. 108–9 (Russian).

122. Engels, F., *Peasant War in Germany,* p. 364.

123. Sunesar, p. 106.

124. Kaminsky, H., op. cit., p. 368.

125. Engles, F., *Peasant War in Germany,* p. 361.

126. Pavlov, V.I., p. 295.

CHAPTER IV

1. Marx, K., *Articles on India,* Bombay, 1951, p. 43.

2. Sarkar, J., *History of Aurangzib,* Calcutta, 1919–24. vol. V, pp. 455–69.

3. Raghuvanshi, V., *Indian Society in the Eighteenth Century,* Delhi, 1969, p. 24.

4. Muzaffar Alam, *The Crisis of Empire,* p. 9; Panikkar, K.N., 'Cultural Trends in Pre-Colonial India, An Overview,' *Studies in History,* Delhi, 1980, vol. II, no. 2, pp. 63–80.

5. Pannikar, K.N., *Cultural Trends,* p. 63. Similar viewpoints on eighteenth-century Indian society and its colonial interpretations have been expressed by a number of other scholars. See for example: Bayly, C.A., *Indian Society and the Making of the British Empire,* The New Cambridge History of India, 1988, pp. 38–41; Washbrook, D., 'From Comparative Sociology to Global History: Britain and India in the pre-History of Modernity', *JESHO,* 1998, vol. 40, pt. 4., pp, 410–43; Gordon Stewart, *Marathas, Marauders and State Formation in Eighteenth-Century India,* Delhi, 1994, p. *IX.* For a critical analysis of India and Western scholars' views of eighteenth-century state models see: De, Barun, 'Problems of the Study of Indian History: With Particular Reference to the Interpretations of the Eighteenth Century—Address of the General President,' *PIHC,* 49th Session, Delhi, 1989, pp, 1–59.

6. Nazir Akbarabadi, *Nazir ki Bani,* Allahabd, 1953, pp. 29–36 (Urdu in Devanagari script).

7. Russell, R., Islam, K., *Three Mughal Poets: Mir, Sauda, Mir Hasan,* London, 1968, pp. 62–8.

8. Vide, for instance, Narpati Nalha's *Bisaldev Raso* (ed. by S. Varma, Kashi, 1951). In this Rajput poem even the Rani upbraided the Raja for lacking lands and wealth and thus provoked him to start war expedition against the Raja of Orissa.

9. Balfour, F. (tr.), *The Forms (Insha) of Herkern,* London, 1804, p. 9.

10. Muzaffar Alam, *The Crisis of Empire,* p. 9.

11. Orme, R., *Historical Fragments of the Mogul Empire,* London, 1905, p. 442.

12. Bhatnagar, V.S., *Life and Times of Sawai Jai Singh,* Delhi, 1974; Ethe, H., *Catalogue of Persian Manuscripts in the Library of the India Office,* Oxford, 1937, nos 2781–3.

13. Dikshit, T.N., *Sant Charandas,* Lucknow, 1953, pp. 35f, 42–5, 54 (Hindi).

14. *Nazir ki Bani,* pp. 160–3.

15. Antonova, K.A., *Soviet Indologists on the Reasons for the Downfall of the Mughal Empire–Essays on the Economic and Social History of India,* Moscow, 1972, pp. 174–6 (Russian).

16. Marx, K., *Articles on India,* p. 67.

17. *Futuhat–i Firuz Shahi,* pp. 5–10.

18. Antonova, K.A., *Soviet Indologists,* p. 175.

19. Nizami, Kh. A., 'Shah Waliullah Dehlavi and Indian Politics of XVIIIth Century', *IC,* 1955, vol. XXV, pp. 137f.

20. *Shah Waliullah Dehalvi ke Siyasi Maktubat,* Aligarh, 1950, pp. 94–6 (Urdu).

21. Nizami, Kh. A., 'Socio-Religious Movements in Indian Islam', *IC,* 1970, vol. XLIV, p. 132.

22. Hidayat Husain, M. (tr.), 'The Persian Autobiography of Shah Waliullah bin Abdur–Rahim al–Dehlavi, its English Translation and a List of His Works,' *JRAS* (Bengal) NS, 1912, vol. VIII, p. 166.

23. Polonskaya, L.R., *Muslim Trends in the Social Thought of India and Pakistan,* Moscow, 1963, pp. 30–59.

24. *Maktubat,* p. 105.

25. Ibid., p. 106.

26. Kishore Das Munshi, *Majmua–e Danish.* Tr. by S. Hasan, Bombay, 1957, p. 20.

27. *Maktubat,* p. 117.

28. Athar Ali, M., 'Eighteenth Century–An Interpretation' *IHR,* 1978–9, vol. V, p. 181.

29. Pandit, Sri Raghunatha, *Rajavyavaharkosha,* Poona, 1880, pp. 1–27 (Parallel text in Sanskrit and Persian in Devanagari script).

30. See also: Barnett, R.B., *North India Between Empires: Awadh, the Mughals and the British, 1720–1801,* Berkeley, Los Angeles, London 1980, pp. 80–1; Nayeem, M.A., *Mughal Administration of the Deccan under Nizam ul–Mulk Asaf Jan,* Bombay. 1985, pp. 229–32.

31. Sen, S., *Administrative System of the Marathas,* Calcutta, 1924, p. 439.

32. Resiner, I. M., *Popular Movements,* p. 195.

33. Puntambekar, S.V. (tr.), *A Royal Edict on the Principles of State Policy and Organization*, Bombay–Madras, 1929, p. 33.

34. Ibid., pp. 15–25, 30.

35. *Poona Akhbars*, Hyderabad, 1953, p. 406; Sen, S., *Administrative System*, p. 462.

36. Kirpatrick, W. (tr.), *Select Letters of Tippoo Sultan to Various Public Functionaries*, London, 1811, pp. LXVII–LXXVIII; Kirmani, M., *History of Tipu Sultan*, Calcutta, 1958, pp. 69, 135.

37. Alayev, L.B., *South India*, Moscow, 1964, p. 139 (Russian). For a description of the agriculture policy of Haidar Ali and Tipu Sultan see: Sheik, Ali B., 'Developing Agriculture: Land Tenure Under Tipu Sultan' in *Confronting Colonialism: Resistance and Modernization under Haidar Ali and Tipu Sultan*, ed. by Irfan Habib, Delhi, 1999, pp. 143–7.

38. *Select Letters*, p. 47.

39. Ibid., p. XIV; Gopal, M.H., *Tipu Sultan's Mysore, An Economic Study*, Bombay, 1971, pp. 15f, 18–24. Sridharan, M.P., 'Tipu's Drive Towards Modernization: French Evidence from the 1780s' in *Confronting Colonialism: Resistance and Modernization under Haidar Ali and Tipu Sultan*, ed. by Irfan Habib, Delhi, 1999, pp. 143–7.

40. Quoted by Choksey, R., A *History of British Diplomacy at the Court of the Peshwas (1786–1818)*, Poona, 1951, p. 47; *Two Views of British India*, The Private Correspondence of Mr. Dundas and Lord Wellesley, Bath, Somerset, 1970, p. 36.

41. Rajayyan, K., 'Dhoondaji Waug and His Endeavour to Establish an Empire', *Maratha History Seminar*, Bombay, 1971 vol. I, pp. 1–6.

42. *Select Letters*, p. XXVII.

43. Pavlov, V.I., op. cit., p. 248.

44. *Modern History of India*, Moscow, 1961, p. 160 (Russian).

45. Pavlov, V.I., op. cit., p. 248.

46. Kirmani, M., *History of Tipu Sultan*, p. 69.

47. Alayev, L.B., *South India*, p. 280.

48. Kirmani, M., *History of Tipu Sultan*, p. 132.

49. *Select Letters*, pp. XIII, LXXML.

50. Fernandes, P., *Storm Over Seringapatam*, Bombay, 1969, pp. 375f. Sajan Lal, 'An Unpublished Letter of Tipu Sultan to a Muslim Divine,' in *Confronting Colonialism: Resistance and Modernization under Haidar Ali and Tipu Sultan*, ed. by Irfan Habib, Delhi 1999,

pp. 138–40; Moraes George M., 'Muslim Rulers of Mysore and Their Christian Subjects', in ibid., pp. 131-7.

51. Hasan Khan, M., *History of Tipu Sultan,* Calcutta, 1951, pp. 375f.

52. *Select Letters,* pp. 295f.

53. Antonova, K.A., 'Tipu Sultan's Struggle Against the British. New Archival Documents', *Peoples of Asia and Africa,* 1962, no. 4, p. 125. (Russian).

54. *English Records of Maratha History. Poona Residency Correspondence,* Bombay, 1937, vol. III, pp, 9–11.

55. Kirmani, M., *History of Tipu Sultan,* p. 70.

56. *Bhushan Granthavali,* Allahabad, In. d., pp. 71-2.

57. Kunju, I., 'Tuhfat-i Mujahedeen. A Historiographical Study', *PIHC,* 1980, p. 318.

58. Pyrard de Laval, *Voyages to the East Indies,* London, 1887, vol. II, p. 248. Tavernier, J.B., *Travels in India,* vol. II, p. 183.

59. Roe Thomas, *The Embassy of Sir Thomas Roe to the Court of the Great Moghul, 1615–1619,* London, 1899, vol. I. pp. 97, 224–5.

60. Qaisar, A., *The Indian Response to European Technology and Culture,* Delhi, 1982, pp. 12–17, 22–35, 72–5.

61. Abu–I Fazl Allami, *Ain–i Akbari,* vol. I, p. XXXV, (A quotation from Akbarnama).

62. Nizami, Kh. A., *Akbar and Religion,* Delhi, 1989, pp. 363–5 (Persian). Haidar, Mansura, *Mukatabat–i Allami Insha–i Abu–l Fazl, Letters of the Emperor Akbar in English Translation, Edited with Commentary, Perspective and Notes,* Daftar I, Delhi, 1998, pp. 8–12.

63. Abu–l Fazl Allami, *Ain–i Akbari,* vol. III, p. 49; Bernier, Francois, *Travels in the Mughal Empire,* London, 1916, pp. 324–5, 353; Bhatnagar, V.S., *Life and Times of Sawai Jai Singh,* Delhi, 1974, p. 319.

64. Tavernier, J.B., *Travels,* vol. II, p. 196.

65. Muhammad Hashim Khafi Khan, *Muntahabu–l lubab,* Calcutta, 1960, pp. 1–2.

66. *The History of Technology,* Oxford, 1957, vol. II, p. 549; Irwin, J. and Schwartz, P., *Studies in Indo-European Textile History,* Ahmedabad, 1966, pp. 104–12. For the beginnings of European Indology and its pivotal concepts see: Inden, Ronald, *Imagining India,* Cambridge, MA and Oxford, 1992; Teltsher, Kate, *India Inscribed: European and British Writing on India 1600–1800,* Delhi, 1995.

67. Puntambekar, S.V., *A Royal Edict*, pp. 31–3.
68. Forbes, J., *Oriental Memoirs*, London, 1813, vol. I, p. 217.
69. *Select Letters*, pp. 462–5. Habib Irfan, 'Introduction: An Essay on Haidar Ali and Tipu Sultan', in *Confronting Colonialism: Resistance and Modernization under Haidar Ali and Tipu Sultan*, ed. by Irfan Habib, Delhi 1999, pp. *XXIX–XXX*.
70. Nizami, Kh. A., *Socio-Religious Movements*, p. 135.
71. *The Private Diary of Ananda Ranga Pillai*, Madras, 1904, vol. I, pp. vii–xi, 284–7.
72. Ghulam Husein Salim, *Riyazu-s Salatin, A History of Bengal*, Tr. by Abdus Salam, Delhi, 1975, pp. 33–5, 414.
73. Sankhder, B., 'Mirza Abu Talib: His Life and Works', *IC 1970*, vol. XLIV.
74. Mirza Abu Talib, *Tafzihul-Ghalifin, History of Asafuddaulah.* Tr. by W. Hoey, Lucknow, 1971, p. 30.
75. Ibid., pp. 30, 72, 78–9.
76. Ibid., p. 72.
77. Abu-l Fazl Allami, *Ain-i Akbari*, vol. III, p. 478.
78. *Tafzihul-Ghalifin*, p. 103.
79. Ibid., pp. 17f.
80. Ibid., pp. 103f.
81. Ibid., pp. 75–7.
82. *Travels of Mirza Abu Talib Khan in Asia, Africa and Europe.* Tr. C. Stewart, Lucknow, n.d., p. XV.
83. Ibid., p. 157.
84. Ibid., p. 173.
85. Ibid., pp. 177–8.
86. *Two Views of British India: The Private Correspondence of Mr Dundas and Lord Wellesley, 1798–1801*, Bath, 1970, p. 17.
87. *Calendar of Persian Correspondence, 1794–1795*, vol. XI, Calcutta, 1969, pp. 318–19.
88. *Travels of Mirza Abu Talib Khan*, pp. 187–8.

CHAPTER V

1. Gurevich, A., Categories, pp. 198–222.
2. Dvivedi, H., *Kabir*, pp. 231, 271.

3. Sazanova, N.M., *The 'Ocean of Poetry' by Surdas*, Moscow, 1972, p. 170 (Russian). Vanina, Eugenia, 'Madhavanala–Kamakandala by Alam: A Hindi Poem of Akbar's Epoch' *IHR*, vol. XX, nos 1–2, July 1993 & January 1994, pp. 73–6.

4. Ashrafyan, C.Z., *Medieval City*, p. 154.

5. Komarov, E.N., 'Ram Mohan Roy, the Enlightener and Trailblazer of the National Movement in India', in *Socio-Political and Philosophical Thought of India*, Moscow, 1962, pp. 6–10; Polonskaya, L.R., *Muslim Trends*, pp. 45–6; Rybakov, R.B., *Bourgeois Reformation of Hinduism*, Moscow, 1981, pp. 7–8.

6. Mujeeb Ashraf, 'Note on Abdul Rahim Dahri, A Forward Looking Muslim Scholar of the Early Nineteenth Century', *PIHC*, 1979, pp. 776f.

Abbreviations

BSOAS	*Bulletin of the School of Oriental and African Studies, London.*
IC	*Islamic Culture, Hyderabad.*
IHQ	*Indian Historical Quarterly, Calcutta.*
IHR	*Indian Historical Review, Delhi.*
JESHO	*Journal of Economic and Social History of the Orient, Leiden.*
MI	*Medieval India, A Miscellany, Bombay, 4 vols.*
PIHC	*Proceedings of Indian History Congress, Delhi.*

Bibliography

SOURCE (PUBLISHED ORIGINAL TEXTS & TRANSLATIONS)

A. Chronicles, Documents, and Letters

Abd al–Qadir Badauni, *Muntakhab ut–tawarikh* in: H. Elliot and J. Dawson, *The History of India as Told by Its Own Historians,* Calcutta, 1961, vol.10 Also portions on Akbar's religious policies incorporated into the vol. I of *Ain–i Akbari* by Abu–l Fazl, published in 1977 from Delhi by Munshiram Manoharlal Publishers. For details see below.

Abu–l Fazl Allami, *Akbar Nama.* Tr. by H. Beveridge, Vols I–III, Delhi, 1979.

Ali Muhammad Khan Bahadur, *Mirat–i Ahmadi.* Baroda, 1931, vols I–II (Persian). Tr. by M.F. Lokhandwala, Baroda, 1965 (Gaekwad's Oriental Series, no. 146).

Calendar of Persian Correspondence, 1794–1795, Calcutta, 1969, vol XI.

Complaint and Reforms in England, 1436–1714, New York, 1968.

Elliot H.M. and Dowson, J., *The History of India as Told by Its Own Historians.*

English Records of Maratha History. Poona Residency Correspondence, General Editors J. Sarkar and G.S. Sardesai, Bombay, 1936–37, vols 1–3.

Further Sources of Vijayanagara History. Ed. and tr. by N. Sastri and M. Venkataramanayya, Madras, 1946, vol. III.

Ghulam Husein Salim, *Riyazu–s Salatin. A History of Bengal.* Tr. by Abdus Salam, Delhi, 1975.

Haidar Mansura, *Mukatabat- i 'Allami Insha-i Abu-l Fazl. Letters of the Emperor Akbar in English Translation. Edited with Commentary, Perspective and Notes.*

Jarric, S.C., *Akbar and the Jesuits*, London. 1926.

Kirkpatrick, W. (ed., tr.), *Select Letters of Tippoo Sultan to Various Public Functionaries*, London, 1811.

Kirmani Mir Husain Ali Khan, *History of Tipu Sultan*, Calcutta, 1958.

Kishore Das Munshi, *Majmua-e Danish*. Tr. by Saeed Hasan, Bombay, 1957.

Lavrenti from Brezova, Hussite Chronicle. Tr. into Russian from Czech by V. Sokolov, Moscow, 1962.

Mirza Abu Talib Khan, *Tafzihul-Ghalifin, History of Asafuddaulah*. Tr. by W. Hoey, Lucknow, 1971.

Muhammad Hashim Khafi Khan, *Muntahabul-lubab. History of Aurangzeb*. Tr. by J. Dawson, Calcutta, 1960.

Munhta Nainsi ri Likhi Marwar ra Pargana ri Vigat (The Historical Description of the Pargana Marwar Written by Munhta Nainsi), Jodhpur, 1974, vols 1–2 (Rajasthani).

Poona Akhbars, Hyderabad, 1953, vol. I.

Review of the Affairs in India from the Year 1798 to the Year 1806 Comprehending a Summary Account of the Principal Transactions During that Eventful Period, London, 1807.

Ruqaat-t Alamgiri or Letters of Aurangzeb. Tr. by J. Billimoria, Delhi, 1972.

Shah Waliullah Dehlavi ke Siyasi Maktubat (The Political Correspondence of Shah Waliullah Dehlavi), Aligarh, 1950 (Urdu).

Sarkar, J. (tr.), *English Translation of Tarikh-i Dilkasha.*, Bombay, 1972.

Two Views of British India. The Private Correspondence of Mr Dundas and Lord Wellesley, Bath, Somerset, 1970.

Zia ud-Din Barani, 'Later Kings of Delhi or Tarikh-i Firoz Shahi', in H. M. Elliott and J. Dowson. *The History of India as Told by Its Own Historians. The Muhammaddan Period. (*Reprint*)*. Calcutta, 1958.

B. Treatises, Descriptions, and Biographies

Abu-1 Fazi Allami, *Ain-i Akbari*. Tr. by H. Blochmann (vol. I) and H. Jarrett, Delhi, 1977–78 (vols II–III).

Ali Muhammad Khan Bahadur, *Khatima-i Mirat-i Ahmadi* (The Supplement to Mirat-i Ahmadi), Baroda, 1930 (Persian).

Balfour, F. (tr.). *The Forms (Insha) of Herkern*, London, 1804.

Banarasidas, *Half a Tale—Ardhakathanaka*. Hindi Text and English Translation by Mukund Lath, Jaipur, 1981.

Callewaert, W.M. (ed., tr.), *The Hindi Biography of Dadu Dayal,* Delhi, etc. 1986 (Hindi text and English translation).

The Dabistan or a School of Manners. Tr. by D. Shea and A. Troyer, Paris, 1843, 3 vols.

Dara Shukoh, *Majmua ul-Bahrain.* Tr. by Malfuz ul-Haq, Calcutta, 1982.

Dara Shukoh, *Sirr al-Akbar* (The Great Secret), Tehran, n.d. (Persian).

Dargah Quli Khan, *Muraqqa-e Delhi.* The Mughal Capital in Muhammad Shah's Time. Tr. by C.S. Sharma and S.M. Chenoy, Delhi, 1989.

Futuhat-i Firuz Shahi (The Victories of Firuz Shah), Aligarh, 1955 (Persian).

Green, Louis and D. Websters (ed.), *Documents on Renaissance and Reformation History,* Stanmore, 1969.

Habib, M., Salim Khan, A. (tr.), *The Political Theory of the Delhi Sultanate,* Allahabad, n.d.

Hidayat Husain, M. (tr.), 'The Persian Autobiography of Shah Waliullah bin Abdur-Rahim al-Dehlavi, Its English Translation and a List of His Works', *Journal of the Royal Asiatic Society of Bengal,* 1912, vol. VIII.

The Private Diary of Ananda Ranga Pillai, Madras, 1904, 3 vols.

Puntambekar, S.V. (tr.), *A Royal Edict on the Principles of State Policy and Organization,* Madras, 1929.

The Saxon Mirror. Tr. into Russian by L. Dembo, Moscow, 1985.

Sri Raghunatha Pandita, *Rajavyavaharakosha,* Poona, 1880 (Sanskrit and Persian in Devanagari Script).

Sukra, *Sukranitisara,* Bombay, 1921 (Parallel Text in Sanskrit and Hindi).

C. Works of Medieval Literature

Barannikov, A.P., *Ramayana or Ramacharitamanasa.* The Ocean of Rama's Deeds. Russian Translation in Verse, Moscow, 1948.

Bahtavar, *Sunesar.* Hindi Text Edited and Translated into Russian by I.D. Serebryakov, Moscow, 1976.

Bedil Mirza Abdulqadir, *Modan-o Komdeh.* Russian translation by L. Penkovsky, Moscow, 1959.

Bhavabhuti, *Uttara Rama Charita.* Tr. by S.K. Belvalkar, Harvard, 1915, vol. I.

Bhushan Granthavali (Works by Bhushan), Allahabad, n.d. (Hindi).

Chaturvedi, P. (ed.), *Sufi Kavya Sangrah* (A Collection of the Sufi Poetry), Allahabad, 1967 (Hindi).

Callewaert Winand M. and Op de Beeck Bart (eds.), *Devotional Hindi Literature*. Delhi, 1991, Vols. I–2.

Devotional Songs of Narsi Maheta. Tr. by Swami Mahadevananda, Delhi, 1985.

Diwan–i Mir (The Diwan of Mir Taqi Mir), Bombay, 1960 (Urdu).

Dvivedi, H. (ed.), *Hindi Premgatha Kavya Sangrah* (A Collection of the Hindi Love Poems), Allahabad, 1953 (Hindi).

Dvivedi, H.P. (ed.), *Kabir*, Bombay, 1960 (Hindi).

Erasmus of Rotterdam, Praise of Folly, Published in Russian in the Library of World Literature Series, 1971.

Faizi, *Nal–o Daman*. Russian Translation in Verse by G. Aliyev and G. Penkovsky, Moscow, 1987.

Gafurova N. B. (tr.), *Kabir-Granthavali*. Moscow, 1992 (Russian).

Gosvami Tulsidas krit sacitr Ramcaritmanas. Samp. Syamsundar Das. Illahabad, n.d..

Glushkova, I.P. (tr.), 'Take God Free! Tukaram`s Poetic Autobiography.' – *Voices from Medieval India*. Ed. by I.D. Serebryakov and E. Yu. Vanina. Moscow, 2002 (Russian).

Gujrat ke Santon ki Hindi Vani (The Hindi Works by the Gujarati Saint Poets), Ahmadabad, 1966 (Hindi).

Jayasi Granthavali (The Collected Works of Jayasi), Allahabad, 1936 (Hindi).

Macauliffe, M.A., *The Sikh Religion: Its Gurus, Sacred Writings and Authors*, Oxford, 1909, 6 vols.

Malukdasji ki Vani (The Voice of Malukdas), Allahabad, 1946 (Hindi).

McLeod, W.H. (tr.), *Textual Sources for the Study of Sikhism*, Manchester, 1984.

Mulla Daud, *Chandayan*. Ed. by Mataprasad Gupta, Agra, 1967 (Hindi).

Nara Israr Singh (tr.), *Safarnama and Zafarnama*, Delhi, 1985.

Nazir Akbarabadi, *Nazir ki Bani* (The Word of Nazir), Allahabad, 1953 (Urdu in Devanagari script).

The Poems of Tukarama. Tr. by N. Frazer and H.B. Marathe, Delhi, 1981.

Ramdas, *Manche Slok* (The Slokas to the Mind), Nagpur, 1953 (Hindi).

Ramdas, *Dasbodh* (The Teachings of Das). Tr. by R. Sharma, Benares, 1956 (Hindi).

224 Ideas and Society

Sazanova., N. M., *There is No Life Without Krishna*. Moscow, 1993 (Russian).

Sazanova, N.M., (tr.), 'Let's Go to the Country Where Beloved Abodes. Select Hymns by Mira Bai. *Voices from Medieval India,* edited by I.D. Serebryakov and E. Yu. Vanina, Moscow 2002.

Selections from the Sacred Writings of the Sikhs, London, 1960.

Sharma, B. (ed.), *Santguru Ravidas Vani* (The Word of the Saint Guru Ravidas), Delhi, 1978 (Hindi).

Singh, M.P. (ed.), *Lal Krit Chatraprasad* (The Chatraprasad by Lal), Delhi, 1973.

Somadeva, *Vetalapanchavimsati.* From *Kathasaritsagara.* Tr. by C.U. Tawney, Bombay, 1956.

Somadeva's *Kathasaritsagara.* Russian translation by I.D. Serebryakov, Moscow, 1982.

Some Specimens of Satpanthi Literature. Tr. by V. Hooda, Collectanea, Leiden, 1948, vol. I.

Sri Dasam Guru Granth Sahibji (The Book of the Tenth Guru). Tr. by Jodha Singh, Lucknow, 1973–74, 2 vols (Hindi).

Strelkova, G.V., (tr.), 'Soul is My Measure, Tongue is My Scissors, Namdev's Hymns from the Adi Granth', *Voices from Medieval India,* edited by I.D. Serebryakov and E. Yu. Vanina, Moscow 2002.

Surdas, *Sursagar* (The Ocean of Sur), Mathura, 1970 (Braj).

Tulsidas, *Kavitavali* (The Collection of Poems). Tr. by R. Allchin, London, 1964.

Ulrich Von Hutten, *Dialogues.* Published in Russian in the Library of World Literature Series.

Vallabha, *Parasarama Charita.* Tr. by N. Wagle and A.R. Kulkarni, Bombay, 1976.

Vidyapati Thakur, *Kirtilata (The Liana of Glory),* Jhansi, 1962 (Maithili Text with Hindi Rendering).

Zelliot Eleanor (tr.), 'A Medieval Encounter Between Hindu and Muslim: Eknath' s Drama Poem Hindu Turk Samvad' – F. Clothey (ed.), *Images of Man. Religion and Historical Process in South Asia.* Madras, 1982, p. 177-187.

D. Travelogues

Bernier, F., *Travels in the Mughal Empire,* London, 1916.

Forbes, J., *Oriental Memoirs*, London, 1813, 4 vols.

Orme, R., *Historical Fragments of the Mogul Empire, of the Moratoes*, London, 1905.

Pyrard de Laval, F., *The Voyage of Francois Pyrard of Laval to the East Indies, the Maldives, the Moluccas and Brazil (1607–1610)*, London, 1887–90, 2 vols.

Roe, T., *The Embassy of Sir Thomas Roe to the Court of the Mogul, 1615–1619*, London, 1899, 2 vols.

Tavernier, J.B., *Travels in India*, Delhi, 1977, 2 vols.

Travels of Mirza Abu Talib Khan in Asia, Africa and Europe. Tr. by C. Stewart, Lucknow, n.d.

Watters, T., *On Yuan Chwang's Travels in India (629–645)*, London, 1904–5, 2 vols.

E. Research Works (Books & Articles)

Abidi, S., 'Talib Amuli. His Life and Poetry', *IC,* 1967, vol. 41.

Alayev, L.B., *South India*, Moscow, 1964 (Russian).

Alayev, L.B., 'Popular Movements in the XVIIth–XVIIIth Centuries India as Seen by the Soviet Indologists' in: *Popular Movements and Their Ideology in the Pre-Capitalist Societies of Asia*, Moscow, 1985 (Russian).

Ambastha, B., *Non-Persian Sources of Medieval Indian History,* Delhi, 1983.

Antonova, K.A., *Essays on the Social Relations and Political System of the Mughal India of Akbar's Times (1556–1605)*, Moscow, 1952 (Russian).

Antonova, K.A. 'Tipu Sultan's Struggle Against the British, New Archival Documents', *Peoples of Asia and Africa*, 1962, no. 4 (Russian).

Antonova, K.A., 'Soviet Indologists on the Reasons of the Downfall of the Mughal Empire' in: *Essays on the Economic and Social History of India*, Moscow, 1972 (Russian).

Ashrafyan, C.Z., *Feudalism in India*, Moscow, 1978 (Russian).

Ashrafyan, C.Z., *Medieval City of India, XIIIth to mid XVIIIth Centuries,* Moscow, 1983 (Russian).

Askari, S.H., 'Material of Historical Value in the Ijaz-i Khusravi', *MI,* 1971, vol. I.

Athar Ali, M., 'Sidelights into Ideological and Religious Attitudes in the Punjab During the XVIIth Century', *MI,* 1972, vol. II.

Athar Ali, M., Eighteenth Century—an Interpretation', *IHR*, 1978–79, vol. V.

Athar Ali, M., 'Sulhe Kul and the Religious Ideas of Akbar', *PIHC,* 1980.

Athar Ali M., 'Towards an Interpretation of the Mughal Empire', Hermann Kulke (ed.), *The State in India 1000-1700.* Delhi, OUP paperback, 1997.

Azimjanova, S.A., *Babur's State in Kabul and in India,* Moscow, 1977 (Russian).

Barnett R.B. *North India Between Empires: Awadh, the Mughals and the British, 1720-1801.* Berkeley-Los Angeles-London, 1980.

Bayly C.A. *Indian Society and the Making of the British Empire.* The New Cambridge History of India, 1988.

Bayly C.A. *Origins of Nationality in South Asia. Patriotism and Ethical Government in the Making of Modern India.* Delhi, 1998.

Bhatnagar, V.S., *Life and Times of Sawai Jai Singh,* Delhi, 1974.

Bhattacharya, S., Thapar, R. (eds), *Situating Indian History for Sarvepalli Gopal,* Delhi, 1986.

Bilgrami, F.Z., 'Mullah Shah Kashmiri and the Mughal Rulers', *PIHC,* 1986.

Blake Stephen P. 'The Patrimonial Bureaucratic Empire of the Mughals', Hermann Kulke (ed.), *The State in India 1000-1700.* Delhi, OUP paperback, 1997.

Bongard–Levin, G.M., Ilyin, G.F., *Ancient India,* Moscow, 1985 (Russian).

Byres, T.J., Mukhia, H. (eds), *Feudalism and Non-European Societies,* London, 1985.

Chandra Satish, 'Historical Background to the Rise of the Bhakti Movement in Northern India', reprinted in *Historiography, Religion and State in Medieval India.* Delhi, 1996

Chandra Satish, 'Reassessing Aurangzeb', *Historiography, Religion and State in Medieval India.* Delhi, 1996.

Chandra Savitri Shobha, *Social Life and Concepts in Medieval Hindi Bhakti Poetry. A Socio-Cultural Study,* Delhi, 1983.

Chandra Savitri Shobha, *Solahvin Shatabdi ke Uttarardh main Samaj aur Sanskriti* (Society and Culture in the First Half of the Sixteenth Century), Delhi, 1986.

Chatterji, A.N., 'Sri Chaitanya and His Sect', *PIHC,* 1980.

Chattopadhyaya Brajadulal. *Representing the Other? Sanskrit Sources and the Muslims.* Delhi, 1998.

Chaturvedi, P., *Uttari Bharat ki Sant Parampara* (The Sant Tradition of the Northern India), Prayag, 1951.

Chaudhury, R., *Mithila in the Age of Vidyapati*, Varanasi, 1976.

Chikolini, L.S., 'Political and Legal Concepts of Janfrancesco Lottini', *Middle Ages*, Moscow, 1984–5, vol. 48.

Choksey, R., *A History of the British Diplomacy at the Court of the Peshwas (1786–1818)*, Poona, 1951.

Chopra, P. N., *Some Experience in Social Reform in Medieval India. The Cultural Heritage of India*, Calcutta, 1969, vol. II.

Choudhary, G., *Political History of Northern India from Jain Sources (c. 650 to 1300 AD)*, Amritsar, 1954.

Classes and Estate in the Pre-Capitalist Societies of Asia, Moscow, 1986 (Russian).

Das B.K., 'Social Protest in Medieval, Orissa', *PIHC*, 1980.

Das Gupta Ashin, *Merchants of Maritime India, 1500-1800*. Brookfield, 1994.

De Barun, 'Problems of the Study of Indian History: With Particular Reference to the Interpretations of the Eighteenth Century. Address of the General President', *PIHC*, 49th Session, Delhi, 1989.

De, Barun, 'Problems of the Study of Indian History: With Particular Reference to Interpretations of the Eighteenth Century', Presidential Address, *PIHC*, 1988.

Dikshit, G.S., *Local Self Government in Medieval Karnataka*, Dharwar, 1964.

Dikshit, T.N., *Sant Charandas*, Lucknow, 1953.

Divakar, K., *Bhonsla Rajdarbar ke Hindi Kavi* (The Hindi Poets of the Court of the Bhonslas), Varanasi, 1969 (Hindi).

Eisenstadt S.N. with Harriet Hartman. 'Cultural Traditions, Conceptions of Sovereignty and State Formations in India and Europe. A Comparative View', A. W. Van der Hoek, D. H. A. Kolff, M. S. Oort (eds.) *Ritual, State and History in South Asia. Essays in Honour of J. C. Heesterman*. London- New York- Köln, 1992.

Elton G.R., *Renaissance and Reformation 1300-1638*. London, 1969

Engels, F., 'The Peasant War in Germany' in K. Marx and F. Engels, *Collected Works in Russian*, vol. VII.

Erasmus of Rotterdam and His Times, Moscow, 1990 (Russian).

Essays on the Economic and Social History of India, Moscow, 1972 (Russian).

Ethe, H., *Catalogue of Persian Manuscripts in the Library of the India Office*, Oxford, 1937.

Faruki, Z., *Aurangzeb and His Times*, Bombay, 1935.

Fernandes, P., *Storm Over Seringapatam*, Bombay, 1969.

Gafurova, N.B., *Kabir and His Legacy*, Moscow, 1976 (Russian).

Ghoshal, U.N., 'A Comparison Between Ancient Indian and Medieval European Theories of Divine Right and the Nature of Kingship', *IHQ*, 1955, no. 3, vol. XXI.

Ghoshal, U.N., *A History of Indian Political Ideas. The Ancient Period and the Transition to the Middle Ages*, Oxford, 1959.

Glushkova I. P. *Indian Pilgrimage. The Metaphor of Motion and the Motion of Metaphor*. Moscow, 2000 (Russian).

Glushkova Irina, 'From Maharashtra Dharma to Maharashtrian Asmita; A Philological Approach to Regional Ideology', *paper presented at International Symposium on Regions, organized by Arizona State University and University of Pune*, forthcoming in *Region, Culture and Politics in India*, ed. by Rajendra Vora and Anne Feldhaus. Manohar Publishers.

Gopal, M.H., *Tipu Sultan's Mysore. An Economic Study*, Bombay, 1971.

Gordon Stewart, *Marathas, Marauders and State Formation in the Eighteenth Century India*. Delhi, 1994

Gordon Stewart, *The Marathas 1600-1818*. The New Cambridge History of India, 1993.

Grewal, J.S., *Essays on Sikh History*, Amritsar, 1972.

Grewal, J.S., *Guru Nanak in History*, Chandigarh, 1969.

Growse, F., *Mathura District Memoir*, Delhi, 1979.

Gupta, P., *Hindi Sahitya ki Janvadi Parampara* (The Democratic Tradition of the Hindi Literature), Allahabad, 1963 (Hindi).

Gurevich, A., *Categories of Medieval Culture*, Moscow, 1984 (Russian).

Habib Irfan, 'Classifying Pre-Colonial India' , T. J. Byres and Harbans Mukhia (eds.). *Feudalism and Non-European Societies*. London, 1985.

Habib Irfan, 'A Political Theory for the Mughal Empire', *PIHC*, Proceedings, 59th Session, 1998.

Habib Irfan, 'Introduction. An Essay on Haidar Ali and Tipu Sultan', *Confronting Colonialism. Resistance and Modernization under Haidar Ali and Tipu Sultan*. Ed. by Irfan Habib. Delhi, 1999.

Hadi Hasan, *Qasim-i Kahi, His Life, Times and Works*, Calcutta, 1967.

Hans Sharsode, K., *Marathi Sahitya ka Itihas* (The History of Marathi Literature), Allahabad, 1950 (Hindi).

Hasrat, B., *Dara Shikuh, Life and Works*, Calcutta, 1953.

Heesterman J.C. *The Inner Conflict of Tradition. Essays in Indian Ritual, Kingship and Society*. Delhi, 1985.

Ideas in History, Delhi, 1968.

Inden Ronald. *Imagining India*. Cambridge MA-Oxford UK, 1992.

Ishaq Khan, 'The Societal Dimensions of the Mystical Philosophy of Nur ud–din Rishi Kashmiri', *PIHC*, 1987.

Jani, M., *Rajasthan evam Gujrat ke Madhyakalin Sant evam Bhakt Kavi* (The Sant and Bhakta Poets of Rajasthan and Gujarat), Mathura, n.d.

Joglekar, D., *Sri Samartha Ramdas*, Bombay, 1951 (Hindi).

Joshi, T.D., *Social and Political Thought of Ramdas*, Bombay, 1970.

Kaminsky, H., *The Hussite Revolution*, Berkeley, 1967.

Kanaka Durga P. S. 'Identity and Symbols of Sustenance: Explorations in Social Mobility of Medieval South India', *JESHO*, 2001, vol. 44, pt. 2.

Kangle, R.P., *The Kautilya Arthasastra. A Study*, Bombay, 1965, vol. III.

Khan A.R. *Chieftains in the Mughal Empire During the Reign of Akbar*. Simla, 1977.

Kohli Surinder Singh, *The Life and Ideas of Guru Gobind Singh*, Delhi, 1968.

Komarov, E., 'Ram Mohan Roy, the Enlightener and Trailblazer of the National Movement in India' in: *Socio-Political and Philosophical Thought of India*, Moscow, 1962 (Russian).

Kosambi, D.D., *An Introduction to the Study of Indian History*, Bombay, 1956.

Krishna Rao, M., *Purandara and Haridasa Movement*, Dharwar, 1966.

Kulkarni, A.R., 'Social Relations in the Maratha Country (Medieval Period)', Indian History Congress, Presidential Address, *PIHC*, 1970.

Kulkarni, A.R., *Maharashtra in the Age of Shivaji*, Poona, 1969.

Kulke Hermann. 'Royal Temple Policy and the Structure of Medieval Hindu Kingdoms' – A. Eschmann, H. Kulke and G.C. Tripathi (etc.), *The Cult of Jagannath and the Regional Tradition of Orissa*. Delhi, 1978;

Kulke H. 'Introduction. The Study of the State in Pre-Modern India', Hermann Kulke (ed.), *The State in India 1000-1700*. Delhi, 1997 (paperback edition, first published in 1995)

Kulke Hermann (ed.). *The State in India 1000-1700.* Delhi, 1997 (OUP paperback edition, first published in 1995).

Kunju, I., 'Tuhfat–i Mujahedeen. A Historiographical Study', *PIHC,* 1980.

Kutsenkov A.A., *Evolution of the Indian Caste,* Moscow, 1983 (Russian).

Lakhpat Rai, *Sarmad, His Life and Rubais,* Gorakhpur, 1978.

Lamshukov, V.K., 'The Principle of "Mobile Perspective"' in *Literatures of India,* Moscow, 1989.

Larus, J., *Culture and Political–Military Behaviour. The Hindus in Pre-Modern India,* Calcutta, 1979.

Lifshitz, G., *The Reformation Movement in Czechia and Germany,* Minsk, 1978 (Russian).

Literature and Culture of Ancient and Medieval India, Moscow, 1979 (Russian).

* *Literatures of India. A Collection of Essays,* Moscow, 1979 (Russian).

Literatures of India. A Collection of Essays, Moscow, 1989 (Russian).

Machve, P., *Hindi aur Marathi ka Nirgun Sant Kavya* (The Poetry of the Hindi and Marathi Nirgun Sants), Varanasi, 1962 (Hindi).

'Madhyakalin dharmik sansar katta nahi tha – Habib' *Amar Ujala,* 17.09.2002.

Mahalingam, T.V., *South Indian Polity,* Madras, 1967.

Maratha History Seminar, Bombay, 1971, vol. I.

Marx, K., *Articles on India,* Bombay, 1951.

Mazumdar, B.P., *Socio-Economic History of Northern India (1030–1194),* Calcutta, 1960.

Medvedev, E., 'Medieval Indian Literature as Sources for the History of Socio-Economic Relations in the Feudal India' in: *The Oriental Historiography,* Moscow, 1969 (Russian).

Menon A.G. and G.H. Schokker, ' The Conception of Rama-Rajya in South and North Indian Literature', A.W. Van der Hoek, D.H.A. Kolff, M.S. Oort (eds.), *Ritual, State and History in South Asia. Essays in Honour of J.C. Heesterman.* London- New York- Koln, 1992.

Metcalf Thomas R., *Ideologies of the Raj.* New Cambridge History of India. Cambridge, 1995

Modern History of India, Moscow, 1961 (Russian).

Moraes George M., 'Muslim Rulers of Mysore and Their Christian Subjects' *Confronting Colonialism. Resistance and Modernization under Haidar Ali and Tipu Sultan.* Ed. by Irfan Habib. Delhi, 1999.

Mujeeb Ashraf, 'Note on Abdul Rahim Dahri, A Forward Looking Muslim Scholar of the Early Nineteenth Century', *PIHC,* 1979.

Mullett, M.A., *Radical Religious Movements in Early Modern Europe,* London, 1980.

Mundy, J.P., *Europe in the Middle Ages,* New York, 1973.

Munshi, K.M., *Gujarat and Its Literature from Early Times to 1852,* Bombay, 1952.

Muzaffar Alam, *The Crisis of Empire in Mughal North India, Awadh and the Punjab. 1707–1748,* Delhi, 1986.

Muzaffar Alam, 'Indo–Islamic Interaction in Medieval North India', *Itinerario,* Leiden, 1989, no. 1, vol. XIII.

Muzaffar Alam, 'Assimilation from a Distance: Confrontation and Sufi Accommodation in Awadh Society' , R. Champakalakshmi and S. Gopal (eds.), *Tradition, Dissent and Ideology. Essays in Honour of Romila Thappar.* Delhi, 1996.

Muzaffar Alam, The Pursuit of Persian: Language in Mughal Politics' , *Modern Asian Studies,* 32, 2 (1998).

Muzaffar Alam and Sanjay Subrahmanyam, ' Witnessing Transition: Views on the End of the Akbari Dispensation', *The Making of History. Essays Presented to Irfan Habib.* Ed. by K. N. Panikkar, Terence S. Byres and Utsa Patnaik. Delhi, 2000.

Nabi, M., 'The Conception of God as Understood by the Early Muslim Mystics of India', *IC,* 1965, no. 4, vol. 39.

Naik, C.R., *Abdur–Rahim Khan–i Khanan and His Literary Circle,* Ahmedabad, 1966.

Narang, S., *Transformation of Sikhism,* Delhi, 1960.

Nayeem M. A. *Mughal Administration of the Deccan Under Nizam ul-Mulk Asaf Jah.* Bombay, 1985.

Nehru, J., *The Discovery of India,* Delhi, 1981.

Nikiforov, V., *The Orient and the World History,* Moscow, 1975 (Russian).

Nizami, Kh. A., 'Shah Waliullah Dehlavi and Indian Politics of the XVIIIth Century', *IC,* 1955, vol. 25.

Nizami, Kh. A., *The Life and Times of Shaikh Farid ud–din Ganj–i Shakar,* Aligarh, 1955.

Nizami, Kh. A., 'Naqshbandi Influence on Mughal Rulers and Polities', *IC,* 1965, vol. 39.

Nizami, Kh. A., *Studies in Medieval Indian History and Culture,* Allahabad, 1966.

Nizami, Kh. A., 'Socio–Religious Movements in Indian Islam', *IC,* 1970, vol. 44.

Nizami, Kh. A., 'The Delhi Sultanate and the Mughal Empire. Genesis and Salient Features', *IC,* 1981, vol. 55.

Nizami, Kh. A., *Akbar and Religion,* Delhi, 1989.

Nizami Kh. A., 'Contribution of Mystics to Amity and Harmony in Indian Society', *We Lived Together.* Ed. by S. Settar and P. K. V. Kaimal. Delhi, 1999.

On the Genesis of Capitalism in the Countries of the Orient, Moscow, 1962 (Russian).

Oriental Historiography, Moscow, 1969 (Russian).

Ozment S. E., *Mysticism and Dissent. Religious Ideology and Social protest in the Sixteenth Century.* New Haven and London, 1973.

Pande, R., 'The Social Context of the Bhakti Movement. A Study in Kabir', *PIHC,* 1986.

Panikkar, K.M., *A Survey of Indian History,* Bombay, 1954.

Panikkar, K.N., 'Cultural Trends in Pre-Colonial India. An Over-view', *Studies in History,* 1980, no. 2, vol. II.

Pavlov, V.I., 'Stadial Formation Characteristics of the Oriental Societies in the Pre-Modern Times' in: E.M. Zhukov, M.A. Barg, E.B. Chernyak and V.I. Pavlov, *Theoretical Problems of the World Historical Process,* Moscow, 1979 (Russian).

Payevskaya, E., *Development of Bengali Literature, XIIIth to XIXth Centuries,* Moscow, 1979 (Russian).

Polonskaya, L., *Muslim Trends in the Social Thought of India and Pakistan,* Moscow, 1963 (Russian).

Puntambekar, S.V., *Maratha Polity,* Lahore, 1942.

Puri, J., Shangari, T., *Bulle Shah,* Amritsar, 1986.

Qaisar, A., *The Indian Response to European Technology and Culture,* Delhi, 1982.

Qaiyum Rafiqi, A., 'Medieval Kashmiri Poet Shaikh Nur ud–din Rishi', *PIHC,* 1987.

Raghuvanshi, V., *Indian Society in the Eighteenth Century,* Delhi, 1969.

Rajayyan, K., 'Dhoondaji Waug and His Endeavour to Establish an Empire' in: *Maratha History Seminar,* Bombay, 1971, vol. I.

Rama Krishna, L, *Punjabi Sufi Poets,* Delhi, 1973.

Ranade, P.V., 'Feudal Content of Maharashtra Dharma', *IHR,* 1978-9, nos 1-2, vol. V.

Index

and institutional legacy of
Muslim kingdoms, 120
polity 2, 23, 24
pollution, notion of 10, 135
see also Hinduism, purity
polyphony 147
Pope 31
Portuguese 167, 168, 171
poverty 131, 134, 177
power privileges 33, 34, 157
Prannath (1618–94) 89–91, 114,
116, 132, 146
Prazsky, Jeronym 138
prejudices 170
Premanand 147
primitivism, primitiveness 94, 105
production
Asiatic mode 13
means, 49
property 49
Protestant 37, 93
proto-secularists 8
Prussia 163
Psalms of David 87
Ptolemy 167
Punjab
economic development 144
Mughal power 149
anti-Mughal movements 18,
121, 128
resisted colonial invasions 157
see also Sikh movement,
Gobind Singh, Guru
Punjabi language 123
Puranas 85, 102, 147
puritans 134
purity 132, 139, 185–6, 189
notions of 187
Purushapariksha, by Vidyapati
115
Pushkin 163
Pushpavati 16
Pushti marg cult 15, 100

Qashi, Mir Sayid Ahmad 76
Qulzum-e Sharif, by Prannath 90
Quran 8, 66, 83, 85, 87, 90, 98,
102, 154

Radha Vallabh sect 136
radicalism 18, 110, 140
Raffaello Santi 1
Rahim *see* Abdur-Rahim
Khankhanan
Rahimiya madrasa, Delhi 152,
190
rahit-namas 128
Raidas 101, 105, 109–10, 113,
185
Raidasis 116
Raj Singh, Raja of Mewar 54
Raja *see* king
rajas, 106
rajniti 26
seven elements 24
Rajputs 38, 48, 64, 128, 137, 149,
150, 152, 156
Rama 25, 29–30, 66, 100, 101,
103, 108, 112, 114, 119, 123,
127
Ramacharita-manasa, by Tulsidas
15, 107, 109, 129, 133
Ramayana 16, 25, 61, 68, 114,
133
Ramdas 15, 84, 105, 119–20,
121, 129, 149
Ramjanmabhoomi Mandir /
Babri Masjid confrontation 7–9
Ramrajya 110, 134
rashtra 24
rationalism 11, 70–1, 74, 78, 80,
153
Ravidas *see* Raidas
Raya Mangal, by Krishna Ram,
85
Reality, realists 13, 16, 88